GRAHAM NORTON

So Me

HODDER

Some names and identities have been changed in order to protect the integrity
and/or anonymity of the various individuals involved.

Copyright © 2004 Graham Norton

First published in Great Britain in 2004 by Hodder and Stoughton
A division of Hodder Headline
This edition published in 2005

The right of Graham Norton to be identified as the Author of
the Work has been asserted by him in accordance with the
Copyright, Designs and Patents Act 1988.

A Hodder paperback

9

A CIP catalogue record for this title is available from the British Library

ISBN 978-0-340-83349-0

Typeset in Linotype Fairfield Light by
Rowland Phototypesetting Ltd, Bury St Edmunds, Suffolk

Printed and bound in Great Britain by
Clays Ltd, St Ives plc

Hodder Headline's policy is to use papers that are natural, renewable and recyclable
products and made from wood grown in sustainable forests. The logging and
manufacturing processes are expected to conform to the environmental regulations
of the country of origin.

Hodder and Stoughton
A division of Hodder Headline PLC
338 Euston Road
London NW1 3BH

Picture Acknowledgements
Most of the photographs are from the author's collection. Additional sources: Steve
Double, chapter openers. Jessica Mallock, 7 bottom. Zed Nelson/Katz Pictures,
10 bottom. Rex Features, 10 top, 14 top left and right, 15. Gavin Smith/Katz Pictures,
16. Darren Sole, 12 centre.

For Billy, Rhoda and Paula
You suffer me, you support me.

Contents

Contents

Author's Note
Important! Please Read!

As soon as I agreed to write this book, I phoned my mother. I explained why I was writing my autobiography now – I'd just turned forty, my career was about to take new and exciting turns – and without actually mentioning the vulgar sum of money the publishers had offered me, I asked her if she'd like to spend her summers in that lovely house we'd seen down in West Cork a few months earlier?

'Write whatever you want,' she said, which was her heavily disguised version of 'Congratulations'.

I wasn't finished.

'One thing though, Mum. Promise me you will never read it.'

There was a long pause followed by a weary sigh that seemed to suggest I'd missed something very obvious.

'No, I won't want to read it, but I'm sure I won't need to. Won't everyone be only too happy to tell me everything that's in it?'

My heart sank. She was right.

This warning is for all of those people in my mother's life – the friends, the neighbours, the girls at bridge, the people from the gramophone circle, the mechanic who services her car, the woman who works in that new place just beside the shop where something else used to be, the officers who check her passport at the airport, and the journalists who periodically darken her doorstep: *my mother doesn't want to know*. All the important stuff she knows already, and all the other stuff she has no desire to know. If you break this perfectly reasonable code of silence just know that deep down you are not nor ever will be a good person.

1

From the Cradle to the Rave

C HILDHOOD: DULL. OH YES, TO the outsider looking in there was the cross-dressing, the bed-wetting, the moving house thirteen times, but for the little boy wearing his sister's dress, lying in a pool of his own piss, in a house that would never be home, there was little sense of thrill.

I wasn't lonely as a child, but at the same time I did spend a great deal of time by myself. This was for various reasons – we tended to live in the middle of nowhere, I was sent to Protestant schools in the south of Ireland so I never knew the other neighbourhood kids, who were Catholic, and of course one can't forget the fact that I smelt of stale piss and sat around in my sister's clothes until I was eight.

I am aware that such early symptoms could (and possibly should) make way for a disturbed and traumatised adulthood, with therapists fluffing up the cushions on their couches, but as a friend of mine, Rose, put it so well, 'People get over things.' My childhood was my childhood. It is only in looking back through adult eyes that I see that all was not as it should have been in a *Janet and John* sort of way. But I don't think I was that different from the other children. Show me a family and I'll show you a dysfunctional one.

What was brilliant about my parents was that they never made me feel like anything I did was out of the ordinary.

Of course they tried to protect me, warning other parents that their kid's room would smell like an old people's home after I had been to visit, or advising me that maybe shorts and a T-shirt might be a better choice for a trip to the shops than several yards of curtain material wrapped around my body and a lace doily pinned to my head. Because they never panicked, and – God knows what worried conversations went on late at night – what they hoped were just phases turned out to be just that. When I headed off to boarding school my slightly stained mattress was as dry as unbuttered Swedish crispbread and I didn't insist on packing any pretty clothes. You can imagine my parents' joy – their good behaviour had been rewarded. Their son was normal and ordinary. Isn't life cruel?

I was child number two for Billy and Rhoda Walker. Their first, a girl, Paula, was already four years old when I was born in Dublin on 4 April 1963. When people ask me which part of Dublin I was born in – and yes, conversation can be that dull – I always say that I don't know, because I genuinely don't. We moved constantly. At first it was just around Dublin, but then my dad got a new job at Guinness as a sales representative and we really got into our stride.

I realise now that all the moving seems to have given me a slightly unhealthy relationship with houses. Now that I have money, I seem to buy them like people buy cans of tuna when they fear an impending food shortage. If the *Big Issue* deals with the problems of the homeless, I need a magazine called the *Tiny Issue* which deals with the problems of the chronically overhoused. Like, where did I leave my favourite sunglasses? To date I have my house in London as well as ones in Cape Town, New York and Cork. Perhaps

I do take after my parents, but I'm just too rich and lazy to actually move.

The first stop on our epic journey around Ireland was Tramore, which means big beach in Gaelic and is a seaside resort. Well, to be honest, and just in case anyone should use this book as some sort of holiday guide, Tramore *is* beside the sea but I dread to think what rough side of hell you would have to hail from in order to consider it a resort. Our house there was the first one I can remember. Twelve more to go.

In 1967 there was Waterford, a small city in the south-east corner of Ireland. Living here was different because we had proper neighbours and, because I hadn't started school yet, the other kids didn't know that I was a freak Protestant boy, and happily played with me. It was around this time that I realised that all families weren't the same. The Connellys next door, for instance, didn't eat the skin off chicken – what madness! I would stand like a small dog outside their back door and they would feed me the unwanted delicacy. The Kennys had to go to bed at six, which I personally blame for the failure of our plan to dig to Australia, and there was another family whose name I forget who put a blue sheet of plastic over their black and white TV screen to make it look like colour (children and adults united in thinking that this was not a great look). The boy of the house gained a certain notoriety when he started declaring that 'his daddy and God were the best drivers in the whole world'. Had no one told him that thunder was God trying to parallel park?

Where else? Kilkenny – that was where I became a choir-boy and the Dean's son told me how babies were made. I refused to believe him. That was what dogs did and surely

God had some higher plan for his favourite creation? Sadly the Dean's son turned out to be right; obviously the Supreme Being had been too busy trying to park.

Despite or perhaps because of the Dean's son's revelations, Kilkenny was also where I had my closest brush with religion. Obviously we went to church every Sunday but for me that had always been just something you did before you got a roast dinner. The Sunshine Club was different. I'm not sure if my parents ever knew how evangelical this after-school club was, but all the other children went, and besides it gave my mother a free afternoon.

We would meet behind the Methodist church and next to the cinema – so close to Satan's lair! Rows of small children in handknitted clothes would sit and listen to larger ladies, who always seemed to be from Scotland or Northern Ireland, tell us stories about children in Africa being nice to their granny or being saved from a lion. These tales of the very expected were illustrated by large, dull monochrome drawings on a flip board. There was, however, one picture that I always looked forward to: Jesus dressed in his traditional drag outside the door of an English cottage. The entrance was overgrown with roses and weeds. Jesus was knocking. This picture, we were told every week, illustrated Jesus knocking at the door to our hearts – all we had to do was open that door and invite him in.

That picture clearly grabbed hold of my imagination, because after a couple of months I decided that the idea of Jesus living inside me sounded great. I sat with one of the big Northern women over a traditional Sunshine Club feast of diluted orange squash and soggy potato crisp sandwiches and told her that, yes, I was going to ask Jesus into my heart.

Given that this woman had been asking us to do this every Wednesday afternoon for almost a year, I had expected a certain positive response: a big embrace like the granny gave the little African boy when he arrived home uneaten; perhaps a simple cry of Hallelujah to the Airtexed ceiling; at the very least she would reach for her tambourine.

What I didn't expect was her bland, 'That's nice,' followed by a pat on the shoulder. It was all right for her, Jesus had been living in her heart for years. I was not accustomed to having any sort of lodger in my body, never mind the actual Son of God. As it happened, Jesus turned out to be a very quiet flatmate. I think it would be safe to say that I never even knew he was there. I assume he moved out at some point, but his departure was as uneventful as his moving in.

My primary school teacher at Kilkenny was a man called Mr Groves. At the time I thought he was about a thousand years old, but in reality he was probably in his late fifties. He lived with his wife in a house next to the school, and each day after lunch he would return to the classroom with a soup moustache. One day in class some precocious child asked him about homosexuals. He happily explained, using the colourful metaphor of pansies in a flowerbed, but then just as he was getting bored of the subject and trying to get back to how clouds are formed, someone called out, 'Can homosexuals have babies?' To this day I have no idea why, but Mr Groves said 'Yes' and then returned swiftly to the joys of evaporation. Perhaps he meant that gay men do produce sperm so that they are able to father children, or perhaps he hadn't heard the question properly, but I am too embarrassed to admit how old I was when I discovered that it wasn't true. For years, whenever I doubted my sexuality

I simply assumed that I couldn't be a homosexual because they could have babies and I could in no way see a baby popping out of me.

Castlecomer was nice. I must have been about ten years old. We lived in the first of our new bungalows there. Bungalow Bliss – not just a state of mind, but also a book of house plans that took Ireland by storm. Everyone wanted one, so all over the country beautiful old farmhouses stood rotting while families moved into their slices of pebble-dashed nirvana. The trouble for our family with building new houses was that we moved so often they were never really finished, and just didn't feel like homes. I remember once we were driving through the countryside late at night when we stopped so that I could go to the toilet – nobody wanted to take any chances with the back seat – and as I stood at the side of the road emptying my tiny bladder into the darkness I saw the lit windows of a cottage in the distance. I felt a sudden and violent longing to have a home. Not the buildings with poured concrete floors and bare light bulbs where we lived, but a real home where the air would be thick with smells and memories.

Bandon, County Cork, was the place where I seemed to collect most of my childhood memories. It was the town we kept coming back to. We had a short stay there early on in our travels, and my parents obviously liked it because that is where my sister Paula and I were sent to secondary school four years later, and it is where they came to build several bungalows when my dad took early retirement from the brewery.

The town has a reputation for being a bit of a Protestant enclave – 'Bandon, where even the pigs are Protestants', as the old saying goes . . . (I'm really not making that up). It is also called the Gateway to West Cork, which is a slightly upbeat way of saying a lot of people drive through it.

The first time we lived there I was about seven years old, and for some reason it was around that period that I became trouble. I remember drawing on a mirror with some of my mother's lipstick and then, being too scared to hang around and face her wrath, I decided to run away. I solemnly packed a small case. All that would fit was a bath towel and my swimming togs. Although my flight to freedom was taking place in mid-November, I figured I'd need them when it was summertime. I strode out towards the nearest town, Clonakilty, but as it got darker and colder, my destination seemed no nearer. I decided to head back to Bandon, where a neighbour found me buying sweets in a petrol station. I still remember my homecoming and how my mother hugged me. All her worry, anger and grief transformed into an electric blanket of love.

On another occasion I decided I didn't want to go to school. I said I felt sick.

'What's wrong?'

'Tummy ache.'

'All right,' said my mother, 'you can stay at home, but I'll bring you to the doctor this afternoon.'

She went downstairs, leaving me lying in bed, petrified as the awful truth began to dawn on me. I had got what I wanted but I was in a state of terror. She had done this to my sister once before. The doctor had told her there was nothing wrong, my mother realised she'd been taken for a ride, and suddenly my sister would have been better off on a school field trip to hell. I knew that I was facing a similar fate, but I had set the wheels in motion towards my own downfall and saw no way of stopping them.

Come the afternoon, a grim-faced mother half walked, half dragged me to the doctor's. I lay down and pulled up my shirt. He pressed his doctor-pink hands into my belly and asked me where it hurt. I felt like blurting out, 'On the back of my legs when my mother gets me back home,' but I played the game, letting out a random selection of 'ows' and 'ouches'. He removed his raw sausage fingers and asked me to wait outside the room for a moment; he wanted to speak to my mother. I left the room with an imaginary rain cloud floating over my head. I sat perched high on one of those hard plastic chairs that only seem to exist in waiting rooms and exam halls, too scared to even swing my legs. I knew what he was saying: he was telling my mother that she was wasting time and money and that she should take her child home and never darken his door again. I would never be able to be sick again. From now on I would be sent off to school carrying my entrails in a wheelbarrow before I'd be allowed to stay in bed.

I stared at a sea of old *People's Friend* magazines while the doctor's voice rumbled on behind the closed door. After what seemed like several hours, the doctor came out of his office and asked me to come in.

'Sit down.'

I braced myself and made sure not to catch my mother's eye.

'Well, you have something called appendicitis.'

I looked up. 'What?'

'It'll mean a small stay in hospital next week and a little operation to take out your appendix.'

10

From the Cradle to the Rave

My mind was reeling. I weighed up the options. I could say that I had been pretending and bring down the wrath not just of my mother but also of a doctor I had just made look like an idiot, or on the other hand, I could go into hospital, get cut open and have a perfectly healthy organ removed. It only took a second. Hospital it was. Tears started to roll down my cheeks as my contrite mother fussed over me and promised me a treat for my dinner.

This is the bit of the story that sort of defies belief – surely, at some point over the next few days, I would have found a way to explain to my mother what had happened and the operation would be called off, but no. A week later my mother and I walked up the driveway to the hospital, with her telling me not to worry and me daydreaming about something going wrong so that I would end up in a wheel-chair like Margaret O'Brien in some black and white tear-jerker movie and everyone would marvel at how brave and sweet I was. In fact the operation went without a hitch, I got several days off school, and I went home with my appendix in a little bottle of brine. It was the perfect ending.

The school my sister and I went to was Bandon Grammar School, and it was founded to provide education for the children of the Protestant community. Set on a farm, it admitted day boys and girls as well as boarders. With hind-sight, I couldn't have asked for a better place to go to school. At the time, I didn't like it very much and the actual academic side of things was fairly poor, but as an education for life it was wonderful. Pupils ranged from kids who lived on remote farms where electricity was on a par with space travel to Fred Astaire's grandson and the three children of a well-known Hollywood stills photographer.

I am grateful to this school for two reasons. The first is that I had two teachers who were inspirational. Typically for teachers who influenced lives, they both taught English. One was called Cally and was feared by all. Her full title was Miss O'Callaghan, and, like all great teachers, she threw her whole being into her lessons. At times we didn't get on – I could be spikey and rude but I think that was probably because I was jealous of her. She was young and sexy and obviously had a life. The rest of the teachers had seemingly uneventful lives like mine and my parents', and who wanted one of those? I knew I didn't. The other teacher was Niall MacMonagle who was a substitute teacher when Cally was off having a baby. Niall has since become a good friend, and it's hard to imagine that he was ever my teacher, but he was and he was brilliant. What Niall brings to the classroom is energy and enthusiasm to burn. He loves books, and his blinking incomprehension of anyone who doesn't share that love is infectious.

What both Niall and Cally gave me was permission to question everything. They taught me that there were no right answers. You simply read the text and you got out of it what you could. They also both encouraged me to perform. There was no tradition of regular school plays or drama clubs; Bandon Grammar School was strictly a rugby or hockey sort of place. I had tried to fit in early on – I had donned my rugby costume and clattered down to the pitch with the rest of them. But of course I was fooling no one. Those boys simply knew that I could not throw a ball. They were like a pack of animals who sensed weakness or who had smelt blood. It doesn't sound like much, but it did make me feel excluded and lonely – it's very hard to understand how alienating it is for a boy who can't do what boys are meant to be able to. And this isn't about being gay or straight, it's just about belonging.

However, once in a blue moon a play would be put on, and this was when I had my rugby moments. Suddenly I did feel comfortable, I felt confident about what I was doing. Whether it was a strange Irish one-act play or a production of *The Importance Of Being Earnest* with furniture borrowed from Niall's flat, I loved being in front of an audience, and although at the time I thought that what I was enjoying was the acting, looking back it was probably more about the laughter coming from the audience. Debating was the other school activity that I did well at. Mind you, it was fairly easy to win. I remember once having a debate against the convent school team about punk rock. Now, as you can imagine, this was not a musical and cultural revolution that had really taken Bandon by storm – we didn't have bin-liners in our bins, never mind in our wardrobes – but I successfully argued that Jesus Christ was the first punk rocker. How I did this I'm not sure, as I don't remember a lot of gobbing in the gospels or any parables about pogoing, but the judges bought it and we won. The girls from the convent were livid: how dare a little Protestant boy teach them the great lesson for living in Ireland? You can't win an argument with someone who has God on their side.

Although it was never mentioned in the prospectus, Bandon Grammar School also provided a rudimentary sexual education. All the boys who boarded lived in a separate building, a large old house called Roundhill, which was full of bunk beds. Out the back there was a room for our tuck boxes and our shoe-cleaning kits, but there wasn't much else. Because my parents were still living in Castlecomer, I was a boarder for my first three years at the school before my parents moved back to Bandon and I could become a day pupil. As I write this I can hardly believe that I spent three years of my life there. I'm sure that in any boys' boarding school a certain amount of sexual activity goes on, and Roundhill was no exception – we 'practised' kissing, and taught each other how to wank. As the years went by the games became more complicated – who could come the furthest was the most popular, a game invariably won by the same boy, who I really shouldn't name, but if you were in the grammar school at the same time as I was, he had curly brown hair and his initials were P.L.

I know it's hard to believe, but even I needed tips. From an early age I had exploited God's great gift, my penis. I had developed an extremely special and slightly medieval way of playing with myself. If I got an erection I would deliver a series of brutal karate chops to my member until I got that 'funny feeling'. This led to great discomfort and some quite bad scarring, so imagine how delighted I was to have that technique made obsolete by the teachings of those wiser than me in the dorm.

It is important to remember what innocent times these were. I can't imagine boys being so open with each other now, but we were like a big house full of puppies. It's only in the telling that it takes on a creepy feeling; at the time it was definitely sweet.

It is against this backdrop that a relationship between two boys, both called Charles, took place. The Charleses were from small remote farms in far-flung corners of the country, and they shared a bed every night for the six years they were at school. It is so difficult to explain why everyone from the cruellest bullies to the teachers' pets at our school indulged this eccentricity. I think in the end most people were just quietly in awe of the strength of their feelings. I often wonder what happened to the Charleses after school. At the time, the only thing these boys might have known about being gay was that it rhymed with hay. I imagine each one is spending his life as a bachelor farmer, living with his mother or sister, working hard all day, maybe having a pint down the pub but not talking to people much. There must be times, though, as they lie awake late at night listening to the creaking of the house, when they can remember what it was like to be wrapped in the arms of another warm body, to be surrounded by love. When I finally told my mother I was gay, her first response was, 'Oh, it's such a lonely life.' For the Charleses I'm sure that is almost certainly true.

It was also in Bandon that I spent my teenage years, mostly watching TV and reading. I loved being whisked off to the highways of California or the glamorous apartments of New York. At the time there was only one television station, called RTE, which started its broadcasts around 5.00 p.m. and then packed up shop around 10.30 or 11 p.m. As a result I watched everything that was on with no content or quality filter. True, I enjoyed *Charlie's Angels* a lot more than *Mart and Market*, the weekly programme that reported the price cattle had fetched in various markets around the country while showing cows walking in a circle, but I watched them both with equal attention. I even sat through *An Nuacht*, which was the news in Irish. The only four words in the whole programme that I understood were '*Agus anois an aimsir*', which meant 'And now the weather' and signalled that the end was nigh and soon I could be enjoying Farrah Fawcett or Carol Burnett.

I wasn't popular at school but nor was I unpopular. Memory has a way of distilling and distorting things, but my overall impression of those times is of waiting – waiting to leave. I had looked through the windows of books and television and immediately decided that the life I was living, this life of marriages, funerals and the price of land, was not my beautiful life. I'm not sure, but I think that if anyone remembers me from school, they wouldn't say I was unfriendly or unhappy, just a bit distant, unengaged.

The first time I felt anything approaching 'life' happened to me was when I ventured out into the world in the summer of '79. The intermediate certificate, the Irish equivalent of the O levels, was over and it would be another year before I left secondary school, so in order to improve my French my parents agreed to have an exchange student to stay with them as part of a school scheme. The plan was that the student would spend a month living with my family, and then I would head off alone with him to spend a month in deepest, darkest, 'this tastes funny' France. I was terrified at the idea.

On the day of the exchanges' arrivals, Cork airport was full of parents with sullen-looking children holding up hastily made name-boards. Mothers conducted hushed conversations ('I just hope they'll eat something', 'I know someone who had one last year and he refused to eat anything but cheese for a month'). When the *étudiants* finally shuffled through the arrival doors we held our breath and gripped our clumsy signs. Leather-jacketed greasy yobs and teenage girls wearing enough make-up to cover the presidents' faces on Mount Rushmore announced themselves to nervous families. There was no sign of our student. But then, like Peter O'Toole in *Lawrence of Arabia*, Jules strode out, blond and clean, as polished and perfect as any model in an ad for Farrah slacks. It seemed impossible that we, the Walker family, had won the French lottery, but we had.

In truth I don't recall much about our month together in Ireland. I'm amazed it was a month, because in fact the only things I can remember are that he ate everything, annoyed me by criticising the way I laid a table and laughed till I thought he might vomit at *The Benny Hill Show*.

But somehow a month passed and it was time for the return visit to France. We went back to the airport ('Weetabix, that's all I could get down him the whole month', 'She went missing for two nights with some fella from Cork city. We had the guards out'). My mother looked very smug as she shepherded St Jules towards the departure gate. My dad gave me a wad of francs, and Mum kissed me and said, 'Eat everything you're given.' I nodded grimly. This was a question of national and family pride. I would be swallowing pig gristle for the Walkers and for Ireland.

I decided that I would keep a diary of my first trip abroad. Now, I can't be certain but I've a funny feeling I might have been reading a little too much Jane Austen before I left. Remember I was seventeen years old and had never been out of Ireland before:

Day One.
We arrived in Lourdes following the plane journey during which I discovered I enjoy flying. Lourdes proved to me once again that Roman Catholicism must be the

least civilised religion in the world. Also, surprisingly, it is falling down. It's quite common to see the Virgin's nose or left big toe missing where lumps of plaster have fallen from the wall. But Lourdes did have one advantage, I met someone who could speak English; an arts student from Hong Kong. Somehow it wasn't quite the same as having a chat.

All of this on Day One!!! I pray this pretentious prig unleashed himself only on the page and that I wasn't quite so bad in reality – surely my mother brought me up better than that. Speaking of my mother, here's another snippet from the diary that she might have written herself.

The house is obviously decorated with taste, but it's not mine. Enough said, suffice to say the stairs don't have a handrail.

And in answer to your question, no, I have no idea what I was talking about either.

The diary documents the month fairly faithfully. In it I describe the heat, moan about the food, and report endless games of ping-pong. There is the odd joke that has stood the test of time, such as:

But now lunch is calling. They might have at least knocked the thing unconscious before we ate it.

There are also frightening violent outbursts about Jules's parents, who I in fact recall very fondly:

*Madame, hang on to your pink bri-nylon dressing gown
'cos you're driving me up the wall! Madame has packed
for me and taken charge of my money and passport,
but still no word about what she intends to do as
regards compensation for the trousers she wrecked.
God bless her little heart, may it break in two and rot
behind her knees. Tra La!*

The father didn't escape my wrath either:

*Jules cooked lunch and there was no noticeable change,
except that there was no cheese for a second time and
I was able to avoid it in the salad. This afternoon I wrote
a few letters because the father more or less asked me
to, and as you know I'd do anything to please the dear
man. Greasy old pig, may he rot in hell!*

It was only a couple of days before the end of the trip
that things took an unexpected twist. The following entries
are exactly as written. Imagine if Adrian Mole had been gay.

August 28th. Night.
*I'm faced with a difficult decision; whether to keep this
a glib record of my little days, or to give an honest
account of what is actually happening. I will choose
the latter.*
*I'm here nervous, tense and terrified. How to write
about this I find difficult to know, I'll just start and
hope it sounds the way it's meant to.*
*This afternoon, changing for windsurfing, Jules
stripped completely and when I took no notice, he*

pointed at his erection and said, 'It is starting.' I gave my usual noncommittal little laugh, but then with the use of gestures and words he asked me if I masturbated and told me every day in school they did it in a group. He virtually asked me to go to the toilet with him. I was surprised by how much this revelation affected me. I suppose it was just the fact of it being clean, proper, smiling Jules. I felt physically sick and my mouth went dry. I just kept asking myself why, why he had to go and do this now the holiday was nearly over? We couldn't be the same again. But it was over now. I prayed we'd have no more.

When we got back to the house I'd recovered a little. I was going to take a shower. Jules went into the loo. I went into the bathroom, but no towel, so I was just about to come out to ask Jules where I could get one, when he called me. I opened the door and there was Jules standing naked on the landing, masturbating.

'Comme ça,' he said smiling.

'Je sais, je sais.'

'You do it?'

'Now?'

'Yes, in the shower.'

He walked towards me masturbating all the time. I shut the door and waited until I heard him go into his room. I felt like crying. It was the most blatant attempt at homosexual seduction I've ever encountered. But why did he do it now? Can it be we are going to have a little group session while camping in Luchon? I pray not. Will he try again in the morning? It is an awful sort of fear because I can't trust myself.

From the Cradle to the Rave

I'm quietly impressed that I had the insight and the nerve to write that last sentence. Of course I was shocked and upset by everything, but part of me was also thrilled. The following day the saga continued:

August 29th. Afternoon.
I survived the morning. During the night I thought of a good way to describe this time; a harrowing experience. In a way it's absolutely hilarious. I imagine him lurking naked behind every corner. Yesterday at the clubhouse when he started to show and tell, all I did was ask him what it was called in French!

Xavier [a friend of Jules'] was here this morning and we put up the tent we have for Luchon. It's a two-man tent; me and Jules! Oh God, what will I do? There isn't room to turn in the damn thing.

This afternoon, tennis – a newspaper took our picture as I stumbled around the court – and then table tennis at the 'Club de Voile'. Things were fine, all was forgotten. When we got back I had my shower without incident. When Jules came into my room he was fairly conspicuous but he did have a towel thrown around him. I was just starting to make up a poem about how discretion was back in style, when I heard a sort of shout. He can't have got dressed by now, I thought, and I was right. He pranced in naked and at his physical peak. He had with him something along the lines of Playboy.

'Have you a magazine like that?'

'Yes,' I lied. It isn't wise to be naïve. I hear that's what they want.

'At your house?'

'Yes. What's the title of yours?'

He showed me and then gaily pranced out again, no doubt scattering scented rose petals all around as he went. I may be flippant, but in reality I do feel sick all the time. It's totally changed my attitude to Jules and to everyone we meet.

Jules and I – how obscene that sounds – dined with Grandmère and Grandpère. Very nice, but I felt a bit tipsy all evening after all the Ricard and wine. We packed the tent and stuff into the car and then played a bit of ping-pong and now I lie here, for the second night, terrified.

Doors that were shut
  Now open sway,
And the happy blue summer
  Is now sweaty and grey.

You know things are serious when the poetry starts, and then the inevitable finally happened.

August 31st. Night.
It is my last night in France and words cannot express how much I'm looking forward to being able to talk English and to the familiar food. I find in the following piece there is no way I can make myself the hero, for I know that I've done wrong. Oh what the hell am I talking about? This is beginning to sound like 'Song of Bernadette'. So what I couldn't hold out in a tent? So I pulled a guy off with my mouth? So I felt like an

infatuated first year? I felt no guilt immediately after, and none now, though a little in between. I don't care, it was enjoyable and I did get my cheap thrills.

Jules wastes no time. I hardly got out of the room in time after collecting a few odds and ends for the morning and already he was on the bed rattling away and I've just found I've forgotten my watch – I daren't go back.

A couple of days later I sat at the desk in my bedroom back in Bandon. At the other end of the house I could hear my mother clinking plates and rattling pans as she put them on the stove. My father was watching the news.

September 2nd. Night.

I have arrived home safely and indeed have already survived an entire day of school. It was wonderful to see Mum and Dad again and see all the old familiar things again. This is the end of my account, no matter what happens after this. I find I have ended up so that I find it impossible to be glib and flippant about Jules any longer. Images of he and I and he alone haunt me. They chase me about in my head and I must jump from one idea to the next to avoid them. I feel decidedly odd, depressed and tensed up.

You the reader must find a tremendous difference between the start and the finish of this, but what could I do? I couldn't predict what would happen.

The bastard, he planned it all. I saw him pack the hankies to go to Luchon and I wondered why so many? Then he handed me one in the tent, so that when we

ejaculated we could mop up. He's packed one for me.
He's known all along, the cold calculating bastard.

Earlier I made too light of that night in the tent. It
was such a long night. Afterwards I cried for hours
without a sob, just a static hot pain in my eyes and on
my face.

You see, I'm no honest writer, I make light so that
it reads jolly. It wasn't, it was a gross and appalling
affair. I cry with the shame of an upbringing as I recall
all this to the page, but what could I do?

Oh dear! A young boy finishes his diary entry, looks out
at the damp Irish fields and writes a poem about weeds.

Things seemed so momentous to me at the time. I had
still to learn Rose's mantra about learning to get over things.
I had lived my life through television and books and so
naturally I was convinced that what had happened between
Jules and myself had to end in some huge drama. Nothing
good was supposed to happen to the homosexual in the story.
I really don't think I had any true moral dilemma about
fumbling around with Jules, I just wanted my own personal
story to have a happy ending.

So many things strike me as I read this old diary, but the
main thing is that, given how I feel now, and if that was
how I felt then, what a very long book this is going be.

2

More French Oral

U NIVERSITY! AND AT LAST I felt like my real life, the one I was supposed to be leading, was about to start. The whole experience with Jules, although completely adolescent and harmless, had upset me and probably made me feel even more distant from those around me. A secret can do that.

On top of that there had been the pressure of our leaving certificate (A levels). I really shouldn't have been going to university at all; God knows my exam results hadn't suggested that I should be. My last year at school had been fairly miserable. I hadn't coped very well. Whenever I'd tried to study I'd just drifted off into panic-filled daydreams about the future. These exams were supposed to mark the start of your adult life, but after France I had the spectre of being gay hanging over me in a much more tangible way than it had before. Now I didn't just have to worry about what I was going to do in terms of a career, I had to consider the possibility that I would never push my kids on a swing in the park or kiss a wife as I ran out the door late for work.

What I really wanted to be was an actor, but sitting in rural Ireland where the only autograph I had collected belonged to a visiting Danish gymnast, that idea seemed too far-fetched even for daydreams. I tried to be sensible and mature. I tried to imagine what the future really did hold for me. I would drive a car and work in an office. I was busy. I was drinking cups of coffee on the go. What was I? I was . . . a journalist! I applied to do a course in journalism in Dublin. They declined. OK. What would I do? I would drive a car and work in an office. My mother suggested I try the bank. My father agreed. So keen were my parents on this sensible career path that a special outfit was purchased for the event. Think brown, think check, think again. Complete with sports jacket and tie I really did look like a banker, but sadly they too turned me down. What would I do? What all the other middle-class losers did – an arts degree.

Having done too badly in my exams to get a grant, my parents had to pay for my tuition. Although never really poor, my father had worked hard and my mother had managed things down to the wire to get whatever money they had. This was going to be a huge expense for them. I suppose that one of the reasons they were willing to give up their hard-earned money was that they were proud: I would be the first person in our family to go to university. My sister had gone the bank route, not enjoyed it very much and so quickly got herself promoted to farmer's wife. I didn't have that option and so I found myself taking the family savings off to University College, Cork.

I loved university. I shared a flat with a boy from school called Billy Forrester. The only memorable thing about the flat was that the living room was wallpapered with gift-wrapping paper, and this was long before that designing pony Laurence Llewelyn-Bowen had shat through a stencil and smeared it on people's walls. We were giddy with independence and cheap lager. For the first time in my life I found myself amongst people I could relate to. They had seen films apart from James Bond, they read books because they wanted to, they gossiped, they preferred coffee to tea – in lots of ways all it really meant was that they were urban, but this was my first exposure to them, and I was dazzled by them.

I immediately fell in with a clique, Mia, Jerry, Carmel, Karen. We wandered around the campus in a self-consciously Bohemian way, our big charity-shop coats flapping in the wind. We spent hours in the vast basement canteen called the Kampus Kitchen (No! You are kidding, that's how they spelt it? – how mad!) sitting at the big round tables, burning holes in the styrofoam cups with cigarettes and watching the coffee pour out. We would dissect what everyone was wearing as they came in, and watch the clock. 'I've got a lecture in ten minutes', 'I've got a lecture in five minutes', 'I'm missing a lecture'.

In that first year we had to take four subjects and I chose mine with great care. English because the plan was I would use this degree to pursue my career in journalism, French because I didn't go through all that stuff in Toulouse for nothing, then it was a toss-up between Geography or History – I went with History because Geography seemed to have a lot of nine o'clock lectures. Finally I took Greek and Roman Civilization because they didn't fail anyone at first-year exams, hoping that someone might go on to take it as a degree.

When I did go to lectures, which wasn't often, I quite enjoyed them. The strictest department was French, as they seemed to notice when you weren't there. The French department was made up of quite starchy ladies, most of whom you suspected had sacrificed their lives for an all-consuming love affair with France in lieu of another human being. The one exception was Dr Esther Greenwood. In her mid-thirties with very long blonde hair, she had lazy, exotic features, dark, slightly hooded eyes, a delicate nose and the sort of mouth that was designed for eating peaches. She drove a bright blue Citroën van, wore large fedora hats, smoked roll-ups and organised exhibitions of Balinese art. In short she was as pretentious and annoying as I and my little clique were. I adored her.

She had managed to get a book of her short stories published by a small publishing house and she announced one day in the middle of a French class that she would be giving a reading at the local arts centre. Having lived in Britain for many years, I know the phrase 'Arts Centre' conjures up something quite municipal, but in Ireland at that time all it meant was a whitewashed basement where you might be able to buy freshly brewed coffee and some woman might know where you could go to get an abortion. Like a little overdressed fly, I was drawn into her creative web. I went to hear her reading. The stories themselves were fairly impenetrable, full of descriptions of leaves hitting windowpanes, but afterwards I bought a copy even though I could ill afford it. I think that's the way I became friendly with her, and we would chat after lectures.

Everyone was making plans for the long summer holiday and I had decided that I would head off to Paris and get a job; I just needed some money to get there. My friend Jerry was in a similar situation. Now Jerry, although part of the übercool and artistic gang at university, was a proper man. This is really what thrilled me most about being his friend. He would talk about the make-up of a wild flower or a T.S. Eliot poem, but equally he would kick around a ball or fix a bike. His one blind spot was that he didn't really seem to notice that I didn't have a masculine side like him. He came up with a money-making scheme. We would do gardening. As deeply unlikely as this seems, I went along with the plan. A professor he knew from the Old English department wanted a fence put up. Jerry & Graham Landscaping to the rescue.

Of course it was raining. Like some sort of bizarre ballet about trench warfare in the First World War, we slipped and staggered around with wooden poles and rain capes. I mostly remember laughing while Jerry got cross with me. A nervous professor peered from his study window. Finally we finished the job, and we were both enormously satisfied, both with our monumental achievement and with the cash. If you would like to go and see this fence I regret to report it only lasted about three weeks – then the winds came or perhaps a slightly overweight bird landed on it, I don't know.

We were on a roll and word was out that no job was too small or indeed too simple. Esther asked us if we could help her build a patio at the back of her cottage. Of course we could! We got on our bikes and headed out into the country. I remember that day was so beautiful. This was the way my books and TV shows told me the country was supposed to be, not dreary and bleak, full of mists and yellow school buses. The sun shone as we cycled along the valley of the River Lee. The council hadn't been to trim the hedges yet and so everywhere we looked was bursting with life and colour. I was young and so happy. I had my friend Jerry with me and we were heading for the inner sanctum of the creative goddess.

Esther's cottage was one of the most perfectly beautiful

homes I'd ever seen. The sort of cottage door that Jesus might knock at, and then inside there was a series of large white rooms that she had furnished very simply but with the sort of style and flair that never would have made it into the Bungalow Bliss house plans. Her home smelled of fresh bread and well-thumbed books. It seemed idyllic to me. It never crossed my mind that this woman living miles from anyone or anything with her unwanted writing might be anything other than incredibly happy.

Jerry and I started work on the patio one Monday. If the professor's fence had been our equivalent of Hadrian's Wall, this was building the pyramids. I let Jerry direct proceedings, but after a while I could tell it wasn't going well. Esther's back garden was really a field, and our ineffectual digging was making as much impact as a plastic spoon in a coal mine. I remember that we did work hard, and that Jerry spent a lot of time moaning about what a slave-driver Esther was, and that of course this was somehow my fault. The vegetarian lunch didn't help matters.

At the end of the day Esther cooked us dinner and we drank wine. It was all so grown-up. We let Esther talk at length about her college days in Brighton and her collection of hats, but most of all she told us about her diaries – her many, many diaries. As I got to know her better it seemed that she really only lived her life so that she would have something to write about in her diaries. It made talking to her all the more interesting, because you thought that what you were saying might be recorded. I'm not sure how we got home that night, but presumably we weaved and wobbled our way back to the city on our bikes.

The next few days went by following a similar pattern,

but on the Friday Esther was going to have a party and we were invited. Jerry had the good sense to be slightly apprehensive, but I was thrilled. I would wear my special green two-tone suit that I had found in some market stall. Somehow it had made its way from a tailor in Hong Kong to Cork. It was too big and smelt of attic, but to me it was sophistication with buttons on. I wore it with a strange silk tie that was covered with what looked like either two melting fried eggs or a couple of vaginas that really needed to see a doctor.

The party was a bit of an anticlimax. The other guests were all thirty- and fortysomethings who were attached to academia or the arts in some way, and they stood around awkwardly with their glasses of wine discussing books they wished they'd written. The highlight was when someone put a Blondie record on. I *loved* Blondie. Off I bopped, but then something happened which I've seen at countless parties since (though sadly now I'm on the other side of the divide): I noticed the other guests dancing too, but not out of pleasure, more in an effort to prove the point that they weren't old, and that they could dance to Blondie even though there were more beats to it than they knew what to do with. I'm the same now at clubs, desperately clinging to a mysterious beat, drowning more than dancing – 'Taxi for Mr Mutton!'

The party slowly wound down. Jerry and I were going to spend the night in Esther's loft room so we waited for the others to leave. Eventually it was just the three of us left, Jerry lying on the sofa, Esther and I on the floor in front of the fire. If I were listening to the conversation again now I would probably throw a brick through the window. We discussed words, the ego and I remember a lot of talk about being self-aware and when it was possible to be lost in the moment. Jerry, and who could blame him, fell asleep. Esther and I talked some more. We danced. She told me she had a crush on the composer Michael Nyman, she told me she had a crush on me, she kissed me, she took me to bed.

The next day was extraordinary. I was full of my secret. This wasn't a terrible oppressive secret like Jules had been, this was a fantastic, glamorous secret. It wasn't grubby – it was scandalous and sexy! Esther gave me a lift home to Bandon and even came in and had tea with my parents. Of course they suspected nothing, why would they? Everything felt electric and almost illegal. As far as I was concerned I was back on the heterosexual team. I looked in the mirror and saw a man in love with a woman, when in reality I was a boy in love with the situation.

I had already booked my tickets to Paris for the following week. Esther announced that she would come with me. We could stay with her old friends Alex and Sarah; she had meant to visit them soon anyway. The plan was that we'd spend a couple of weeks together and then I could start my Parisian adventure on my own when she went back to Cork.

She flew off to Paris first and I was to follow a few days later. In the meantime I sat in my parents' bungalow watching TV, but in my mind I was as decadent as any opium eater. The day of my departure I said goodbye to Mum and Dad, who were both terrified about what might happen to me in the leg-waving, bare-breasted hell that was Paris. I don't think they would have felt any better if I'd told them I was going to be under adult supervision throughout, and that in fact I'd be sleeping with it.

When I got to Paris, Esther and her friend Alex met me

at arrivals. She took me to one side. The news was not good. Yes, we would be staying with Alex, but Sarah wouldn't be there. Sarah had died the week before of cancer. Now, there are many ways of responding to a friend who has lost a loved one from cancer: you could give flowers, make a donation to a charity, perhaps cook a meat pie, but I didn't think a particularly obvious one was showing up with your toy-boy lover. To make matters worse Alex had lost his voice through shock. He rasped hello and led us to the waiting car.

The apartment was no longer a home. Alex was a photographer and had transformed the place into a shrine to his dead wife. The children had been sent to stay with some relatives, so Esther and I slept in the nursery. Perhaps there was another spare room, and Alex was just trying to point something out to Esther.

I can't say I was very comfortable in my role of toy-boy lover. I sat awkwardly at dinner while friends of Alex whispered and giggled in the sort of French that was way beyond me. I remember once as we walked by Notre Dame cathedral, Esther tried to take my hand. I was appalled. I can only imagine what a grotesque couple we made.

Alex had two lovely friends called Pierre and Christine who photographed food for a living. They worked and lived in an amazing apartment overlooking the Seine – large white rooms that led to more white rooms, all with windows framed by billowing curtains. We visited them one afternoon and chatted while we ate everything they had finished photographing. Somewhere in a conversation that I couldn't follow they invited Esther and me to spend the weekend with them in the country, presumably to leave Alex alone with his grief. Esther thought it was a good idea, so we accepted.

To this day I don't know where we went. It took hours to get there and it was either to the north or the south of the Massif Central. The house itself was an old farmhouse that they had started renovating but never finished. Esther and I slept in a room upstairs that could only be accessed by a ladder just outside the front door. The front door led directly into the kitchen and another bedroom led off that. As far as I recall that was all there was to the house. It had a long-drop toilet full of spiders with a rather incongruous pile of back issues of *Vogue* next to it. Still, always quite pleasant to wipe the smile off a model's face, no matter what the circumstances.

The days were spent sunbathing or helping to weed the big, seemingly empty vegetable patch. It was at night that the place came alive – various friends of Pierre and Christine would show up with copious amounts of wine and some local moonshine. Esther hated these evenings. She didn't see the simple pleasure in getting drunk, finding everything very funny and then going to bed. These parties were nothing like hers, where the wildest thing was a Blondie record. I would really look forward to these mad nights and would choose to stay up sticking cutlery to walls or trying to lift cars long after she had sniffily said goodnight. The sun was nearly always up when I finally climbed the ladder to my bedroom of bliss. I felt like a teenage Andy Capp returning to a very grumpy Missus.

The sex between us was . . . well, I'm guessing it wasn't great because on one of these nights in the strange room upstairs she told me that she thought I was gay. Two thoughts: couldn't you just throw my dinner in the bin like any normal pissed-off girlfriend, and secondly – *of course* I was gay. At the time I still hadn't realised this, but it must have been so obvious: how could she ever have thought I was straight? The fact that the rest of the world could tell I was gay didn't help me, of course. I was furious. How dare she presume to tell me what I was? But at the same time I was sort of delighted that someone was helping me face up to the truth. Back in Paris I began to look at men and wonder if I was attracted to them. It all seemed so seedy – and that was to a boy shagging a woman in her mid-thirties in the flat of her dead friend.

One night after dinner in a restaurant with Alex and more of his friends giggling in French – *'Il est un pouf!'* – we got back to the flat and Esther took me to one side. Did I mind if after I went to bed she spent some time talking to Alex, because she felt he wanted to talk about Sarah? Of course I didn't. I said goodnight and headed off to bed with my diary. As I filled the pages with long descriptions of French trees and reflections on the Seine, I was aware that things in the flat had gone very quiet. The music had stopped. I could just about hear whispering. Then total silence. I lay there listening to the sound of my own breathing. Then some creaking floorboards and the clicking of light switches. A door closed. I couldn't quite believe what was happening. I'd agreed to Esther giving Alex a shoulder to cry on, not a vagina to stick it in. I felt in my own childish way that she had once again misjudged her response to a friend in mourning. Didn't she know it was possible to buy special sympathy cards?

My mind was racing. Lying in a bunk bed surrounded by pictures of Babar the elephant and a dead woman, I considered my options. My thoughts froze when it came to what

I should do, but the one thing I was certain of was that I didn't want to be here in the morning. No croissant could be buttery enough to tempt me to that particular breakfast *à trois*. So that was a sort of decision – I would leave. As quietly as I could I packed my things back into my summer-of-adventure backpack. Then I turned my thoughts to the note I was going to leave for Esther.

The fact that I made a duplicate copy of the note for my diary says quite a bit about my excruciatingly self-absorbed state of mind at the time. The note itself tells you everything you need to know about my relationship with Esther: a little bit of sexual frisson topped by catering portions of pretentious wordy nonsense. When I rooted it out and read it again after all these years for this book, I was appalled. My hand is itching to give myself the most enormous slap. I really hope I wasn't the person who wrote this note and that it was written by the version of me that went out with Esther. I'm probably wrong – I'm sure friends would say that I not only was but still am the kind of person who wrote this:

Dear Esther,

My leaving like this may seem a bit childish and hypocritical but let me explain . . . Actually I can't so let me say that all of this has been marvellous! Back to Paris, the twist in the plot, my cinematic departure, long may such silliness continue!

I'll write to you again but then I say that to everyone but I think to you I will. My leaving like this is quite unusual for me. I've wanted to do something a bit peppy like this for ages and never bothered. What a time to choose to start! What a way to start my French adventure! This should be a long epistle clarifying everything but you know me (better than myself, you know me) and how I couldn't clarify a steamed up window. I think I've said all I can. I don't know if the affair is on or off. I think I'll just put it on hold for a few months. When I ring again I think I'd prefer to get an engaged tone rather than 'number disconnected'.

From the boy you were/are/will be fond of –

Thanks for everything,

Graham (who lives as far away from Poland as Passion is from Graham)

- *Count the number of 'I thinks'*
- *Lots of exclamation marks*
- *This letter will infuriate you I know*
- *Say thank you to Alex. He's really a gem. Give him a kiss for me. He'd really be quite fanciable if it wasn't for those dreadful trousers he wears.*
- *Say thanks to Pierre and Christine aussi. They're both adorable.*
- *And now the experience starts. Do you think a tourist office will tell me where the gay quarter is?*

Nothing to add or subtract, though I could easily divide or multiply.

Graham.

Writing this letter out for the third time in my life I can sort of forgive myself a little. I was only nineteen, and it was three in the morning.

But where could I leave it to be sure Esther and Alex would find it? Only one place sprang to mind – the toilet bowl. I genuinely didn't think they would read any extra subliminal message into the location. Sweet boy. It really was just the one place where I was certain they would find it. I shut the door and headed off into the silent wet streets of Paris.

If this were a film, this is the point when I would get myself into all sorts of adventures with drug dealers and prostitutes, perhaps hook up with a travelling circus, but all I really remember was doing a lot of walking. I found a youth hostel and left my bag there. While having imaginary angry conversations in my head with Esther, I tramped the streets wondering what I should do. Obviously I needed a job. I wandered into shop after shop and wandered out again, unable to pluck up the courage to ask for one. I walked past the Pompidou and it struck me that I could busk. Odd, when I think back, that I never thought further as to what sort of busking I would do. I bought a long bolt of some material, and that was about as far as that plan got.

One evening around dusk a couple of days later, I was walking along the banks of the Seine when I suddenly looked up. There, high on a balcony over the far bank, were Esther, Alex, Pierre and Christine having a drink. I couldn't make out their faces clearly but I liked to imagine that they were having a good old laugh at my expense. The music swells, the camera pulls out to show Graham as a tiny dot in the vast teeming city of Paris. Cut to:

A bus heading from Paris to London. A friend called Julie from university was spending the summer there and I'd worked out that whatever chance I'd have of getting a job, it would be marginally higher in a country where I could speak the language.

I've now lived in London for nearly twenty years. It is still my number one favourite city in the world, so I'm slightly surprised at how disappointed I was by it that first time. After the scale and grandeur of Paris, there was something very domestic about London. All the legendary landmarks, Westminster Abbey, Trafalgar Square, Piccadilly Circus, they were all so . . . well, so small. Dublin had places that looked this good.

I tracked down my friend. She was living in a squat in West Norwood. If you haven't been to West Norwood, and I can think of no good reason why you would have been, it is one of those seemingly endless bits of south London with semi-detached houses and rows of shops like Radio Rentals and Clintons cards, and if you're really lucky a Greggs pie shop. It was exactly the same in 1982.

It turned out that the first thing Julie and her new English boyfriend Harry had done was discover that instead of getting a job, you could go on the dole – free money! This country left France in the dust. I immediately signed up for some. Sadly, somewhere along the line I must have told the wrong lie or, perhaps, cardinal sin, the truth, because I never got any dole money. Part of me felt like giving up and just heading back to Ireland, but because I was so sure that money would be shoved into my hands, I had spent all that was left of my summer savings, so I was, in effect, trapped in London. I would have to get a job.

This was at the height of the troubles in Northern Ireland and there had just been bombs in London, so it really was not a great time to be Irish and looking for work. Place after place turned me down. I don't know what possessed me, but I finally went into a restaurant called Rockwell's American Diner on the piazza in Covent Garden and announced in a strange accent that I was Canadian and my name was David Villapando. It worked, I got a job. I would start the next night. I never thought I would actually look forward to wearing a stripy apron and a paper hat.

The name was not pure invention. David Villapando was the name of one of the pen pals I had in school. While all the Malaysians and Germans had fallen by the wayside, I did still correspond with David. He lived in Whittier, California and, surprise, surprise, was struggling with his sexuality. What complicated matters slightly when I showed up at the restaurant for work was that nearly everybody who worked there seemed to be from Canada. Where was I from? Where did I go to school? Did I know Cindy Bloggynuts? This was going to be slightly harder than I'd thought. Being a consummate liar, I used the age-old technique of distracting people from one lie by admitting to another. I confessed I wasn't Canadian. I was in fact from Whittier, California but had to lie because I didn't have a work permit. My secret was safe with them, they assured me.

For the next six weeks I had the time of my life. With money in my pocket and an extended Canadian family, I went out drinking and clubbing every night. I bought bright orange clothes and had my hair cut in a 'Salon'. Truly this was my beautiful life. Sadly it was someone else's. I was going to have to go back to Ireland to start my second year.

On my last night in the restaurant I was put on washing-up duty. I couldn't have been more upset – washing-up was boring and you couldn't chat to anyone. My glorious summer and career shouldn't be ending like this. So it didn't. I didn't do any washing-up. I simply hid the dirty dishes and pots and pans all over the restaurant. Even as I did it I felt guilty for the poor sods who would come in the next day and find an old lasagne tray in the laundry basket, but this was my special night.

When I got back to Cork, it really was a case of 'How you gonna keep them down on the farm after they've seen Paree?' I was miserable. What had seemed glamorous, exciting and fun to me in the first year just a few months earlier was now, in comparison with my summer, dull and wretched.

The months dragged by and I did nothing to help myself. I moved into a rancid bedsit that was in the attic of what was essentially a derelict building in the centre of Cork. People would break in to have sex in the hall out of the rain. Once I came home to find a rat lying dead on the stairs about halfway up to my flat. If it had been on the ground floor it wouldn't have upset me so much but its early grave proved that rats were capable of climbing stairs. It was just a matter of time before I would wake up staring into the tiny beady eyes of one of its fitter relatives.

It was also in this flat where I started finding hundreds of flies – big heavy winter flies that seemed punch-drunk. I killed them systematically and then – and this is the slightly weird part – kept them in a small styrofoam tray on top of one of my stereo speakers . . . and I would count them every day. I can't remember the death toll, but it was well into triple figures by December. This was also the time in my life that I decided mirrors were bad. I didn't have one in the flat. If I needed to shave I used the reflective surface of the kettle.

I positively pursued loneliness. I stopped phoning people and practically dropped out of university. It's hard to describe my state of mind, but I remember being shocked and saddened when I had a small party in my flat and nobody came. A normal reaction, you might think, except that I hadn't actually invited anybody.

The moment when even I fully realised something was wrong came in a very unexpected place. I was struggling with my French. I had just scraped through into the honours programme in the first-year exams and it was now February and it looked like I was going to fail in spectacular fashion. One of the French professors called me to her office after a lecture one day. Madame Lafarge was a classic French academic, with a serious bob and large glasses that took up most of her pale face. When I went in she had one of my essays in front of her. Unless a red pen had exploded while she had been reading it, I was guessing I hadn't done very well. She started to go through the mistakes. I was listening to her drone on, watching her thin lips and wondering if she ever wore lipstick, when I got an odd feeling. I was going to cry. I was going to cry now, this very instant. I made to leave, to mutter something about feeling *malade*, but it was too late. I burst into tears. I never knew what that phrase meant until that moment. I was like a salty water balloon that had hit the ground from a great height. Bawling uncontrollably I sat back down.

Madame Lafarge looked suitably appalled and tried to reassure me that there weren't as many mistakes as it seemed and that they weren't very serious. I told her the one thing of which I was certain: 'It's not the essay.' I repeated this again and again through huge gasping sobs. Madame opened her handbag to find a tissue. She pulled out a large pile of paper napkins that even in my state of distress I recognised as ones she had stolen from the staff canteen. After I had rendered all those to a grief-filled pulp, she finally gave up the gold: a foil-wrapped moist towelette from Aer Lingus that looked like she had been hoarding it since 1965.

I finally managed to stop crying and I started to leave, thanking Madame Lafarge for her kindness. There was awkwardness in the air, the sort of tension you get between strangers who've had sex. I wondered if she knew about Esther.

I walked back towards the fly-filled hovel. Of course it was raining. Every hundred yards or so I would start to cry again. Off and on this torrent of tears continued for days. Perhaps if I behaved like this now it might be described as a minor breakdown or a bout of depression. Maybe I would seek professional help and take a pill or two to get over it, but at the time all I knew was that my life couldn't continue like this, and it was up to me to change it.

3

Hippy Replacement

EVERY SUMMER IRISH STUDENTS WERE given the opportunity to apply for J1 visas issued by the American government. This meant we were allowed to travel to the States with a temporary work permit. I applied, got it and then told my parents about my plan to go to America for the summer. Obviously they had received a highly edited version of my trip to Paris, but as far as they were concerned I had proved I was responsible. I could go to America, and they even lent me the money for my ticket. On top of that I had another two hundred pounds which, we budgeted with supreme optimism, would last me for at least four weeks while I looked for work. I know this was a long time ago, but even if it had been pre-Revolution America I doubt if that would have been enough.

My plan was that I would go with the other J1 students to New York and then I would travel by bus to California to see the man who had given me my happy alter ego, David Villapando. In the year of misery after Paris and London, David had taken on a strange importance in my life. When I couldn't talk to anyone because 'they wouldn't understand', for some reason I felt free to pen page after page of rambling soul-searching to David. In fairness I think he was pretty miserable and confused himself, and he used me in the same way. The plan to meet was hatched and, although unspoken, I think we both sort of thought we would fall in love and that would solve all our problems in one fell swoop.

My parents drove me to Dublin airport and waved me and all the other Irish students off as if we were a pack of Paddington Bears. We flew in a jumbo jet! Our excitement knew no bounds, but wait, yes it did – we had landed again in Shannon. We had been in the air for about half an hour when we were brought down to earth due to technical difficulties. The hours dragged by and the ground crew kept giving the passengers tokens to use at the buffet. Of course, this being Ireland all the tokens went straight behind the bar. When we finally took off I have never seen a drunker group of people sitting in rows. The air hostess abandoned her safety demonstration, presumably because she felt, quite rightly, that if anything happened to this plane these sodden idiots were all doomed.

Slightly hung-over but still wildly excited, we arrived at JFK. We were all huddled on to a bus which was to take us to the YMCA for our first night in America. Like children outside a toyshop at Christmas we pushed our faces against the windows of the bus. 'The cars! Will you look at the size of the cars.' When we came out of the mid-town tunnel into Manhattan, the driver announced over the microphone in a deep New York growl, 'Welcome to the Big Apple!' We cheered and clapped. Glittering skyscrapers, yellow taxis, Walk/Don't walk, it was everything we had dreamt it would be.

The next morning we were gathered in a big room and some nice man gave us a talk which might as well have been called 'How to not get killed in New York'. I listened intently and to this day follow his advice. Don't look up, walk next to the kerb not the buildings, and if you have to look at a map go into a store. Thank you and goodnight. He wished us a pleasant stay. We stepped out into the canyons of New York like Stepford Wives with backpacks, staring into the middle distance, walking in a straight line and expecting to be attacked by a gang of gun-wielding thugs at any moment.

I spent the day in New York, and then made my way to the Port Authority bus station for my journey to California. I knew that travelling across America by bus would take about four days and my unlimited rambler ticket lasted for seven, so my journey could be quite leisurely – at least that was the plan. Because I was heading off on an adventure I didn't want to organise a route or an itinerary. I would be spontaneous. Looking back, I realise now that a map would have been pretty useful. My guidebook didn't have one so I found myself planning a journey of thousands of miles using the little diagrammatic routes that the bus company had on their leaflets. I knew I was looking for ones that ran right to left across the page and not top to bottom. This slightly simplistic approach to orienteering meant that I ended up in places I never would have visited in other circumstances. I decided to take in a visit to Kansas City because my guide-book told me it had more fountains than Rome. I have never found out if the guidebook was joking or if I just hit a very dry part of town, but unless you count a tramp pissing I don't think I saw one public fountain. I do remember that it was hot, really hot – over 100°F, but for a boy from Bandon that might as well have been Centigrade. I went for a walk around the city streets that seemed to be deserted. The only things I remember were turning a corner and finding a gospel choir singing and sweating for a small crowd, and then on the way back to my flea-farm hotel a man stopped me and asked me if I wanted to go to the movies with him. 'It's air-conditioned,' he promised. I politely declined.

When I arrived in Salt Lake City, the place was *en fête*. A jazz festival combined with a celebration of foods from around the world was taking place. Sounded good, but the reality was a crowd of couples with prams listening to tune-less saxophones wailing slightly louder than the babies, and eating bowls of rice from planet bland.

I could tell my plan to get to LA was going wrong given that by late on day five I had yet to see a bus leaflet that had LA marked on it. Late on day six I saw one that said San Francisco. That was in California, and a woman who had given a guest lecture at college had given me some numbers there. The City of Angels would have to wait.

The bus pulled into San Francisco early on a crisp and cloudless Sunday morning. My first port of call was the youth hostel. Now that I know how far it is from the bus station I can't believe I walked all the way, but walk I did. I tramped off in what I hoped was the right direction. Suddenly, scream-ing split the air and from around a corner came a truck full of drag queens. I stood and stared as it disappeared as quickly as it had arrived. As I walked on I reflected that everything I had heard about this city must be true.

What I didn't know until later was that I had stumbled into the rainbow city on the very day of Gay Pride. After I found the youth hostel I went back into the city in time to see some of the parade. Lesbian grandmothers, Native American drag queens, Grace Jones singing on the back of a truck, it all rolled by. People were also handing out leaflets about something called AIDS. Looking back we were like those people in historical dramas who say things about a spot of bother in Germany and how it will all be over by Christmas.

My first priority was to find somewhere more permanent than the youth hostel to stay. I rang the numbers the visiting lecturer had given me. Most of them led to answerphones or people awkwardly stuttering their apologies and silently cursing the stupid bitch who had given me their number. I had one more number to call. What had seemed so simple – 'Just call any of these people. They'll be more than happy to help' – now seemed like a joke. Unless I stepped out of this phone booth dressed as Superman I couldn't see myself succeeding. Trying not to panic I dialled the last number and waited. A woman called Gail answered the phone. I calmly explained who I was and who had given me her number. She began to tell me why she couldn't help (yeah, yeah) but – What was that? Did she say 'But'? – but she did have a number for a place called Stardance. It was a hippy commune near the Haight-Ashbury district of town and they had a hostel room they rented out by the night. This didn't help me very much, but at least it was cheaper than the youth hostel.

After further phone calls I went to dinner at Stardance so that they could vet me. I felt like such a fraud as I sat cross-legged eating grilled tofu listening to the commune members tell me about their vision of utopian housing. I replied with a harrowing tale of Irish poverty and incredibly evil landlords. They lapped it up. I could have kissed the dead rat on the stairs. The next night I moved in for a week. I left over a year later.

The patriarch of the commune was Geoph. He was in his

late thirties, calm and kind of handsome in a boyish way. He had founded the house with Erica. Originally they had been a couple, but now no longer shared a bed. In fact Geoph tended to sleep in an odd loft that he had built in the ceiling of the hallway. This was so he never referred to any room as 'his' and also because with his hidden view of the comings and goings at the front door, he was always first with the gossip.

Erica was forty and not to be messed with. She was all for the concept of communal living, she just loathed living with actual people. She was back at college studying nursing and was raising her young daughter Mindy. At nine years old Mindy was oddly subversive. She attended a regular school and spent her time with normal middle-class children. It was Mindy who smuggled the plastic perfection of Barbie into the house, it was she who put Coca-Cola in the fridge. It was a bit like *Alien* with an enemy egg growing up on the inside of Stardance.

The other permanent residents were Obo and Jem Help and their three-year-old daughter Faith Shines Help. Obo and Jem had been in a group marriage but had eloped when she became pregnant. It was only after Faith was born and turned out to be black that Jem realised she had eloped with the wrong member of the group marriage.

Slowly over the year I became extraordinarily fond of these people. I quite liked the whole communal living thing. There was always someone to talk to, it was cheap and you shared all the dull household chores. Most of these I didn't mind. The one that I dreaded, though not as much as the rest of the housemates dreaded me doing it, was cooking. I had come from the great student tradition of Pot Noodle, and suddenly I was expected to prepare a vegetarian feast for around eleven people. What do vegetarians eat? Salad. Well, I knew how to make that, I'd seen my mother make it. You take a couple of leaves of lettuce, a quarter of a tomato, two slices of cucumber, egg and beetroot and then you pour salad cream all over it. If I had squatted on the table and carefully coiled my own turd in front of them, I don't think eleven vegetarians could have looked less impressed.

To make money I returned to the restaurant business. Down in the financial district was Vie de France, a brand new themed bakery/café/restaurant. I got a job working there as a lunchtime waiter. I began living a very schizophrenic existence. At home a vegetarian recycling utopian, and at work a camp, bleach-haired party boy.

This was also the time when I began to drink in earnest. Now, don't worry, this isn't going to turn into one of those stories of alcohol problems followed by reform. My only problem with drinking at the time was that I didn't have the stamina and I would end up vomiting quite often. One night I came home and as I lay on the floor of my room (even getting on to the bed seemed life-threatening) I had the wheelies. The room was spinning around and I knew it wouldn't stop until I satisfied its lust for vomit. I obliged, and then I didn't move – I just lay there in my own mess. Finally I came to some time during the night, took off my clothes and went to bed. In the morning as I sat eating my Cheerios (God, how the young can bounce back!) everyone who came into the room looked at me in a slightly quizzical way and asked me if I was all right. Weird. I was fine. However, the mystery was solved when I went to brush my teeth and looked in a mirror. I had dried vomit all down one side of my face where I had smeared it taking my jumper off in the middle of the night.

On St Patrick's Day a film crew was in the bar we were in near Vie de France. The people I was with brought the camera over because I was Irish. They asked me how I was planning to celebrate the saint's day. Full of lager and confidence I replied, 'I'm going to drink and drink and then go home and get sick!' Well, I learnt a valuable lesson about programme making. When it was broadcast on the news it turned out the piece wasn't about St Patrick's Day, it was about new tougher drink-driving legislation and by the time they had edited my comments into the piece I looked like some sort of crazed killer. Thankfully, I don't vomit any more.

The year I spent in San Francisco was by far the most formative in my life. I was already twenty years old, but in rural Irish years that made me a sort of international four-teen. Yes, I had travelled a bit already, but somehow I'd always had an invisible umbilical cord to home. Here on the west coast of America I was unconnected to anyone or anything. I suppose that is why it was quite easy for me to live my strange double life. I wasn't being untrue to myself, I was simply inventing new versions of 'me' and keeping the parts that felt comfortable. To this day I'm a borderline alcoholic that recycles his bottles.

Being somewhere where nobody knows you and there isn't anyone to judge you means that all normal constraints on your behaviour are removed. I know the following story did happen to me, but I have no idea why.

Given that my only sexual experiences up to this point were a fumble in a French tent and a short-lived affair with a woman nearly twice my age, it seemed a teeny-weeny bit sexually ambitious of me to apply for a job as a rent boy, but that is what I did. I saw the ad in some free newspaper, called the number and was given a rendezvous. I was to go to an apartment for an interview after my lunch shift the next day. Perhaps I thought it would be a sort of *Reader's Digest* course in sexuality, so that I could make up for all my lost time growing up in Ireland, perhaps I wanted the money, perhaps I just wanted people to want me and in my clumsy, emotionally stunted way I thought this was how I could make that happen. Perhaps I just wanted to have sex with a man. I didn't tell a soul what I was planning to do, but if I had and they'd asked me why, I'm pretty sure that even back then I couldn't have told them.

The next day I left work as normal in my black trousers and white shirt. However, even I knew that really wasn't a great look for a hustler, so I went into the toilets of a McDonald's on Market Street and changed into some 'casual' clothes. I can't imagine what I had in my wardrobe that I thought fitted into hooker wear, but, the makeover complete, I headed to the address I'd been given. It turned out to be an enormous apartment complex, almost like an hotel. Numb with fear I went in, got in the elevator and headed up. When the elevator doors opened I was in a very long, dimly lit corridor with what seemed like dozens of identical dark wooden doors. I was hyperaware of everything: the sound of my shoes on the carpet, the dull reflections of the lights on the fake wood panelling, the drums in my head telling me that this was a big, a really big, mistake. I knew I could stop, turn around and take the elevator back to the bright sunny street – no one would have thought any less of me, no one knew I was here – and yet I kept walking towards the door. I promised myself that I wouldn't have sex or take off my clothes.

I paused, and then watched my hand knock on the door. Several centuries went by and then I heard a voice. Footsteps and then the door was opened. The man was in his late forties, I would guess, with grey hair. The hair on his body was also grey. I could tell this because he was only wearing a pair of wet shorts. He apologised, he'd been in the pool. Come in, sit down, would you like a drink? No? OK, what's your name? We chatted. He was English and seemed charming. No mention was made of why I was there. This might have been a job interview for anything, it could have been a tutorial, I could have been in a waiting room.

He stood up. Would I like to come into the other room? I followed. The other room was a large bedroom with a wall of mirrors at the far end. I noticed that both pillows had been slept on. For some reason I found that disgusting. He asked me to take off my clothes and told me he'd be back in a minute. I stood there and like some stooge in a hypnotist's show slowly unbuttoned my clothes. I left them in a small pile on the floor and stood there naked. The situation was spiralling way out of control. I had promised myself that this wouldn't happen and yet it had and I was the one making it happen.

The English man came back in. He looked me up and down.

'Turn around.'

I turned around.

'Now, treat me like you'd treat one of your clients.'

I walked over to him and put my hands on his hips and kissed him. I pulled down his wet shorts. He had a hard-on.

This was as far as I'd ever gotten with a man. I hesitated. In that moment the English man lifted me up and carried me to the bed. The sudden appalling reality of being naked on a bed with some older man who had a raging hard-on finally jolted me back to my senses. Like some convent schoolgirl lying in a field after the village dance, I looked up at him and asked, 'Are you going to go all the way?'

Without missing a beat he said, 'Well, if you apply for a job as a secretary, you're expected to write a letter.'

It was such a slick prepared line that I thought of all the other boys he had said it to, all the other boys he had had sex with.

'Hey, if you'd like to stop, we can.'

Another line, but this one was the brake I'd been looking for. It was like a verbal version of those little red boxes that say, 'In case of emergency break glass.' I broke it.

'Yes! Yes, I would like to stop!'

As I got dressed I felt fantastic. At the time I thought I felt great because I had said 'No' to this man and was somehow empowered. I think the more likely truth is that it was because I had got away with doing such an incredibly stupid, risky thing. I did not deserve to be leaving this apartment not screaming and crying, but that says everything about what is brilliant and terrible about being twenty. As I left, the English man was washing his hands. You could almost hear the cry of 'Next!' hanging in the air.

When I got back to Stardance there was a letter waiting from my mother. Seeing the small blue sheets of Basildon Bond paper with the familiar writing was strangely reassuring – I hadn't abandoned all normality, it was still going on and there if I needed it. My mother was concerned because she had received phone calls from someone called David Villapando who was very worried about me! I had forgotten all about him because I no longer needed him and I suppose I thought he would somehow be feeling the same.

Of course he wasn't. I phoned his number and waited for him to pick up the phone. It was odd because despite our lengthy correspondence I had never heard his voice.

'Hi, Graham! I'm so glad you called.'

I nearly blurted out 'Eugh!' David Villapando was a queen! His voice was a stereotypical high-pitched whine and suddenly all the letters meant nothing. I recoiled and immediately just wanted to get off the phone. I know this sounds awful, but in my defence it was all to do with how I was feeling about myself at that moment. Of course I'm sure I sounded exactly the same on my end of the phone, but I didn't know, or want to know, that.

Promising to come and see him, I hung up, determined that I would do no such thing. I felt tainted by just speaking to him. I ignored his future letters and calls and soon they stopped. As I've got older and come to terms with being a big sissy queen myself, I have felt very guilty about David and on several occasions have tried to track him down, but Internet searches and phone books have never turned him up. I'd just like to apologise for being such a dick. As this story unfolds I think you'll find that I have very few regrets in my life, but the way I treated David Villapando is one of them.

Life settled down into a routine of work and communal living. Of all my housemates I was becoming very close to Obo Help. When I was cooking he'd come and chat to me and sometimes play his guitar, singing lilting ballads about the Revolution. One night he asked me if I wanted to go and see a movie. Sure. I remember we went to see Woody Allen's *Zelig*. The cinema was packed and we ended up sitting in the front row. I remember it was a warm night and Obo took off his sweater and just sat there in his undershirt. I was sort of proud to have this 'proper' man as a friend, just as I had been of Jerry.

Because it was such a beautiful night we decided to walk home after the film. We talked about this and that, about people from the house, people from his past. Then, as we were coming down the hill towards Stardance, he asked me if he could ask me a question. Well, I knew what was coming next. I'd heard that tone of voice before: he was going to ask me if I was gay. I said, 'Of course you can,' and geared myself up to give my standard reply about how I wasn't sure and I thought people fell in love with people not gender and all the other crap that I hear young guys not ready to come to terms with their gayness still spout now. He paused and said, 'Would you like to spend the night with me?'

If he had literally taken a large wet fish out of his pocket and hit me around the face with it I couldn't have been more surprised. He had missed out all the conventional stages. This was the first time that someone had not asked any questions but simply presumed I was gay. Just then a car full of lads drove by and out the window one of them shouted 'Faggot!' God, the heterosexual bush telegraph was effective. I was only just finding out the news myself, and already they knew. I asked Obo about Jem and how she would feel, but he explained that they had an open relationship and it would be fine. I was unsure. I found Obo sexy but I didn't want things to be weird in the house, and besides this was a big step. We went inside the front door. I told him I'd think about it and we kissed. Somewhere high above us God and Geoph were watching.

Unlike my brush with prostitution, this was an experience I discussed with everyone and anyone who would listen. At the Vie de France I think there were probably customers I told about my quandary in between listing the *soupe du jour* and our vegetarian special. Obviously most people didn't care, but one woman at work I was very close to called Elizabeth took it all very seriously. She thought I would be making a big mistake – she thought Obo was too old, there were all the messy complications of the other relationships in the house, and besides, maybe I should give heterosexual sex another chance, she said. In theory I agreed. I wouldn't have minded sleeping with more women, but frankly they weren't asking, and as for me approaching them, the situation could be summed up by one of those novelty badges I'd just bought that said, 'So many women, so little nerve'.

I argued that Obo was a good choice because I did fancy him but felt fairly confident that I wouldn't fall in love with him, and on top of that he was older so he'd know what he was doing. I decided that Obo was the one for me. It makes me laugh that I thought I was in control or was listening to anyone else's advice. Obo had shone his light on me and I was thrilled and blinded by it.

We chose an evening and went out for a date. I climbed into Obo's VW van, which I worked out was the same age as me. The other slightly worrying bit of maths I did was to work out that the age gap between me and Obo was greater than the age gap between me and his toddler daughter. Oh well! I remember we went to a couple of gay bars. I can't imagine what the rest of the clientele made of us – some bright-eyed and bushy-tailed kid dancing with a shaggy ageing hippy. Maybe it was San Francisco, maybe it was Obo, maybe it was being with a man, but despite everything I didn't feel as awkward or embarrassed as I had done with Esther.

That night I slept with Obo. He had tidied up his room specially and lit candles. He was so sweet to me and, of course, breaking the very first promise I had made to myself, I began to fall in love with him. There was one major stumbling block here and that was that, although I didn't understand it, I was really just a statistic to Obo. Political attitudes being what they were in the house, no one was allowed to object or show they cared, but Obo slept with practically everyone who moved into the house. Shortly after we had slept together a girl called Mary moved in with her son Jasper. One night I walked into the kitchen when Mary was cooking and what do you know? There was Obo and his guitar. Mary was admiring his fingering and I felt like the biggest fool on earth. Due to my lack of a vagina I was slowly moved to the back of the sleeping rota until I finally faced facts and took myself off it.

The thing is, I don't think Obo was ever gay or indeed even bisexual. He had grown up in a wealthy East-Coast school and attended an Ivy League university, but somehow it had all ended and now he was a mechanic with one failed group marriage behind him. He told me later that he had spent some time in therapy and that at one point the therapist had latched on to the idea that Obo was in love with his best friend from college and even made him phone him to tell him. I'm guessing that the guy really was a good friend, because the two are still close to this day.

At the time, though, I was upset. People in the house were very kind and concerned about me. They recognised that I was young, this was not my world, and while it meant almost nothing to Obo this was obviously a big deal for me. Of course the odd thing was that it didn't make my sexual preferences any clearer for me. Yes, I had now had sex with a man, but I didn't feel any different. I know now that that is the great lesson to be learnt – you don't. What should be about who you are sleeping with isn't necessarily so. Most of what defines being gay, whether we like it or not, is lifestyle – it is the bars we go to, the clothes we wear, the people we hang out with. All I knew was that I had enjoyed sex with Obo, but I was still a long way off understanding why men wore leather and hung around the Eagle.

Meanwhile, life went on. One day while we were in the middle of a busy lunchtime at Vie de France, I suddenly felt very peculiar. I turned to the rest of the people in the little service area between the kitchen and the dining room and was about to say something, but everyone else had reacted at exactly the same time. The floor was moving! An intense woman called Patty Paris who was training to be a biological illustrator behaved as if she had been reading some 'what to do' manual every day since her first birthday. She threw her arms up and pushed her whole body against the shelves of glassware to prevent them from falling. 'Earthquake!' she cried. The rest of us looked at her for a beat and then all screamed 'Earthquake!' and ran out into the restaurant.

All the customers were standing and silent, and then, defying all logic, a large rippling wave went through the wooden floor. Ignoring every bit of Patty's advice to stay where we were we ran out into the street and looked up to see the tops of the buildings swaying like trees by the side of the road. Just as the excitement was beginning to turn into the genuine fear that this wasn't just a severe tremor, it stopped. The city shuddered back to its old self and we went back inside. Everyone was talking at once, and no one was really that interested in what the specials of the day were for the rest of the afternoon. In the service area, there was Patty still holding up the shelves waiting for the all-clear. We peeled her away and told her about the amazing buckling floor and how we had seen the buildings move. She gasped in horror, 'What about falling glass?' As it turned out, despite being the worst tremor the city had experienced for over twenty years there was only one casualty. A guy skateboarding down a hill had been thrown off course and had skated straight into a wall. Hard to feel that sorry for him really.

San Francisco has an odd way of making you feel like it is the centre of the universe, and I can remember how shocked I was, when I phoned my mother to reassure her that I wasn't dead, to discover that our earth-moving experience hadn't even made it on to the news there. Back at work when I told my new best friend Elizabeth about our global snub, she too gasped in disbelief. It must have been especially hard for her to understand because her family were firmly entrenched in the 'old money' part of the city. They were involved with the opera and ballet, and if what went on in San Francisco didn't matter then their lives were meaningless.

Perhaps it was because of my experience with Obo that I was so drawn to this woman who inhabited such a different world from Stardance. Blonde and beautiful in that waspish

American way, Elizabeth lived with her grandparents in a huge house near the Presidio, an area that was effortlessly tasteful – the sort of place that families in TV movies live in until someone kills the babysitter.

Elizabeth, too, was effortlessly tasteful. Although only in her early twenties, she had strict rules for life. At nineteen, a young woman should choose a hairstyle that would serve her for life – she had opted for a short bob. One should never order a drink that had a name – the one exception being a Bloody Mary. These are just the ones I remember, but there were many more. I don't want to give the wrong impression about her because she was also very bright and funny and fiercely independent. She had been doing a degree in English at Berkeley for what seemed to me a very long time and supporting herself by doing various restaurant jobs.

I can't quite explain what happened with Elizabeth. What began as simple meetings as friends – a picnic in the park, an art house movie, coffee and cake in some trendy café – slowly became dates. I think some of it stemmed from the stupid badge I had bought that had the slogan about too little nerve. Elizabeth seemed to see it as some sort of challenge, a way of me asking her to make the first move, and so late one night I found myself standing outside her house kissing her. I'm sure a few curtains twitched, but they only saw a nice young white couple making out before the gentleman headed home. Given that this was San Francisco, it is extraordinary that no one looked out of their window and saw the reality of the situation: a young gay man in denial clinging to the deluded desires of a love-hungry girl.

It seems incredible to me now that not only did I have a relationship with this woman, but also that it lasted for a little over a year. The Esther affair can be explained or understood because I'd loved the drama of it all, and although it hadn't involved hairy chests and cocks at least it had had the frisson of forbidden love attached to it. This was entirely different. A young woman my own age, a perfectly pleasant, pretty woman going out with me – me! If the gay world gave out prizes I was in with a very good shot of getting 'Most promising newcomer'. For me I suppose it was my last-chance dance with acceptability and a simple straightforward life with the Sunday papers, corduroy trousers and a dog.

More than that, though, I did love her. Of course we should have just remained very close friends, but my cock was not the brightest beast on the block and, as I've discovered many times since, it sometimes finds it hard to get a grasp on the concept of friendship when it can stick itself into people. The real question is what was going through Elizabeth's head? Why did she do this? Well, as my friend Carrie Fisher explains when people ask her why she didn't spot that she had married a gay man, we were having sex, lots of sex.

I don't spend a great deal of time thinking or talking about my straight experiences, but if people find out about them they always want to know about the difference in the sex – is it better with men, can a woman give a blow job, that sort of thing. This is just one aging homosexual's opinion, but I really don't think there is much of a difference.

I once knew a friend of a friend called Jackie. Jackie lived in Canada and was a transvestite, and while I'm sure he didn't consider himself a hooker there did seem to be a fairly direct link between dollars and sperm in his life. Jackie had wanted to have a full sex change for years, and saved all the money he could until finally the day arrived when he could afford it. My friend received a phone call late at night. He groggily answered the phone to hear an hysterical Jackie at the other end of the line screaming from his hospital bed that he couldn't go through with it, he was too scared, etc. etc. All very moving I'm sure, but sadly his emotional tug of war isn't that relevant to the point of the story.

These second-thought cries from the heart began to happen about once every couple of months for a year. Jackie wanted to be a woman, but he wasn't man enough to go through with it. Finally, silence. Word reached us that Jackie had bitten the bullet and let go of the smoking gun. Jackie was a woman. She was thrilled. Finally the time came for her to earn an honest dollar and try out her new womanhood. She chose a handsome Canadian trucker to do the honours. Like a burly version of our own lovely Queen launching a new cruise ship, he splashed his salty champagne down her new slipway. She lay there flushed with her own sense of achievement. The trucker, however, just lay there, breathing hard, but not being very forthcoming with the reviews. Jackie could bear it no longer – this was the moment her whole life had been leading up to. How had it been for him? Well, the story goes that the trucker rolled on to his side, looked at her with a mixture of puzzlement and impatience, and in a deep Canadian monotone replied, 'A hole's a hole.'

Now I don't mean to be as crass as our trucker friend, but I sort of know what he means. You can't really compare straight and gay sex because sex is simply about mechanics, what feels good, what doesn't. Sexuality, however, is all about emotional responses. In truth, vaginal sex is probably physically better than gay sex, but for me sleeping with men is about their strength, the feel of their body, the stubble of their kiss. I do realise that I'm slightly pissing on years of research done by very clever men and women in white coats, but as far as I'm concerned, the difference between being straight or gay is as simple as whether you prefer dogs to cats, or coffee over tea. There is no better or worse, no right or wrong, and if there is a why, who cares?

End of lecture. Back to Elizabeth.

My memories of the time I spent with her are like one of those long montages you see at the end of a weepy romantic movie just before the heroine finally loses her battle with some mysterious disease that prevents her heart from working properly, but leaves her just enough energy to constantly reapply make-up. We walked all over the city hand in hand, went to the movies, battled the wind on the beach, laughed as her scarf blew high across the trees. Mostly we talked, and talked, and talked. It felt good to be in the heterosexual gang. Maybe we would get a dog.

About eight years ago I saw Elizabeth again. She was in London with her boyfriend (whose wife, interestingly enough, had left him for a woman) and we went out for dinner as some sort of weird masochistic demonstration of how all right we were with our past. I'm not sure what I think my relationship with Elizabeth is now, but that night she treated me like an ex-boyfriend, which of course I am, but it still took me by surprise. When her current boyfriend slipped away to the toilet, she looked at me and, almost to underline the awkward silence his departure had left, said, 'You know, you were the only one who ever talked enough for me.' This, of course, was true because I had been her best friend in lover's clothing.

I was having a great time with Elizabeth, but at the end of my year in San Francisco, I felt it was time to go home. I'd given up on university and had failed to get a degree, and there was nothing concrete to go back to, but it was something I felt I had to do. The hippies all piled into Obo's old blue van to see me off, and we posed for pictures in the airport. On the plane during take-off I stared out of the window at San Francisco and started crying. I could see the green flag of Golden Gate park, and from there I could work out exactly where Stardance was. So small and getting smaller. The tidy elderly lady next to me asked why I was going home. I answered that I was going home for my parents – they were worried about me being away for so long, etc. – but then I remembered that my teacher and friend Niall MacMonagle had given me some very harsh but sound advice years before: 'Never do anything just for your parents; after they're dead you are still going to have to live your life.'

So why was I really going home? I knew that the year I had spent in San Francisco had marked some sort of beginning in my life. The slightly frayed jumble of hippies had taught me so much. I had finally learnt what my mother had meant on a good luck card for my exams when she had written, 'You can only do your best, but do it!' There is no shame in failure; the only shame is in not making the attempt. These are all obvious platitudes, the sorts of things you can read in any third-rate self-help book, but to be twenty-one and fearless is a very powerful combination. I decided then and there that I would head back to London, I would go to drama school, and then I would become a respected member of the acting fraternity – actually, fuck that, I would be a star!

4

Acting Out

LONDON IN NOVEMBER 1984 WAS really not very different from what it is now. As a city it doesn't really grow, it moves in circles. The trendy neighbourhoods may change, but there are always trendy neighbourhoods. When I arrived, the place to be was just north of Covent Garden. It was called Neal Street and it was a Mecca for the cool kids. The restored cobbles would be teeming with screaming girls from the suburbs desperate for a glimpse of Bros., whose management had offices there. Horny teenage boys soon caught on to this and started hanging around dressed up as the boys from the band in the hope that a lazy groupie might think to herself, 'A tribute band in the hand is worth two nowhere near the bush.' Today it is an odd area where you can only buy fashionable trainers or kites. Mmm.

When I arrived in London I headed back to my old friends Julie and Harry. They had now moved into a squat in Camberwell that was struggling to become part of a housing association. The house was wedged up against the railway line, and sitting in the bath you were almost able to read the headlines of a commuter's *Evening Standard* as the trains rumbled by. The vibrations gave the water a sort of low-tech jacuzzi effect. The lack of privacy was compounded by the lack of a door or indeed a wall on the other side of the room.

Similarly the stairs just seemed to hang from the wall with no visible means of support. Mattresses of mysterious origin were the only recognisable pieces of furniture, though I was assured that a large wooden electricity cable spool in the kitchen was a table.

I lay on my mattress that first afternoon looking through old copies of *City Limits*, a sort of politically correct version of *Time Out*, and two weeks in a row I noticed an ad in the gay section for a restaurant called Smiths on Neal Street. Now, I was still supposed to be going out with Elizabeth at this stage, even though she was still in San Francisco, but for some reason that idea of making money out of my sexuality had lingered on in my mind (never mind that I didn't know what my sexuality was). I made my way to Smiths and discovered it was a large basement restaurant, all tastefully decorated in white and red with a huge collection of art on the walls, exactly the sort of place, I thought, that two rich old queens might start up. I asked about the job and was told to sit and wait for the manager. An obviously gay man came up to me and introduced himself as Mike Belben. He clearly liked me and the job was mine. I would start as a busboy the next day.

While the job was real, everything else turned out to be all in my imagination. It was just a weird coincidence that the ad had appeared in the gay section. The restaurant was in fact owned by Christina Smith, an imposing woman who had made a small fortune speculating in property in the seventies and who was now trying her hand at catering. Mike Belben was one of the most heterosexual men I had ever come across and was just being friendly.

I was soon to discover that Mike wasn't hard to work for,

he was *impossible* to work for, but, mysteriously, for every employee who thought he was an unreasonable fanatic there were ten who despite themselves adored him and would have defended him to the death. I was with the ten. Over the years he has been incredibly loyal and supportive towards me, and besides having become a great friend himself has, by some very fine hiring of staff, provided me with several of my best friends in the world.

Mike staffs restaurants as if he is casting a play. When I started at Smiths, there was David Eyre, now a very successful chef and restaurateur in his own right, who told us stories of his childhood in Africa. I listened with the blinking incomprehension of a dog. All I could hear was 'posh, posh, posh, posh, posh'. Phineas and Orlando Campbell were young eccentrics in training, and Eileen McGowan was a red-haired bolt of Scottish energy. Soon after, Helen Smith arrived, breezing in like a breath of fresh air from Salisbury, full of headscarves and tales of her recent stay in New York. All blonde hair and huge blue eyes that nearly exploded at the mention of champagne, she was my sort of replacement Elizabeth, except that this time my penis respected the boundaries, and as a result we are still very close. A girl called Nicola Reeder also worked there. Nicola hails, rains and shines from Leeds. She is without doubt the funniest person I know and has a heart the size of one of those freak vegetables that get seen at country fairs. Again, twenty years later we are as close as ever.

However, the one who really rocked my world was a gay man called Syd. That was the way he spelt it. He was part of a group of Canadians all working in various restaurants around the city, and for some reason, especially given that

Canada's chief export now seems to be dullness, they all seemed extraordinarily cool – in fact they were the ones who knew Jackie, the man who would be Queen.

Syd was many things, but what he was, mostly, was beautiful. He had a smile that defied you not to fall in love with him, and eyes and a walk that made you blush, they were so sexual. All thoughts of Elizabeth – and indeed women in general – flew out of my head. I developed the most enormous crush on him and would spend most of my time analysing every word and glance he addressed to me. In my heart I knew I didn't stand a chance, but in that desperate way of the unrequited lover, I secretly enjoyed my love-spurned role. I became consumed by my feelings for him, and I remember one late night walking drunk all the way from Covent Garden across Waterloo Bridge and on through the concrete plains of South London to Camberwell shouting nonsense into the streets full of nothing but wind. What were my feelings? Did I love Syd? Why couldn't life be simple? For what seemed like hours I trudged southwards, wailing and flailing. Of course it was raining.

Desperate, I went to a tarot reader around the corner from work. Perhaps the cards could tell me what I should do about my feelings for Syd. I walked into the small room at the back of the shop full of crystals and books that had unicorns on every cover, and found a very pedestrian-looking woman – less mystic gypsy, more Countryside Alliance. I resolved that I would tell her nothing specific about my problem, I would simply listen impartially to what the cards had to say. I sat down, she said 'Hello', and when I opened my mouth, instead of a similar greeting out came a tidal wave of emotional sewage. I told her everything, things I hadn't told anybody. 'Sometimes he cuts enough bread for my tables as well.' 'He hangs around the cash desk when I'm doing my bills . . . sometimes.' My sensible footwear soothsayer made a half-hearted show of shuffling a couple of cards and then went straight into counsellor mode. 'You must tell him how you feel, or you'll never find out how he feels.' As advice went, it was simple and sound. Putting it into practice, however, was a whole different ball game.

Sometimes Syd and I travelled on the same night bus home. He lived in Peckham a couple of stops beyond where I got off in Camberwell. We would sit upstairs to get away from the people who were so drunk they couldn't manage to climb steps. The charming Adonis in his perfect uniform of baggy Levis and white T-shirt sitting next to me, the small grey potato with sprouting hair on my head and espadrilles on my feet. My mind was racing. I had to say something. This was it. Of course I knew the answer, of course I didn't really need to ask, but in some weird twist of logic it is always the hopeless that dare to hope.

My initial pick-up line isn't quite as bad as it sounds.

'Would you like to be my cousin?'

A couple of nights earlier Syd had picked up a man who had been eating in the restaurant, and when Helen had asked him why they were leaving together, Syd had told her that his companion was his cousin from Canada. She had believed him, and to be someone's cousin had become our new favourite expression. However, Syd, presumably desperate for me not to have meant what he thought I meant, looked at me and just said, 'What?'

The agony continued. I braced myself and went for the direct unprotected approach, devoid of cutesy armour.

'Would you like to spend the night with me?'

As embarrassed as I was at the time, I can only begin to imagine how mortified Syd must have felt. He looked at me. Judging from the expression in his beautiful eyes, I might as well have asked him to hold my vomit for a moment while I nipped to the loo.

'I don't think that's a very good idea.'

A pause to assess just how humiliated I felt. 'Right.'

For a couple of stops I attempted to recreate an attitude I'd heard of called 'nonchalant'. Finally it was my turn to get off. I turned to Syd, dear, kind, sweet, beautiful Syd who had not done one thing to encourage me or bring about this festival of shame, and said, 'Goodnight, sleep well,' and then clattered down the stairs past a thicket of drunken limbs and out into the wasteland of minicabs and kebab shops. By now I was crying again, and I think you can guess what the weather was doing.

Now that I am forty-one, I like to think that one of the few perks of being older is that I have learnt how to deal with the demands of my heart and cock a little better, but the sad, laughable fact is I haven't. I don't believe anybody does. We learn to be frightened of love and the terrible havoc it can inflict on our lives, while our hearts take such pleasure in mocking our brains. 'Yes, that's right, that is the way you should behave, that would be the sensible course of action, but watch now as I make you do something so reckless and self-destructive, it will take you several years to re-establish even a basic form of self-esteem.'

Weirdly, however, the tarot reader had been right, because although the bus journey to hell via Camberwell had been awful beyond belief, it did jolt me back to reality. The air was cleared. I could get on with my life, and Syd and I could get on and become the friends we were meant to be.

I was beginning to come to terms with London and myself. Life seemed good. I was making friends and money, and I had the time to focus on the reason I had come to the city in the first place: drama school.

I applied to East 15, LAMDA, RADA and Central. I prepared my Shakespeare pieces and my modern, reciting as I polished cutlery in Smiths or waited for the bus. Hamlet was a particular favourite, 'How all occasions do inform against me . . .'

I can't have been completely useless because I got recalls wherever I went, which are a big deal when you are on the drama school audition circuit. East 15 were the first to reject me, which did set my confidence back a little since they were the least prestigious of the schools I had applied to. In a way, though, I was rather relieved because they had a very serious, worthy reputation. If you were playing the role of an Eskimo, you'd have to go and spend the afternoon squashed between the cheddar slices and the fruits of the forest yoghurts in your fridge – that sort of thing.

LAMDA felt very grand when I went to the recall. A long panel of God knows who sat behind a trestle table. I did my monologues, and when I finished there was a long silence. Sometimes after a dramatic piece that can be a good sign, the air emotionally charged, the panel welling up with tears. Or it can be, as it was in this case, the panel thinking,'Sweet Jesus in heaven, what are we going to say to this poor fuck?' A lady at the end broke the silence. 'Do you think your Shakespeare went better at the first audition?' I had no idea, but I thought I'd better err on the side of caution. 'Yes, yes, I think it probably did.' The thin lady removed her glasses and studied me for a moment. 'Pity.' I didn't get accepted to LAMDA.

RADA was the big one, the one everyone wanted to go to. My first audition was fantastic. The second audition was brilliant. Now I only had the one-day workshop to get through. RADA was mine. This was where I was meant to go.

The night before the workshop I went out for one drink with Syd. The next day would be the beginning of the rest of my life, so surely I deserved a quick glass of wine. We perched ourselves at the bar in the front of another restaurant in Covent Garden and began ordering cocktails. I don't want to bog you down with all the details, not least because I can't remember any of them, but I'm fairly certain we ended up being asked to leave and never return. The next thing I can remember is waking up on the floor of a friend's flat in West London. I felt like something that would normally be found under a pile of piss-soaked newspapers in a documentary about animal cruelty. I peered at my watch and very slowly worked out that I was late for the rest of my life.

Now, I still maintain that they should have accepted me at RADA. OK, so on the day it may not have seemed obvious why they would have wanted a sweaty, greenish-grey lump in trousers that smelled of smoke and a few late-night chips to join their elite troupe but on the other hand they never knew just how awful I really felt all day, and believe me, not letting on required a great deal of acting on my part.

RADA rejected me, and I knew it was my own fault.

The Central School of Speech and Drama was my last hope. I stopped drinking for a month and polished up my audition pieces. Now, what they do rather cleverly at Central is that they give people so many recalls that even if you never wanted to attend the school, by the end of the process you would feed your Granny into a wood-chipper in order to get a place. Rumours abound about the audition process. There is one story about a poor woman who was doing a speech by Glenda the Good Witch for her modern piece, who was so bad that they kept giving her recalls so that other members of staff could get a chance to see her. As you read this she is probably icing a cake, telling her children about how close she got to attending a top drama school. Some jokes are too cruel.

My own auditions at Central were fairly uneventful – it was just that there were so many of them. In the end I was recalled to be on a waiting list. I could almost feel the leg warmers, I was so close. At the end of the day I was called into a room, and George Hall, the principal of the school, broke the news: I wouldn't be going to Central. Did he say 'would not'? I couldn't believe it. This was not my wonderful life. It was the set speech from *Measure for Measure* made real: 'To whom should I complain?'

I had told myself when I got back from America that I would only follow my dream to be an actor until I hit a full stop. Of course life is never that straightforward. There is always doubt, there are always choices. Being turned down by every major drama school should have given me a clear sign to give up, but stupidly the people auditioning me had encouraged me enough to make me want to try again. I retied the strings on my waiter's apron and resolved to give it another go, ignoring my mother's adage, 'If at first you don't succeed, you mustn't be very good.'

*

Since coming to London I had been more or less celibate. Elizabeth had made a brief visit early on, but by now she was dating a Persian prince back in California. I don't think I was all that devastated by the news because when she broke it to me all I can remember saying is 'I think you mean Iranian'.

I had never really discussed my sexuality at the restaurant, but one by one all the people who worked there just assumed I was gay. By the end of a year, although I hadn't slept with anyone, I was de facto a homosexual. My first brief affair was with a friend of Syd's from Vancouver. His name was Philip, and to save on lengthy physical description, let's just say he was a tall queen. I think what seduced me was how flattering and attentive he was to me. He took me out to dinner, to the movies; he treated me like a boyfriend. Amongst the Canadians he was a figure of fun, and I think Syd setting me up with him was really his revenge for the night bus of shame, but I remember Philip as being sweet – a big, queeny fool, but a sweet one.

One night we went for dinner in the sort of restaurant I wasn't used to somewhere in Fulham. We drank wine and I ordered a goat's cheese salad. They apologised, there was no goat's cheese but they could do it with Brie. 'That'll be fine'. What arrived was an entire Brie – I don't even remember it being sliced – sitting on top of a large leaf of lettuce. I ate it.

More wine, liqueur coffees and I was very drunk and a bit queasy. We walked back to Philip's expensive bedsit at the World's End bit of the King's Road. Along the way I managed to lose his favourite cashmere scarf that he had lent me, and then, just to make the evening complete, when we were just starting to have sex I vomited all over him and his tiny apartment. I lay there groaning while Philip washed down the walls and took care of me.

The next weekend, leaving some party north of Baker Street, the situation was reversed. Philip was legless and falling over in the snow. Did I return the sweet care and affection that I had received? No way! I tramped through the snow towards the main road, listening to my designer scarecrow crashing around behind me. I was simply furious with him. I resolved to get in the first cab that came along Baker Street, and if Philip hadn't caught up with me, tough luck. It began to dawn on me that this wasn't love.

Back at Smiths a new Australian waiter had started work. Blond and handsome in a sort of forties movie-star kind of way, Ashley immediately caused speculation amongst the rest of us. Helen was very impressed. 'Look at the way he pours champagne.' I didn't really know what that meant, but at the time I knew it was a good thing.

Falling in love with Ashley was the easiest thing in the world. We just clicked. Laughing, flirting, it felt like this could be the big one. Syd was a mad crush, Philip was a fling, Ashley was going to be the love of my life! The only obstacle in my way was that I had no idea how to make a move. The direct bus route was not an option, so all I could do was make myself available. Like some slutty gazelle hanging around the water hole faking a limp and hoping that a lion would eat him, I put myself in Ashley's way as much as possible. Now I have a television show to lure prospective suitors with, but then I had nothing. My one claim to coolness was that I had moved in to a houseboat – a small, freezing, floating hut – but it provided me with a plausible invitation. 'Would you like to see the houseboat?' He said he would. The gazelle was smothering ketchup all over himself.

The tension was palpable – the accidental brushing of hands against legs, the laughing at every little joke, the no mention of leaving. It was exciting, but it was going on for ever. Any sort of gay God would have just screamed through the clouds, 'Get on with it,' but it seemed we were as bad as each other, both terrified of rejection, refusing to read the 'sure thing' signs stuck on our foreheads. What a long, seemingly pointless evening – chatting on the deck, drinking wine in the kitchen, wandering out on the deck again because it was warmer outside than in, and finally venturing into the bedroom 'to look at some photos'.

We talked some more. It is odd, but even after all these years, first date conversations between gay men, a bit like Nana Mouskouri's taste in eyewear, are always the same. There is always a first sexual experience story, then an optional 'Have you ever had sex with a woman' segment, followed by the mandatory 'Do your parents know?' section. We had covered all of these when finally Ashley could bear it no more.

'What would happen if I kissed you?'

A brave start, but a rather awkward question. Was I actually supposed to tell him? He might as well have asked me 'What are you into?' or 'What's your favourite drug?' The lion was about to strike. I didn't want to be covered in cling film and popped back in the fridge for later, and yet all I could think of saying was, 'I don't know'.

Would the lion phone a taxi? No – he was hungrier than that.

'Well then, is it a good idea?'

This was more like it. This was a question I could answer. 'Yes,' I said as clearly as I could with a mouth full of another boy's tongue.

The next morning we walked up to the King's Road from the river to get some breakfast. I was so full of the love drug that I didn't notice where we were walking. Just too late I realised where we were – opposite Philip's apartment. I looked up and in an awful, impossible coincidence my eyes met Philip's looking from behind his curtains. Silly, camp Philip looked like a puppy that had been kicked by its owner. The message was cruel but clear. I was no longer going out with him and all he was left with was a faint smell of sick and a space on his shelf where his favourite scarf had been.

I was in love for the first time in my life. Romance had blossomed and taken over the entire garden. I hope not everyone falls in love the way I do, because for me it is close to a state of madness. Like some sort of chemical imbalance, the smallest thing can set it off: a smile, a haircut, the way he orders a drink – that's what I fall in love with, and then, like an emotional tarpaulin, I'll stretch that one thing I love to cover over all the things that I don't like or that don't fit. Finally, after a while, that tarpaulin of love starts to rip and all the things that were there all along are revealed and I realise that I'm going out with an arsehole who has nice hair. In Ashley's case, however, the tarpaulin never got a chance to wear out, he pulled it off himself.

Initially we couldn't have been happier. We worked together and pretty soon we lived together. The flat was in a great neighbourhood and nicely decorated, and there were always loads of people around. Australians come from a country with unlimited space, but for some reason when they travel abroad they are happy to live like cotton-wool balls packed into a plastic bag. The flat Ashley and I shared had one bedroom, but in the year and a half we lived in it there were never fewer than five people calling it home. What this cost us in terms of privacy was more than made up for in the spice it added to our sex life, and the fact that there was always something in the fridge to eat. By and large our other flatmates tended to be wine-guzzling Australian women who worked in offices and were in love with Ashley. He ruled the roost and declared the living room as our domain. Like plebeian royalty we sat up in our battered sofabed eating party-size packs of mini sausage rolls and watching daytime telly before dashing off to work.

I totally embraced the idea of being in a couple, and friends were put on a back burner while I got busy spending lots of 'we' time. I would have been quite happy for us just to sit around playing with each other's hair, but Ashley was determined to see a bit of Europe, so a holiday plan was hatched. We would go to Turkey.

We flew into Turkey's third largest city, Izmir, thus carefully avoiding Istanbul, the only place I had ever heard of or had any desire to see. Never mind. The first night we headed out for a meal and then back to the hotel where after sex we fell into separate single beds and I slept right through the night. In the morning Ashley didn't look great. It turned out he had spent most of the night on the toilet with an upset stomach. We wondered what might have caused it because we had eaten exactly the same thing. I tried to make the right cooing noises, but really I just felt very smug.

Ashley got us into some sort of shared taxi thing and we

This is a screen grab from a home movie of me as a baby.

Big girl, age 15.

This picture was taken the day we started building Esther's patio.

Me, age 19, with my landscaping friend, Jerry.

That bohemian set from Cork University, 1982.

Me with some very dodgy hair outside Vie de France in San Francisco, 1983.

The outside of Stardance.

Elizabeth and me on
our way to Alcatraz.
No, really.

Serving someone
in Smiths.

Syd and me.

Ashley and me on holiday in Turkey in 1986
– can you smell something?

Nicola and me at Helen's wedding.
Why am I dressed like a jockey?

My desk in
Cockroach
Towers.

Portrait of the artist on the eighteenth floor.

Stephan trying to speak English at Melange.

Mother Teresa coaching a member of the cast of the nativity play.

My retro shoebox flat near Columbia Road.

Scott and our convoy.

The large hole in the middle of America.

headed off to the bus station to catch a ride to Effes to see its famous Roman ruins. Whatever. As the taxi rolled and shuddered around dusty corners I became aware of a slight rumble in my stomach. Oh-oh. By the time we got to the bus station, the Vesuvius of my ass was in danger of turning the inside of the taxi into a poo Pompeii. I ran from the car and found the public toilet. Although I couldn't read the Turkish signs it wasn't that hard to find, since my nose knew what it was looking for and a helpful swarm of flies were flapping their shit-covered wings and buzzing encouragement about the place. I didn't care. I squatted over the hole in the ground and my insides promptly fell out.

I stumbled from the scene of the grime and found Ashley. By this time he was fully recovered and hurrying me to get on the bus for Effes. We were the only tourists on it, and since we were the only English speakers I'm not sure how we knew this, but the route was non-stop and took about three hours. I put on my Walkman and Ashley got out a book. The engine started and the doors closed with a hissing noise. Literally the moment the bus started to move and there was no escape my ass went into spasms. It seemed my insides had not all been left behind – there was lots still in there and it wanted out. I clutched the seat in front and broke into a cold sweat. I battled each new wave of spasms like some woman not wanting to give birth to her sticky brown baby. I kept saying to Ashley, 'I'm in bits, I'm in bits.'

'Hang on, just hang on,' he said.

Well, I did hang on for what must have been at least a couple of hours until finally it wore me down. A spasm too far and suddenly the battle was over. I sat very still, feeling so much better but horrified by what had just happened.

Like a dog sitting by a steaming sin, I looked at Ashley and said simply, 'I couldn't hold it.'

'Don't move and hopefully no one will smell it, and when the bus stops we'll just get off as quickly as we can.'

A good plan.

The bus continued on its merry way with upbeat Turkish music blaring from the radio. Ashley and I were poised like Olympic athletes ready to fly off the starting blocks the minute the doors opened. Finally the bus began to slow down. We clutched our bags. It stopped, the doors opened and we sprang up. As one, the rest of the bus started waving at us to sit down – this was not our stop. It seemed that the non-stop bit wasn't entirely true. Appalled, we slowly sat back down.

'Shit,' Ashley said.

Quite. I looked down at the lino-covered aisle where I had just been standing, and there, like a tiny piece of melted chocolate, was a drop of my poo. As I raised my head, my eyes met those of the man across from me who was also looking up from the floor. He stared at me as if I had just tried to clean his ear with my cock.

At Effes, the whole bus told us that now was the time to leave and we took them at their word and fled. Under Ashley's instruction I leant against a wall to hide a rather unattractive dark brown map of South America that had appeared on my trousers. He went to find us somewhere to stay. I hung my head in shame and felt very far from home and holidays both. Some man came up to me and in broken English tried to sell me a day trip to where the Virgin Mary had either been born or died, I can't remember. The force of my 'no' frightened us both.

Acting Out

Ashley wasn't just a waiter, he was also a fully trained nurse, and once we got into our hotel room he went into full care mode. He showered me and put me to bed, he washed my clothes, he nursed me. I lay there wondering why, if love was blind, it couldn't have lost its sense of smell as well.

The rest of the holiday went by without a hitch. In week two the travelling stopped and we stayed in a small village on the south coast. I had worried that two men travelling together might raise a few Turkish eyebrows, but no one seemed to care or suspect a thing. One night, though, as we ate our dinner, an oiled and groomed moustache appeared above our table. He noticed that we were eating lobster; in fact he seemed fascinated by the idea of us eating it. We tried to chat back and laugh at what he was saying.

'After lobster, later you will have to astable.'

'Sorry?'

'Later you will have to musible.'

'No, we don't understand.'

'Have to marsibo.'

'No.'

By now he was becoming quite heated and was clearly annoyed by our poor grasp of English.

'Matuba!' He was getting louder.

We shook our heads. The other people in the restaurant were begining to look over. It was at this point that he almost exploded with frustration, and as he did a very graphic mime we suddenly heard very clearly 'Masturbate! Masturbate!' It turned out he was the local pimp trying to interest us in his ladies after the seafood aphrodisiac effect had kicked in. We giggled nervously as every other customer stared at us and our strange wanking friend. Finally he got the message and sloped off into the night. Of course the irony was that he was quite right – we did nothing but 'mastuba' for hours when we got back to the hotel.

Returning from holiday I took a deep breath and entered the drama school fray once more. This time it was all a bit of an anticlimax. I went to Central, did my speeches and was then asked into George Hall's office once more.

'I'm very pleased to say that you have a place at Central next year.'

'Oh.'

After all the trying and dreaming, I had expected this moment to be accompanied by fireworks and an Oscar ceremony intensity, but instead I felt a bit flat. I thanked him and got the tube back to Covent Garden and went to work. I told Ashley, Helen and Mike, and they were so excited they started to tell customers. Even they seemed more pleased than me. I felt like I was listening to my favourite record underwater.

5

The Deepest Cut

THIS WAS MY BEAUTIFUL LIFE. I was going to go to one of the top drama schools in Britain, and I was living with a man I loved. It almost felt uncomfortable. I was so unused to things going my way that I just assumed that this couldn't last. I was right. Well, as a pessimist once said, 'a pessimist is never disappointed'.

Shortly after I got accepted by Central, I was hanging around the Australian dorm we called home, heating up more sausage rolls, when Ashley casually mentioned something about booking his ticket home. Now, I knew that when we had met he was only staying in England temporarily, but I had somehow assumed that meeting me had changed his plans. Home is where the heart is, and surely that was in London with me. For some reason at moments of emotional shock I tend not to cry but instead to get very angry, and this was no exception. I turned into a windmill of tea towels as I stormed around the flat. 'Do I mean nothing to you? Don't you think you should have discussed this rather than just present it as a done deal?' As far as I was concerned, he was a selfish bastard and I was a heaving, bosomed heroine wronged by her man.

I stomped out of the flat and went to the Oval in South London where I was taking part in some awful fringe play about the Irish in Britain. Ashley couldn't come because he was on nursing duty through the night for a rich old lady in order to earn some extra money – presumably to help pay for his airfare.

After the play the cast went across the road to the pub, and I got talking to a very cute man who was a friend of one of the other actors. As closing time approached, one by one everyone started to say their goodnights. Finally there was only me and Cute Guy left. I remember looking around, wondering who he was waiting for, and then the impossible dawned on me – I was the one he was after. This was the biggest sexual compliment I had ever been paid. Thank God I was still in a foul mood with Ashley so that I could somehow morally justify this bit of adultery. 'Well, if he doesn't care about me, etc.'

Cute Guy took me back to his flat. We got into a big wooden bed which for some reason he felt he needed to tell me had belonged to his now dead Granny. As we rolled around I became aware that something very unusual was going on. For I think the only time in my life, my cock seemed to be talking to my heart, and between them they had decided that cheating on Ashley was not the thing to do – I could not get a hard-on. What a great night; what else could go wrong? What indeed . . . After he managed to come, Cute Guy burst into tears because I was the first person he had been with since his boyfriend had left him. I lay there with a limp cock and a stranger sobbing on the pillow next to me and thought about Ashley and the dead Granny who had owned this wooden nest of sadness. Adultery hadn't been like this on *Dallas*.

I went back to Ashley the next day and we discussed the situation. Ashley's plan to go home would go ahead, but now it was slightly modified. I would follow him during my long summer holiday from drama school, and then Ashley would return to London and we would set up home together properly without the lost tribe of New South Wales sharing with us. Things returned to normal.

Finally the day dawned when I would start at the Central School of Speech and Drama. Ashley gave me a packed lunch and waved me on my way. After all the anticipation, it was a strangely underwhelming moment when I actually saw the other twenty-five people I was going to spend the next three years with. I'd spent hours wondering who my contemporaries were going to be, and suddenly this was it. I had two shocks. The first was that someone I knew from Cork was in my year, Dan Mullane who I had met through the drama society at university in which I'd dabbled. I thought this was wildly unfair. Central was supposed to be my new beginning where I could reinvent myself. Dan and I looked at each other and I'm sure he felt exactly the same. The other shock was that the vast majority of the boys were straight. Only four of us fitted into the theatrical stereotype.

We sat in the tiny coffee shop making small talk and looking at hundreds of fading 8 × 10 photographs of ex-students. Although we all pretended to care about the craft of acting, it was obvious that all any of us really wanted was to be famous, so it was slightly worrying that we only recognised about four of the students. The only person who seemed to know all their names was Betty, the tea lady who served behind the counter. It seems deeply ironic that sweet, unassuming Betty is now more famous than most of the school's past pupils.

Once I got into the rhythm of going to school every day

and working a couple of nights a week at Smiths, I loved it. There is no doubt about it, drama school is the most self-indulgent thing in the world. Each morning I'd wake up and wonder what I would be doing that day and then remember, 'Oh yes, thinking about myself.'

Ashley left on a Sunday night. We had a big gathering of our friends at lunchtime and then Ashley and I headed out to Heathrow. Airports are so deceptive. On the surface they are just vast, impersonal concourses full of shiny floors and bland art, but they are in fact enormous emotional hotpots. Everyone who walks into an airport is in some sort of heightened emotional state. The terror of flying, the excitement of a holiday, the sadness of leaving, there seems to be an amnesty for dressing and behaving like the cast of *One Flew Over the Cuckoo's Nest*. I don't think Ashley actually laughed, but he couldn't disguise how thrilled he was to be going home. I did well in the 'keeping it together' department until the very moment when I waved him through the departure gates and turned to leave. I walked through Heathrow bawling like a baby who has just realised that its favourite toy has fallen out of the pram. The tears lasted off and on for most of the tube ride home.

Of course most people would have dragged themselves to work the next day and stared numbly at a computer screen for eight hours, but I was going to drama school. We were doing a poetry performance showcase that morning, and with my freshly acquired grief I knew I was going to be marvellous. I practically skipped down the road. Sure enough, about three lines into Auden's 'Stop All the Clocks' (long before Simon Callow's funeral in *Four Weddings*), I was in tears. Every cloud . . .

The Deepest Cut

By now I was twenty-four and one of the older people in my year. The other students my age seemed to have spent their whole lives in education, and so I found myself feeling very worldly and, because of my restaurant job, relatively rich. I had to keep reminding myself that I wasn't happy and that I was living my life in mourning for Ashley, who had morphed in my memory into the first Antipodean saint.

I was now renting a huge room in a flat in Swiss Cottage with two women who had put up a card on the school noticeboard. It became clear that one of the women, Ann, was very much in charge. She had lived in the flat for years and we all abided by her slightly eccentric rules. She was deeply committed to healthy living and was a strict vegetarian. She religiously used her water filter jug, in fact she used it so much that she had never had a chance to wash it. The grimy, scum-covered plastic jug sat on a shelf, and the other lodger Helen and I would walk past it pulling faces of horror. When my mother came to visit, she took one look at it and summed it up perfectly: 'A water filter? A fish couldn't live in that.' Also Ann had a budgie that lived in the living room. I don't know what sort of Herculean bird this was, but it seemed to be capable of throwing food and shit nine or ten feet across the room so that the room was less like a lounge and more like an enormous birdcage. It wasn't ideal. Added to that was Ann's very long red hair, strands of which turned up all over the flat. It's hard to describe the full horror of stepping into a bathroom that looks like it was last used by a pony with a hair-loss problem.

Soon it was time for me to visit Ashley in Australia. Now, I do like Australia. It is a very nice place; however, I don't think anyone could argue that it is nice enough to warrant the journey. If Australia was where France is I'd go all the time, but it seems perverse to put yourself through airplane hell for days simply to arrive somewhere that is really just America, but with most of the population missing. Most places one visits take on the quality of the centre of the earth simply because you are there. In Australia it is very different. It feels like the edge of the earth, and even Australians who have never lived anywhere else seem to know that they are living very far from the action. Of course none of this mattered to me at the time; I was going to be reunited with the love of my life.

Ashley had promised that by the time I got there he would have moved out of his parents' house. When I arrived I found that he had been true to his word. He had moved out of their house – into the garage. Oh, he'd done it up with long drapes of material and nice pieces of furniture that he had been keeping in storage, but no amount of interior design could save me from the embarrassment of having his father walking in on us lying in bed while he looked for a hammer or an elusive drill bit. I wasn't out to my parents, but Ashley couldn't have been more out to his. He seemed to think that the only way for his parents to prove that they accepted his life and truly loved him was to have them sitting at the bottom of the bed while we had sex in it.

Obviously honesty is a good thing in any relationship, but sometimes it strikes me that coming out to your parents can be quite a selfish thing to do. Kids and their sex lives are never going to be welcome topics of conversation for parents. I remember when, a couple of years after my sister was married, she announced that she was pregnant: we were delighted for her, but there was also a feeling of embarrassment lingering in the air because we now knew for sure that she was no longer a virgin. As for my sexuality, I felt that Ashley sobbing in front of my visiting parents as he watched Audrey Hepburn in *Roman Holiday* and gasping, 'Her dress . . . her dress is so beautiful,' was as close to coming out as I wanted to get.

Ashley's parents, Mr and Mrs Eccles, were very sweet and couldn't have made me feel more at home. True, I was on a major charm offensive, and made sure to help with chores, drink 'stubbies' with the father and compliment the mother profusely on her signature dish, 'curried sausage casserole'. By the time I left Mr Eccles was patting me on the back and saying that it was like having another son. You can imagine how annoying Ashley found that.

Although we had a few arguments ('The fucking garage!!') for the most part we lived well in each other's pockets. His friends liked me and I was surprised by how much I liked them. I will mention Jenny McCarthy, just because I know she will read this and be very upset not to find her name anywhere. Overall I headed back to London believing that I would spend the rest of my life with Ashley. Had there been gay marriage at the time, I would have been popping the vol-au-vents in the oven and arranging bits of old net curtain on my head, as I had in my former life as a toddler transvestite.

The next few months were spent trying to find a one-bedroom flat for us to share when Ashley got back. Finally I found one a bit further away from Central, over in Queen's Park. Now I just needed to pay for it. Mike Belben, my catering mentor, had moved to a small restaurant around the corner from Smiths called Melange. It was incredibly busy, and the waiters got to keep their own tips. I said farewell to the ordered calm of Smiths and stepped into the lucrative madness that was Melange. Anyone who ate there would not have forgotten it in a hurry. It was owned by a Dutchman named Freddy who had only ever worked in one other restaurant. He had been fired from that job after one night. This might have given some people an indication that catering was perhaps not the job for them, but Freddy took this initial discouragement as some sort of challenge and opened his own place.

Melange was unique in so many ways. The interior looked like a designer had lost a bet. Holes that had been knocked in walls during a drink-induced fit of DIY enthusiasm sat gathering dust, islands of mosaics glistened hopefully, bits of scaffolding held up the bar and most of the stairs. An estate agent might have described it as looking distressed. The food was equally eccentric, but for the most part delicious. David Eyre had quit Smiths as well and had discovered somewhere along the way that he was a great chef. The customers piled in and the small band of waiters ran up and down stairs with trays and attitude. Melange became my extended dysfunctional family.

My life was back on track – Central was going well, I had settled into a group of friends, I was earning more money and I had found my love nest. That was when a letter arrived from Ashley. It lay on the mat in its innocuous airmail envelope. My heart leapt when I saw it and I couldn't wait until I got to school to read it. I ripped it open as I walked up the hill to Finchley Road. 'This is the hardest letter I've ever had to write.' I slowed down. That didn't sound good. My eyes dashed across the words, desperate not to believe what this letter was, scrabbling to find something positive I could cling to like a drowning man reaching out for a stray plank of wood. 'I can't love anyone until I learn to love myself . . . Please try to understand.' I felt myself slip under the water.

Because of the time difference I had to wait all day before I could call him. As the day dragged on, my shock and grief turned to anger. The selfish little shit! Fuck the relationship, I had signed a lease on a flat that I couldn't possible afford all by myself. The phrase 'learn to love myself' kept popping back into my head. Well, it's going to be hard to learn to love someone who behaves like a snake in the ass! That first day I didn't tell anyone else what had happened because I felt like such an idiot. There I was, all kitted out in my wedding outfit but it turned out it was dress-down Friday.

When we finally spoke I pleaded my case. 'This isn't fair. You've got to at least do it to my face, give us one more chance.' He in turn rambled on about some self-help group that he had been going to. Later Ashley sent me a copy of the book that explained the philosophy behind it. I flicked through its crisp pages that were full of platitudes and strange declarations like 'we don't choose our parents'. So what? That may or may not be true, but what is also true and far more important is that it doesn't alter the fact that these two people are your parents and you'd better just deal with it. A long chapter on jealousy could have been edited down by any provincial junior reporter to read: 'Don't be.' Ashley had written on the inside cover 'I hope this helps you understand'. All it helped me understand was that my lovely, funny, handsome boyfriend had been turned into a howling loon by some group that was claiming to help him.

After a couple of days I managed to tell some friends, and

they were as confused as I was, just not as humiliated. It's one thing if your boyfriend leaves you for someone else, but Ashley was declaring to the world that he would prefer to be with nobody rather than be with me. I kept calling and pleading and even got friends to call. I don't think I ever admitted it at the time, but I can see now that my aching heart was gradually overshadowed by a real sense of panic about how I was going to pay the Queen's Park rent. Eventually Ashley agreed he would return and give me one more chance.

When he got back, the first thing he gave me was crabs. It seemed he had been learning to love a few more people than himself. I leafed through his bible but failed to see a chapter entitled 'Be a big lice-ridden slut'. Ashley was gone; this creature that had returned from Australia was an unbearable, sanctimonious bore. The love nest began to look like a hamster lived in it as piles of tiny pieces of paper started to appear everywhere. These were Ashley's affirmations. Obviously I read them to see if they said anything about me. Mostly they were things like 'I deserve to be rich' or 'I deserve to live in a flat with a shower'. I longed to tell him what I thought he deserved.

His madness was catching, and I found myself behaving in a really erratic way. He told me he had a date with a man he had met in the shop of the English National Opera. When Ashley wasn't home by midnight I sat on the floor ringing central London hotels describing him. When that drew no results I started phoning major European Opera Houses trying to find out if anyone who worked there was visiting London. This is why love scares the shit out of me. No matter how many days are spent having picnics and laughing over brandies, this awful day always arrives. Like a dirty ball of farmer's twine, love tightens its grip around your heart until you end up sobbing on the floor of a tiny flat in North London, hardly able to breathe because your happiness has simply wandered off holding the hand of a stranger.

The couple of months I spent with Ashley at that time were by far the worst of my life. Love had turned into cruel hatred and pettiness. If he said something about the noise of a neighbour mowing a lawn, I would argue that it was a chainsaw cutting wood until one of us had to end up screaming and running out of the flat. I hated him for throwing away our old life, and he hated me because I wouldn't let him get on with his new one.

Isn't it surprising that whenever you think things can't get worse, something comes along to point out the obvious – they can.

I went to a party at Central at the end of the summer term. It was a Friday night and warm. We stood around in the small garden of the school, drinking and shrieking as drama students are prone to do. By the time I left it was late and I was tired. I had just about enough money for a taxi, but I decided that I wanted some Kentucky fried chicken more, and besides, I was in no rush to get home to Ashley fast asleep under his snow-white duvet of spiritual superiority.

I trudged up Finchley Road, got my chicken and chips and munched away as I walked through a deserted Kilburn and on towards Queen's Park. I was just walking along the north side of the park when I became aware of a boy walking quickly in the shadows on the other side of the road. He overtook me. Then, almost running, he doubled back on himself and headed towards me. This wasn't good. I turned to flee in the opposite direction, only to bump into another guy who had been walking behind me. I was trapped. Like in a horror film when the inevitable happens, I cried out a thin, 'No. No, please don't.' Then they were hitting me over my head. I heard a strange echoing noise and assumed they were using some sort of plastic pipe. It was only later that I worked out that it was the sound of wood against the bone of my skull. They told me to give them my wallet. I did. They told me to lie on the ground. I did. They emptied my small rucksack. I noticed my chequebook fall to the ground along with the couple of credit cards I had in my wallet. They took only my cash, which was about six pounds fifty. I almost wished I had more to give them, and felt bad that I had thrown away so much on the chicken and chips. Their work seemed to be done. I was told to keep lying there face down for five minutes. I nodded my agreement as vigorously as I could with my head pressed against the ground. I heard their footsteps clattering down the road as they ran off into the night.

Silence. I lay there breathing heavily and thought about Ashley. He was going to be unbearable because I knew he would tell me that on some level I had attracted this attack, that I had wanted it to happen, or needed it, or some such pointless shit. I had been mugged. Couldn't I just be a victim, please? Then I noticed I had a cut on my wrist. They must have had a knife that I hadn't seen. Fuck, Ashley would go into full Angel of Mercy mode. This was going to be awful. I felt a slight chill go through me and thought I had better gather my stuff and get home, which was just around the corner. As I got up off the cold pavement I was aware that I was peeling myself off the ground. Odd. I looked down. My chest was covered in blood. My blood. I was bleeding profusely. I pulled back my T-shirt and there, almost in the centre of my chest, was a small, dark, wet hole. I had been stabbed. I started to gather up my books and bag, but I had to lie down. I was suddenly tired, very tired. I lay my head upon the rucksack and breathed in the familiar smells of books and pencils, only now mingled with the warm stickiness of my blood. I knew that all I really wanted to do was lie there, but a tiny glimmer of panic managed to force me into standing up again. I tried to pick my bag up once more, but the books just slipped from my hands. I wasn't in control. Even my cries for help felt like small wet towels falling out of my mouth.

I managed to drag myself up to a house that had a light in the window and rang the bell. I leant against the door, whimpering. Nothing. With a huge effort I began to stumble down the street shouting 'Help' over and over again, because that was what I urgently needed. A door opened and an elderly man stood there staring. I walked down the short path towards him. I lifted my blood soaked top and pointed at the hole and explained helpfully, 'I've been stabbed.' I was like one of those characters in Shakespeare who declare, 'I've been run through!' I'd always thought they said it for the audience because there were no bloody special effects in those days, but, no, you say something like that because you are so surprised to find a hole in yourself.

Without waiting to be asked I lay down on his doorstep. He said he'd phone the police. His wife arrived in a bright cloud of dressing gown and stared down at the bloody mess.

The bloody mess looked up at her and without thinking asked, 'Can you hold my hand, please?' For a moment I thought she hadn't understood, but then, slightly awkwardly, she reached her cool, calm hand out to me. I held on to her hand like a baby grabs hold of a finger. It was pure instinct – I didn't want to die alone.

From then on, I started to drift in and out of consciousness. I had always imagined that if I found myself in a situation like this I would 'fight for my life', but of course when you are bleeding to death, as I was, your very life force is seeping out of you and it's very difficult to fight. You're tired, you want to sleep, you want to let go and drift away. Somewhere there were sirens. A man's voice floated above me. 'We better wait for the ambulance. There'll be hell to pay if he dies in the back of the van.' I was a bit light-headed by then and I thought to myself without a care in the world, 'Oh, this must be quite serious.' Then I was in an ambulance and a man was saying, 'All right, son, we're just going to take your strides off.' In my cosy fog I can remember translating 'strides' into 'trousers' and feeling rather clever.

Then a lady was standing at the end of a trolley. We were in a room now. She was holding a thin tube. 'This is a catheter and I'm just going to insert it into your penis.' In a slow flash I was seven or eight years old and pouring salad cream on warm boiled beetroot. My Aunt Hannah was explaining a procedure they had performed on my Uncle Cecil in hospital. I remember at the time thinking that whatever it was that having that cured I didn't care, I'd prefer to die. Now, all these years later, they were about to do it to me and I couldn't do a thing to stop them. I couldn't do a thing.

Bright sunlight woke me, streaming in through tall windows the next morning. Fans turned slowly on the ceiling. This might have been the St Charles hospital somewhere in the tropics. I didn't feel like moving much, but I could see that I was attached to a bag of blood and some other tubes were coming out of my side and of course there was the Uncle Cecil special coming out of my cock. I had to ring Mike to tell him I would probably be late for my shift in Melange that night. Just then a nurse approached and asked me if I wanted to phone anyone. I gave her Mike's number. She looked at me as if we were talking at cross purposes.

'Would you like us to call your parents?' she asked.

I processed this question. If they phoned them they would panic and get on a plane and come to London. What a waste of money if I was going to be all right. I looked up at the nurse and asked what I thought was a perfectly reasonable, straightforward question.

'Am I going to die?'

The nurse did something before she replied that I really don't think was great in terms of bedside manner. She hesitated, and then almost stumbled over the word 'No'.

Oh my God, I might die. This is serious; I may not get to Central on Monday to be in our second-year showing of *A Winter's Tale*.

Another nurse came up.

'Someone called Ashley rang,' she said.

I gave a weak smile. Ashley knew and cared.

'He said he'll be in to see you later, he's busy today,' she continued.

Of course he was busy. Today was the day of his self-help group seminar. What could be more important than that?

Your lover lying with less than half of his blood left inside him in a hospital bed maybe? What blood did remain was boiling.

Mike Belben and my friend Helen from Smiths had started dating, so they turned up together. Rather helpfully, Helen walked in, looked at me and burst into tears. In her defence this turned out to be a fairly common visitor reaction. I obviously didn't look great.

I slept as people stood around whispering. At six o'clock, handsome Ashley walked in and lit up the room. I hated myself, but I was thrilled to see him. He sat by my bed and, fighting back the tears, explained to me in as much detail as he could what I should have known he would say all along – that this was about him. It was about him collapsing in the hallway when the police came to bring him the news in the middle of the night. It was about him standing up at his fucking self-help conference and telling them all about what had happened and asking them to focus their healing energy on me. I can only imagine the expression on my face, and still he asked me with the wide-eyed glee of the truly deluded, 'Did you feel anything?' I had lost half my blood and all of my boyfriend.

I didn't make it to Melange or Central. I lay in that ward for two and a half weeks as they drained blood off my lungs. Visiting me was pretty much on the timetable of every drama student in my year. Large groups with leggings and scarves gathered by my bed and made a note of how they were feeling at that moment so that they could remember the emotions later when they got a part in *Casualty*. Other people came too, policemen, ladies with forms explaining how I could get counselling, others with forms explaining how I could get compensation. For the first few days the people I really wanted to visit me were world leaders. As I lay there I felt like I knew the answer to everything – world peace, hunger, history. I was like Solomon with a tube coming out of my cock. Sadly, this feeling faded quite fast and I went back to wondering if we'd get cream or custard with our pudding.

When I finally got out I was back in the flat with Ashley, but not for long. We had given notice, accepting that we and the flat were over. I was moving to Brixton to live in a room in a house, and Ashley was going to Hawaii on borrowed money for a conference on immortality. By now I found it hard to look at him without spitting. Immortality? I wanted to shake him. 'Save yourself some money, you fuckwit – you are going to die, but hopefully not before you pay the money back to the stupid bitch who lent it to you!'

For some reason Ashley wanted us to remain friends. To stop his mindless rambling, I promised we would be. As he headed off to the airport for Hawaii, he made a great show of hugging me and crying. Dry-eyed I patted his back and thought to myself, 'You'll have to live for a fuck of a long time before I'll ever want to see you again.' He shut the door and I didn't see him for fourteen years and when I did it was the sort of meeting you fantasise about having with an ex. I had lost weight and gained money and fame. All the things that normally embarrass or annoy me like fawning waiters or kids banging on the restaurant windows to attract my attention gave me a truly deep satisfaction. I'm not proud of the feeling, but I cannot deny the pleasure it gave me.

6

The Feeble
Has Landed

I WASN'T ALLOWED TO WORK, and Central had broken up for the summer break. I wasn't good at simply hanging around, so I decided to take full advantage of my new single status and post-stabbing skinniness. I booked a flight to Athens and decided I'd head to Mykonos, which was at that time the only gay haven I could think of apart from San Francisco.

Unfortunately, I hadn't booked my accommodation, nor had I realised it was a state holiday. I ended up having to do the unthinkable: camp. I didn't have a sleeping bag let alone a tent, but I didn't have a choice either, and so as the moon shone down and a gritty wind blew across the island, I was to be found lying on a towel, wearing most of the clothes that I had brought with me and a sweater wrapped around my head.

During the day I would leave my bag with my passport and traveller's cheques sitting in an unlocked zip-up holdall on the campsite. Perhaps it was a sort of post-stabbing fatalistic attitude to life, but remarkably that bag sat there for the next five nights untouched. Sadly, so did I. Bronzed, beautiful gay guys from all over the world roamed the island oblivious to the very needy boy with a fresh scar on his chest. Apart from ordering drinks or meals, I did not speak to one other person for five consecutive days. Looking back this seems extraordinary for me, but I must have been much more emotionally bruised by the mugging and by Ashley's behaviour than I had realised.

On the last day a Canadian jewellery designer spoke to me on the beach. As he approached me I actually did that thing of looking behind me to see who he was walking towards. Would I like to meet him for a drink later? We chatted a little. He was quite sweet and we talked easily, although I was a bit on the defensive. He walked me back to the entrance to the campsite and asked me if I'd like to have dinner with him. I shrugged my shoulders and said, 'Well, I've got to eat.'

He looked a little taken aback. I thought an apology explaining that this was the first time I'd spoken to someone in a week wouldn't help.

I still don't know why I didn't sleep with the jewellery man. I ended up bunking up with him in his hotel in town, we rubbed copious amounts of aftersun on each other, I imagine I even got a hard-on. To the cynical, sex-starved man who is writing this now, it makes no sense, but maybe I didn't want casual sex, I wanted to fall in love again. If I had known how many years that would take to happen, I'm sure I would have happily accepted a designer pearl necklace that night.

Back in London with the sort of tan that you usually only see in a sample book at World of Leather, I was starting over again. No Ashley and a new home. I'd moved to Brixton, and the man who owned the house, Henry, was one of the sweetest, gentlest men I'd ever met. The house was one of those classic three-storeyed terraced houses with a small back garden leading out from a tiny lean-to kitchen. Thanks to Henry the whole place had a rural, Bohemian feel full of piano music and bubbling pots of red cabbage.

My final year of drama school was great and mainly consisted of a series of full-scale productions that were open to the public and, far more importantly, agents. This was what the whole process had been about, and tensions ran very high around casting time. People crowded in front of the noticeboard to see who had got which part, and every so often someone would run, shrieking with frustration and disappointment, into the ladies' loo. A gaggle of actresses who wanted to explain how much they wished they hadn't got such a big role, and, of course, to check out the quality of the crying, would usually follow. I know that if it hadn't been for the stabbing I would have got sucked into the whole drama, but somehow my ambition had never reached the same level again. I got a good range of parts and tried to do them as well as I could, no more, no less.

Sadly, this sometimes wasn't quite good enough. Dame Judi Dench came to the school to direct *Macbeth*. I have no idea what possessed her to do this, and as she stood in front of the assembled cast, the expression on her face seemed to suggest that she didn't know either. Dan Mullane, the man I knew from Cork, got the lead and Saskia Wickham got to give her Lady M. I was stood at the notice-board for some time before I found out what my parts were. A lucky public was to enjoy my Donalbain and my Second Murderer. I don't mean to imply that I wasn't memorable in these roles, but years later, when I was on the radio show *Loose Ends*, Ned Sherrin asked Judi, who was a guest, who had played the best Donalbain she had ever seen.

'Donalbain,' she laughed. 'Isn't that part normally cut?'

More laughter. Ned explained that the person who had played the role in her production at Central was sitting at the table. A panicked expression came over her face and her eyes darted around the group. She turned to the man on her right. 'Of course, how . . .'

'Not him!' barked Ned.

It took her three guesses before she stumbled upon me. I like to think that had he asked about the Second Murderer, she would have immediately remembered me.

The biggest lesson I learnt during that final year was that I couldn't play a serious role. Try as I might, through no choice of my own, people only saw me as a clown. I remember once while rehearsing Ibsen's *Ghosts*, the director was putting me through my paces as Oswald. I was supposed to be positioning someone so I could draw their portrait. I was fully into the part as I tilted the woman's face towards the light. I grabbed an imaginary brush. Suddenly I was wrenched back to the harsh reality of the classroom. The director exploded, 'You're supposed to be an artist, not a fucking window dresser!' At first I was crushed that I couldn't do heavyweight, but then I noticed that the light, silly roles that I found relatively easy some people couldn't do at all. I had always been the funny one at work in the restaurant or at home, so it made sense.

In the summer of 1989, as we said farewell to Central, it would have been a brave bookie to take odds on who would become successful. A remarkable number of us are still working, and even more remarkably are still friends, but very few of us have names that the average reader would recognise. Perhaps that is no bad thing; perhaps it is just shallow me who judges success in terms of fame.

The Feeble Has Landed

The really lucky ones left with jobs already lined up. Sadly, that didn't include me, but I was still relatively confident because at least I had managed to get an agent. Barry Brown was the perfect agent: loud, brash and very pragmatic. I had a meeting in his house and was suitably impressed by the furniture and paintings on the wall. If he was this rich on ten percent, imagine being the person who held on to the ninety percent. I sat back and waited for the auditions and the money to come flooding in.

There is a lot of talk in drama schools about agents and what role they play in an actor's career. 'When you get one, don't forget that they are working for you – you are calling the shots,' is what you usually hear. Of course the reality is very different and you soon realise that as a client they are doing you a favour by representing you. I quickly learnt this and stopped expecting the phone to ring. In fairness to Barry, I did get my first job quite quickly. In September I was temporarily rescued from waiting tables and whisked off to, if not exactly star in, appear in *Shadow of a Gunman* by Sean O'Casey at the Liverpool Playhouse. I was thrilled. I would be playing the parts of Tommy and of an English soldier. Thanks to Equity, the actor's union that said that no two members could have the same name, Graham Walker was no more. From now on, I was Graham Norton, working actor.

I read the play, I marked my lines, I worked on the text. No matter that these were tiny parts – they would be perfectly performed. I got on the train full of shock and excitement that I was going to be earning money doing the one thing I had always wanted to do. When I got there, I found that a couple of other actors were nearly as inexperienced as me, but that for the most part the all-Irish cast were old hands who took it all in their stride. I quickly discovered that my new friend in the cast would be a man called Desmond Jordan. Funny and handsome, with a heart that contained just the right-sized streak of mean, he was exactly the sort of man I would fall in love with. The slight complication was that he was in his early seventies. Still, I had a new friend and it gave my heart hope that there were other people out there who could be just as nice and interested as Ashley had been before his transformation.

Home was a big boarding house near the cathedral. The other people staying there seemed to be mostly unhappy women who ate nothing but toast and silent young men who never did laundry. Also in residence was the city's mice population. Tiny furry friends were everywhere you looked: on top of the TV, jumping out of the grill when you turned it on to make toast . . . Once there was even one floating whiskers down in someone's bath water.

I spent time in the few gay bars the city had at the time – really just dimly lit rooms with mysteriously sticky carpets that smelt of poppers and aftershave. The only man I met was very beautiful but had a chronic problem with premature ejaculation. By a bizarre coincidence, a friend of mine has slept with him since and apparently his problem was all to do with a tight foreskin, but thanks to a circumcision later in life, my friend assures me that the situation is much improved. A nation rejoices.

I spent two months in Liverpool and had a great time – that much I know. How, is the mystery. The play was fine but hardly changed the world, and while my Tommy was a triumph, my English soldier left quite a bit to be desired.

Night after night he would burst angrily on to the stage and kick over a chair. Night after night an audience would suppress a giggle. Now I was not just a window dresser, I was an irate one. If the English army had contained many soldiers like this one I think Ireland might have achieved independence quite a bit sooner.

Back in London, it was back to working in the catering asylum that was Melange and to waiting for my agent (how grand it still sounded!) to phone me. In between carrying plates, I managed to squeeze in a BT training film where I played a corpse. For any actor this is humiliating enough, but they made me audition. Mind you, at least I got the part; imagine being the poor creature who was rejected. Now I could add to my list of roles: dead window dresser. I also got a small part in a Fay Weldon television series called *Growing Rich* through Caroline Harker, a brilliant actress and friend who was playing the lead. I played Henry who, and this may surprise you, was not a window dresser – no, he was a waiter.

Something, however, didn't feel quite right in my life. Drama school had been great fun, but I was beginning to wonder whether I really wanted to do acting as a career after all. I kept plugging away, doing all the things I was supposed to do – writing to casting directors, sending CVs to regional theatres – but the truth was my heart wasn't really in it. I hated the lack of control, waiting for the phone to ring, being grateful for being allowed to work. It seems to me that the main difference between a successful actor and an aspiring one, as I was, isn't so much to do with talent as with patience, and no amount of training at drama school can give you that.

Frustrated by both life and career, I was spending more and more time alone. Part of this was self-inflicted. The idea of dating anyone after what had happened with Ashley wasn't very appealing, but also lack of money was another big factor in my finding myself sitting hunched over a small black and white television nursing a glass of red wine. More and more I had the house in Brixton all to myself, because Henry had got several jobs with opera companies abroad.

Although I never felt particularly unsafe in the house, while I lived there we were broken into twice. The first time they took the small black and white television. The second time they didn't take anything – presumably they just went, 'These poor shits have less than we do.' But what really freaked me out was what happened to me one night after I had gone to bed in my room, which was at the top of the house. It was a very hot night and I lay naked on top of the duvet. I went to sleep. About two or three in the morning I suddenly woke up. An old woman with grey hair was standing at the foot of my bed. She was wearing what looked like a shapeless nightie and seemed to be rubbing her eyes. I remembered I was naked and pulled the duvet over myself. In a quick-fire round of deduction, I worked out that this must be the woman from next door who had been given an extra set of keys by Henry in case of emergencies, and I assumed she was most probably sleepwalking.

'Hello,' I ventured quietly.

Nothing. Still she rubbed her eyes.

'Hello,' I said, a little louder.

Again she failed to react. I began to doubt myself. I looked away and looked back. She was still there. Without making a sound she moved away from the bed towards a chair by the door. She began to sit down, but she did so just to the right of the chair, as if it had a ghost replica of itself by its side. Odd. Then, just as she reached the level of the seat, like a switch being turned off she disappeared. I was thrown into a state of terror and covered my head with my duvet. If she had evaporated like a shifting mist I might have convinced myself that she had never been there, but her sudden disappearance made it clear to me that I had seen a ghost.

Telling this story is a bit like me talking about having had sex with women – I know it happened but I still find it hard to believe. I have told very few people about it because it makes me feel like such a fat daytime television loser, but it did happen. Strangely, when Henry came back he was talking to this woman who lived next door and discovered that on the night of my visitation she had been seriously ill. Perhaps, and I know I'm sounding like Shirley MacLaine here, it wasn't a visit from beyond the grave, but instead some sort of transferred energy from next door. Or perhaps I should drink less. Ah, wine! The truth is in there.

As a result of spending all this time on my own, my love life was uneventful. Although Ashley had left my heart squashed like romantic road kill, I still hoped that the man of my dreams would come along. I would look at men on the tube wondering, *à la Sleepless in Seattle*, if they were the one. There was a dark-haired boy I saw a few times on the Northern Line who always returned my glance. Then, one night I was having dinner in Melange and he was at another table with a large group of friends. We stared at each other for most of the evening, but neither of us did anything about it.

A few nights later I was in a South London gay bar called

the Two Brewers. It was late and the dance floor was heaving to a disco remix of 'Don't Cry for Me Argentina' (I have cancer, let's dance!) when I saw him again. This time something had to happen. We walked towards each other, eyes locked, and within minutes we were kissing, within hours we were in bed, and by morning we were going out with each other.

A week of my new romance went by. I had met his flat-mates, he'd stayed over at mine, and on Saturday night I took the rather big step of taking him with me to a friend's party. This was the unveiling of 'Graham's new boyfriend'. All was going well and we were standing in one of those party circles, chatting. The new boy – who, you must have guessed by now, does have a name, it's just that I can't remember it – took it upon himself to start up a new strand of conversation:

'What's your favourite film?'

People who ask questions like this tend not to be actually interested in anyone else's answer, they simply want to tell the group what their favourite film is. I was appalled that when it came time for him to do just that, the words *The Color Purple* fell out of his mouth. It's one thing to be forced to admit to such an appalling lack of taste, but to actively want to share it with others seemed completely unacceptable to me. My 'new boyfriend' was rapidly becoming 'some man I know'.

He then volunteered to the group that on the following Monday he was going to have a tattoo done. What? I had been going out with him for nearly a week and he hadn't mentioned anything about this. Where was he going to have his tattoo? On his arse. Hmm. What was he going to have done? A picture of Winnie the Pooh holding a balloon. 'Some man I know' had just become 'some man'.

A couple of years later, a friend who had been at the party bumped into him in a bar and asked him about the tattoo. Apparently on the Monday he had gone in to have it done, but it had hurt so much that he made them abandon the whole thing. Now, when he gets lucky and goes home with someone, he takes off his underpants to reveal the tattooed outline of a balloon. Presumably to avoid embarrassment he tells people it's ringworm or a rare form of scabies.

All of my friends seemed to be moving on with their lives. People from Central were getting jobs and starting careers, my friend Helen had split up with Mike and then moved to Paris to be with her new boyfriend Remy, Nicola was going back to College . . . In comparison, I was just treading water.

I was still seeing lots of Syd. I loved being his friend and we had become close when I had stayed with him for a couple of weeks. His flat was on a large, bleak council estate in Peckham: taxis would drop visitors on the main road and they would make their way past abandoned shopping trolleys, broken glass and burnt-out cars towards Syd's front door. Once inside it was like a tasteful monastery in its simplicity. Slowly Syd came to trust me as a friend and began to share the secrets of his past. To me, the life of a beautiful person seems so straightforward, but for Syd it had led to all sorts of complications and conflicts. His father was a truck driver, his mother his defender, he had run away from home (Canada) to live in Hawaii, he had worked as a model, he had played around the edges of prostitution. He was a very special man, a sexual angel – pure and debauched, sexy and sweet, all at the same time. He was loved by everyone, and

I'm terrified that mutual friends who read this will think that somehow I've let him down.

During the couple of weeks we lived together, I noticed that he'd stopped drinking, and that he'd become very careful about what he ate. He became obsessed with bulking up. He would drink cans of condensed milk and then creep to bed very slowly and carefully to prevent vomiting. None of this was particularly remarkable to me – he looked great; of course he took care of himself. Then one day he announced that he was going back to Canada to visit his family. Fair enough. We bade farewell and I presumed I'd see him again in a few weeks.

One Saturday, while Syd was away, Sandy and David, two Canadian friends who knew Syd from Vancouver, arranged to have lunch with Rebecca, another good friend of Syd's, and me. We met in a restaurant on St Martin's Lane and chatted about where we had been, who we had seen, who was earning what, which clubs were good and which were crap. It was coffee time before David and Sandy went serious, and after many awful, awkward silences, reluctantly told Rebecca and me in the best way they could that Syd, special, sweet, sexy Syd, had AIDS and had gone back to Canada to be cared for by his parents.

Apparently he had written to his parents to tell them about his condition, had posted the letter and then had a dramatic change of heart. He had waited for hours by the postbox to get his envelope back, but the postman, the poor man, had to explain to a sobbing, pleading Syd that once posted, all mail became the property of the post office and couldn't be returned. Once his mother knew the truth there was no resistance – he had to go home.

The Feeble Has Landed

There was a lot of crying, and the waiters must have wondered what weird love pact at the table had just gone hideously wrong. Suddenly a lot of things and nothing made sense. We coped with the news as best we could over the next couple of weeks. At Melange the phone would ring late at night. Sweet, drug-fucked Syd would be calling from the hospital to tell us that he loved us. We'd hurriedly shout down the phone that we loved him too. Then his money would run out and, red-eyed, we'd have to deal with some customer who didn't think their white wine was cold enough.

It was maybe a couple of months later when David phoned me with the news. 'Syd's gone.' All across London I swear a thousand hearts were breaking.

Thousands of miles away, somewhere on the outskirts of Vancouver, a heartbroken mother couldn't fulfil her son's dying wish to be cremated. She couldn't bear it, she had to keep him for as long as she could, so now there is a gravestone with Syd's name on it. During all my crying, I had decided one thing – if God did exist, he wasn't a very nice person.

7

I'm So Hungry
I Could Eat
the Hind Leg of the
Lamb of God

S YD'S DEATH FORCED ME TO reassess things. I was
working hard and making good money, but somehow
I always managed to spend most of it on the way home. Life
was fun sometimes, and the people I worked with were
great, but on the whole I wasn't enjoying it, or at the very
least wasn't enjoying the person it was turning me into. Every
restaurant has a bitter old queen working in it, and somehow,
without me noticing and against my will, I had become that
person. When I had started work at Smiths there had been
waiters who were twenty-seven, and I remember looking at
them with pity and wondering where their lives had gone
wrong. Now here I was, nearly thirty, with no end of my
catering career in sight.

I was approached for a part, and I decided to have another
proper go at acting. In fact, I welcomed the distraction. I
think it will tell you how low I had sunk when you learn
how delighted and overjoyed I was to learn that I had been
cast in the Harrogate Theatre's production of *Puss in Boots*.

Harrogate, I have been known to say on occasion, is where
they invented the lace doily. It is the capital of twee. It has
endless shops – or should that be 'Ye Oldye Shoppes' –
selling pot-pourri and stencils, but try buying a Fray Bentos
pie or a packet of Smash instant potato. Before I got there

everyone gushed on to me about a tea shop there and how wonderful it was. When I arrived I found overpriced tea being served on a bad BBC set for some low-rent *Miss Marple*.

The only highlight of the town as far as I was concerned was the Victorian Turkish baths: vast steamy halls covered in beautiful intricate tile and mosaic and full of towel-clad men of various degrees of attractiveness. Most men in there I presumed were straight, and of the obvious gay ones, there was only one elderly local man who was overt or aggressive about it, and he was only tolerated because of his age. If he did take a fancy to you, you simply walked to the pool at the other end of the room and it took him so long to follow you that by the time he arrived you were ready to move on to the next bath. I did speak to one man, though, who hadn't seen this plan through properly. He had gone upstairs to the chill-out room to get away from the old man; however, he had made the fatal mistake of falling asleep on one of the mattresses there. He awoke to find a mysterious liquid deposit on his chest and saw the old man shuffling away with what might have been the slightest hint of a spring in his step. Turkish delight.

I was playing Rollo. Surely you remember Rollo? He is one of the evil brothers who inherit the mill and the donkey while the good brother just gets the cat who turns out to have a slight Imelda Marcos complex. Puss was played by James Dreyfuss, who went on to have great success with *The Thin Blue Line*, *Gimme, Gimme, Gimme* and various films. He was very funny and charming in the part, despite having to wear a very odd costume that made him look like a giant toilet-roll holder.

I'm So Hungry

Yet again the excitement of getting the part soon faded as the reality of living in Harrogate and dragging two members of the local youth theatre dressed as a donkey around the stage every night slowly sank in. I discovered that a comedy henchman with a Yorkshire accent was outside my range – I was awful in the show, but extreme boredom meant I didn't care. One night I was under the stage killing time before my next entrance when high above me I could hear one of the actors going, 'Oh Neddy!' I thought this was odd because I couldn't remember a single scene that Neddy appeared in that I wasn't in as well. Hmm.

Fuck!! I rushed on to the stage from the wrong side to find my evil brother staring at me with all too convincing menace. I helped drag the members of the youth theatre draped in grey furry car-seat covers into the wings, and as I apologised profusely to my brother, they shuffled away like a couple of fur balls sicked up by a giant cat, saying, 'And he's supposed to be the professional.' What made it worse was that they were right.

Catering seemed to be the only profession that would have me, and that I was moderately good at. However, when I got back to London after panto hell ready to pick up my apron, I discovered that even that wasn't going well.

Melange was in trouble. As is the case now, the London eating scene was very fickle and our trendy crowd had simply grown tired of expensive anarchy and moved on. Fewer shifts meant less money and the very real possibility of no job or money at all. I thought about finding a job in a different restaurant, but that seemed like I would be making a proper career move and finally admitting to myself that I was a professional waiter rather than an actor.

Luckily I was still living in Brixton with sweet Henry and paying very little rent, but even this stability in my life was rocked by one Stephan Deraucroix.

To meet Stephan is to have strong feelings about him. Many, myself included, adore him, others have an almost allergic reaction to him. He is originally from Strasbourg, but when I first met him he was living in Paris with his boyfriend Jean-Jean. The two of them had decided to come to London to have some fun and make some money. Jean-Jean ended up washing dishes somewhere and Stephan found himself scampering around Smiths, which is where I'd first met him. We got on immediately because I could speak a little French and he liked talking about sex as much as I did. He is handsome in a sort of French cartoon way, with big dark eyes and permanently puckered lips.

Stephan makes me laugh like no one else I know. Sometimes this is because he is being consciously funny, but mostly it is his Stephancentric view of the world that is hilarious. The way he communicates is very hard to describe. He does speak English, but with what must have taken supreme effort on his part, he has managed not to improve at all over the last twenty years despite living for long stretches in London.

One night at Melange, a table asked Stephan for broccoli. I can only assume Stephan fancied the guy because normally if something wasn't on the menu we would take great delight in substituting 'fuck off' for a string of 'sorries' and 'only the freshest blah blah blah'. On this occasion Stephan abandoned the rest of his section, went to the kitchen, found some broccoli, chopped it up, whisked it into the microwave and finally, several minutes later, appeared breathless at the table proudly brandishing a small dish of the green vegetable. The customer looked at him blankly.

'You asked for some broccoli?'

'No. I asked for a bottle of beer!'

Merci et bonne nuit.

Stephan expects the world to take care of him, and so it does. He had decided to come back to London and needed a job and somewhere to live. Mike gave him some shifts at Melange and I was in charge of accommodation. Beside me on the top floor of the house in Brixton was a much smaller room that looked out on the back. This was empty and Henry needed another lodger, so Stephan moved into it. Unfortunately, Henry turned out to be one of the aforementioned people who have an allergic reaction to Stephan. They did not get on. Although I still liked living in the house, weeks after moving in Stephan began to plot our departure.

With an obsessive determination he began to talk to everyone about his quest for a flat for us. I let him get on with it because it's very hard to take Stephan seriously. Then one day he announced that he had found us a place to live. A friend of another waiter in Melange was leaving his council flat, but he would sublet it to us if we paid off his back rent. At least, I think that was how it was supposed to work – all I really remember was that it all sounded quite dodgy, but to all our friends at the time getting a council flat was like finding the holy grail. I think this excitement blinded us to the fact that some council flats aren't worth having.

We headed off to Hackney to see our prospective new home. At the time I didn't know East London at all, so as the bus pulled away from Old Street, the nearest underground station, it was the start of a great adventure. Past Shoreditch town hall and then north towards Dalston to Queensbridge Road. It was a tree-lined avenue stretching for a couple of miles through north-east London, and it contained that fairly standard mix of rundown Victorian villas and council estates within the bombed-out gaps. About two-thirds of the way along on the left-hand side it suddenly opened up into a long stretch of balding grass, and there stood the four tower blocks of the Holly Street estate. The third grey lump of unwashed concrete was Grange Court, and on the eighteenth floor was our new home. On one side of the building there must have been great views back towards the river and the city itself, but the view from our windows was of the featureless vastness of Hackney, Stratford and beyond into Essex.

Our very own council flat! We took it. I know I was sad to say goodbye to Henry and Brixton, but I was genuinely incredibly excited to be moving into the eighteenth floor of a Hackney tower block. Perhaps Stephan had put me under some sort of French spell.

Actually, the flat itself was lovely. With two bedrooms, a lounge and a kitchen, it was spacious and bright. We painted walls and borrowed, begged and bought pieces of furniture. We loved it. As far as we were concerned, people who gasped in horror when we told them where we lived or refused to visit us were simply mad or jealous. Of course, as Stephan and I sat up late at night watching the first Gulf war unfolding on television, we couldn't help noticing that the Baghdad landscape the scud missiles were lighting up bore an uncanny resemblance to the view we had over East London.

One Sunday I was lying on the sofa idly watching police

search helicopters hovering outside the window and flicking through the pages of the *Sunday Times* magazine. A photograph caught my attention. It looked like a picture of our beloved tower block. It was. Why was it in the news? I read the caption. 'This building has more cockroaches in it than any other in Europe.' I froze. We had been there about a month and I hadn't seen a single cockroach, but in that moment I expected to hear the sound of a tiny marching army of them coming down the hall to carry our fridge and cooker away. People in the article talked about finding them crawling over their babies' faces and up their own legs. I decided that if I ever saw one, I would have no choice but to move out. Then, as I read on, almost in passing the journalist casually mentioned that parts of four different human bodies had been found in the bathroom of one of the flats by police investigating some gang war. I stared down the hall at the front door that only moments before had seemed solid and secure.

To make matters worse, a fire in an empty flat on our floor meant our landing was all blackened by smoke and none of the communal lights worked. Night and day we came and went through Stygian gloom. To see another human being was to scream. Mysterious water started to run down the walls of the living room. Light switches and plugs sizzled and popped and then died.

It really was a dump. On the ground floor, an archaeologist could have just about pieced together what the entrance must have looked like twenty years earlier. Broken hinges hanging withered on the wall were all that remained of the security doors. A large, gouged-out hole to the side of the entrance had become the empty grave of what had been the intercom system. Anyone could come and go and have access to the lifts and the flats beyond. I was waiting for the lift one day with an elderly lady, and I felt for her as she stared around her at the empty beer cans, graffiti, and suspect puddles. She shook her head and said sadly, 'When we's moved in, it were like an hotel . . . an hotel.'

Every night, coming home was like running the gauntlet, creeping around corners, freezing at the sound of a voice or a footstep, praying for the lift to come with a little extra prayer that there would be nobody in it. There were two lifts. One served the even floors, the other the uneven numbers. In all the time we lived there, I think both lifts worked at the same time about three times. Depressingly often neither of them worked, and then the long climb up began. I often thought about the old lady and her hotel.

Once, late at night, I came home to find only one lift working again. I waited for it to come to the ground floor. Finally it arrived, the door creaked open, and there stood a very large white German shepherd dog. It looked at me. I stood back to let it out, but it just stayed where it was, breathing and staring. I weighed up my options: get into a small confined space with a large, potentially dangerous dog I didn't know, or climb eighteen flights of stairs. I stepped into the lift. The dog looked at me, the doors closed and up we went. I pushed every button, and each time the lift stopped and the doors opened, I looked at the dog and he looked at me. Finally, on the eleventh floor, the dog looked up, nodded his thanks, and wandered off down the corridor like a pale, hairy ghost.

Another night, the one working lift arrived. Nobody in it, not even a dog, just a small fire burning cheerily. Again I weighed up the options. This time, however, I had some slight concerns about suffocating. I decided I couldn't get into a lift with a fire. For the first and only time in my life, I proceeded to piss in a council lift. Sadly, my bladder was not a big enough reservoir to extinguish the flames. Eighteen flights of stairs, but at least I wasn't bursting to go to the toilet.

Mostly the people who lived in the block were all as scared as and of each other. As the lift doors closed I always felt like a kitten thrown on to a busy motorway. Who might get in on another floor? One day, Stephan and I were going down in the lift and a bunch of real East End lads got in. We started to speak in voices several octaves lower and stood in as butch a way as we could. As we walked from the lift with the lads following behind, we really felt we had got away with it – they hadn't detected for a second our extreme level of nelliness. Suddenly a whole cooked chicken landed with a steaming fleshy thud at our feet – a row over Sunday lunch must have reached a crescendo several floors up. Stephan and I jumped out of our skins and screamed like two fat virgins seeing the Chippendales for the first time. Game over.

The most important survival rule I knew about living in the tower block was not to draw attention to oneself. When I bought myself a smart new outfit, I was very worried about wearing it in the lift because it made me look like such a rich person. One day I couldn't resist: I put on my black trousers with a grey jacket and waistcoat made of a blanket material that was very trendy at the time, and finished the outfit off with a white shirt and a black satchel. The whole outfit screamed media millionaire. I crept out of the flat and scuttled into the lift. As it slowly descended I repeated my silent prayer for it not to stop until it reached the ground floor. My heart sank as the lift stopped at the tenth floor and a woman got in.

'Hello,' I said.

She didn't say anything. I could feel her staring me up and down. Doubtless she was wondering to herself, 'What is this rich bastard doing in here?' We reached the ground floor, and just as the doors opened she could resist it no more – she turned to me and spoke.

'Excuse me, are you the postman?'

Going down.

Pretty soon the cockroaches heard that we had moved in, and after the initial skin-crawling horror of seeing them around, we got used to them. I stalked them around the flat armed with sprays and rubber gloves as I had done on my fly safaris during my student days. I was forbidden from squashing them because Stephan, a cockroach expert (he had lived in Paris after all), explained that in their death throes the last thing they did was lay all their eggs. It seemed that cockroaches were the Cilla Blacks of the insect world – they knew how to survive. Occasionally men from the council would knock on the door. They stood there dressed like astronauts and wheezing through huge face masks and explained that although the stuff they were about to spray all over your home was lethal to cockroaches it was completely safe for human beings. Once they called at lunchtime, and as they left one of them noticed me pouring out a bowl of soup that I had been heating up. 'Are you going to eat that?' he asked through several layers of charcoal filter. I looked at the bowl of what had been delicious tomato soup before their intervention and then back at my visiting spaceman. 'Yes.' He blinked through his mask. 'I wouldn't,' and with that he was off on his mission to stamp out all the multilegged Cillas on planet Hackney.

The rather obvious question surrounding all of these stories is why didn't we leave? Why did I live there for nearly five years? Why did I live there longer than I have lived anywhere else? I suppose the answer is to be found in a variation on Rose's wise words about people getting over things: people also get used to things. The other main reason was, of course, that financially it was impossible to move.

Melange had finally closed down. When it happened it was almost a relief. Better to have no job than to pretend to yourself you have one even though you are earning practically nothing. On our last night a few of us sat around the bar staring at the empty tables and telling stories that would have made poor Freddie's hair stand on end.

'Remember the time you pissed in the man's coffee but someone else drank it!'

'Oh, what about the lady with the nut allergy and we forgot to tell the kitchen and her lips blew up like big purple dinghies and she had to go to hospital.'

'What about those people who left their camera behind and we took lots of pictures of ourselves pointing at their shitty tip and then they came back for the camera.'

We took it upon ourselves not to serve any customers that night – it was going to be our special night. I don't know who came up with the idea – maybe me? – but we put a sign on the door saying, 'Please use other door.' We became almost hysterical watching people walking up and down outside the window searching for the elusive 'other door'. When we got bored of that we put up another sign that simply said, 'Please use Neal Street Entrance.' That sent people around the block and left us in peace to enjoy our wake. I told that story on the radio once, and apparently Freddy the owner heard it and was very upset. He didn't understand that it was something we did only once and on the last night. I think he felt that I had single-handedly carried out a cruel vendetta against him and caused his beloved restaurant to shut down. Freddy, if you ever read this, the truth is there was no reason Melange failed in the end, and its success, like all restaurants that do well, was mainly due to a huge streak of freakish catering good luck.

So there I was, with no money, living in a dump and unable to move. And then the council got in touch and told Stephan and me that we weren't legal tenants. I explained that we had been paying the rent and using the rent book. I was called in for a meeting where I met a man sitting in an office no bigger than a phone box. He had the sort of moustache that was so groomed and pampered that one assumed he preferred it to his penis. I stared at it as he explained that there was no record of our rent and he didn't know where it was going. When I asked him if we should stop paying rent, he paused and said, 'Well, I would,' and licked his moustache.

I walked back to Grange Court, went up to what was now my free home on the eighteenth floor and wondered what I should do. I had no job, but I had no rent to pay. I realised that I could live on very little indeed and somehow use my time to pursue other ambitions. I knew I had to broaden my horizons as far as my career was concerned, and not rely on the few acting roles thrown my way. I decided that I would write something for me to perform. It was as simple and spontaneous as that.

In many ways, the moment we stopped paying rent was a turning point for me. I suddenly had the luxury of having the time and the means to develop my own projects. I still had to make some money to survive, of course, so I did various bits and pieces. A friend of mine called Gill Sheppard had an interior design PR company, and every few weeks I would go in to her office for a day, or sometimes just a couple of hours, to stuff envelopes and answer the phone to journalists who wanted photographs of taps or sofas. In the evening I broke my rule of never working in another restaurant ever again. But at least the place I ended up in was a bit different. It was a pub on the Farringdon Road called the Eagle. Mike Belben and David Eyre had left Melange and without knowing it had started the first ever gastro-pub. The idea seems so obvious now – a bare bones pub with an open-plan kitchen to one side serving restaurant-quality food at cheap prices and with no fuss – but back then it was radical, and a huge, howling success.

Mike had always backed me in my ambition to be an actor, working my rota around rehearsals or auditions, and now he came up trumps again. He was fine about not giving me a regular job, just the odd shift when I wanted the money or he needed the help. The Eagle was an incredibly liberating experience. I was doing more or less the same job as I had been doing at Melange, but this time I wasn't relying on or even expecting tips. I saw one huge, glowing advantage to this system – I could be as rude as I liked. While he didn't exactly encourage this behaviour, Mike had worked in catering long enough to have learnt that the customer was not only usually wrong but also annoying.

'A smile costs nothing,' a customer who'd been ordering

in dribs and drabs and therefore irritating me would say.

'And intelligence can't be bought,' I'd retort. Why nobody rabbit-punched me I don't know.

I was at a dinner party recently and a female journalist turned to me and asked if it was true that I had worked at the Eagle.

'Yes, I did.'

'I'm sure you won't remember this, but I used to be barred from that place!'

She then told the party about how she had been barred from the Eagle for absolutely no reason in 1991. She had simply tried to order a drink from the wrong end of the bar, she claimed. Polite titters ensued. I stared across the table. Of course I remembered her. She'd been a vile, drunken bitch, and we had taken huge pleasure in telling her that she could never come back. I was disappointed for two reasons: one, that Mike had now relented and let her back in, and two, that somewhere along the line I had made decisions in my life that meant I was now sitting next to her at a dinner party.

I felt for the first time that I had a bit of a life plan going. Often, when I wonder about my inexplicable success, I think back to my years on the eighteenth floor and realise that on some level I had to succeed because failure really wasn't an option. I didn't know exactly what plan A was, but I definitely knew that there was no plan B.

Stephan was spending longer and longer stretches in France with his boyfriend, and our television had been nicked months before, so there were few distractions. I sat on the wheelchair I had got from a local junk shop and stared at my typewriter. I knew that what I wrote had to be funny, but the whole idea of stand-up terrified and appalled me. I absolutely did not want to do stand-up, but I did want to do a show. Characters? Maybe I could do Alan Bennett-like monologues? I tried a few but they all petered out. I ate a lot of Smash potato and did a great deal of wanking.

For some reason, Mother Teresa of Calcutta had always struck me as funny. There is something ridiculous about anybody who is considered completely one thing, be it good or evil. When I was working at Melange, I would often pop a tea towel on my head and pretend to be the sainted old lady. It seemed to amuse the other people at work, but really it was just one quick visual gag and I had never thought of expanding it into anything else. Then, one day, in between the spuds and the spunk, a title for my show came to me. It would be called 'Mother Teresa of Calcutta's Grand Farewell Tour'. I still had no idea what was going to be in the show, but I knew that I would buy a ticket to a show with that title.

I started writing, assuming that Mother Teresa would simply be the first character in a sketch with other characters, but I just kept thinking of things for her to say. In my mind she was like a tough old Irish housewife. The sort of woman who would consider herself a Christian beyond reproach, but who would think that anyone who actually believed in the Virgin Birth was more than a little naïve. I knew hundreds of women like this.

I was on a roll, and before it was in any way structured or even fully written out, I asked Mike if I could perform it in the gallery space above the pub. He agreed, but said that he needed a date. I plucked a date out of the air five weeks ahead. It seemed suitably far off and vague. No pressure. Then, when I was working behind the bar, various people started saying to me that Mike had told them about the show and that they were really looking forward to seeing it. Suddenly it had all become very real and very soon. Pressure.

Maybe it was because I was used to performing with others, but there was something about the act being just me, by myself, that made me uncomfortable. So I wrote in parts for two little sisters. My friend Nicola Reeder would play one, but I thought it would be handy if the other one could play a musical instrument, perhaps a guitar. It seems incredible, but we didn't know anyone who could play an instrument. I guess we'd all been too busy carrying plates and planning our fabulous futures to find time to actually learn how to do something. Finally Nicola came up with Lorne Widhal Madsen. She was half Danish, model pretty with long blonde hair and she played the clarinet at professional level. It wasn't exactly the happy-clappy folk mass kind of sound I had been looking for, but the very oddness of it appealed to me. I decided that she should deliver all her lines in Danish with Nicola interpreting them. I suppose I was trying to create a show that was quirky and unlike anything anyone might have expected. I hoped it was going to be funny, but if it wasn't, at least it would be bonkers.

When I had finished the script I had a read-through with some friends. Such was their keenness to get a sneak preview that they even made the trip to the eighteenth floor in the council estate. They seemed to like it. Rehearsals with the little sisters revealed they had so little to do that in actual fact they made it look more like a one-man show than ever. Oh well, it was too late now.

I'm So Hungry

I went on a PR blitz to promote this tiny one-off show above the Eagle. I had photographs taken of a faceless Mother Teresa looking at a London A–Z, I got press releases printed and (my favourite) I made business cards with just the name of the show and a small scrap of tea towel stuck to it like a holy relic. I sent this eccentric press pack off to everyone I could think of. The fact that I had no idea what I was doing coupled with the very real fact that I had nothing to lose gave me an extraordinary confidence. *Time Out* wrote a little feature about the upcoming event, and then on the day the Radio 4 show *Loose Ends* called. A producer called Alison Vernon Smith thought it might make a good feature for the show. I told her as much about the show as I knew, and she seemed to think it was funny. She would be down and she would bring her reporter for the piece, Emma Freud. Emma Freud! She did stuff on the telly! There was going to be a celebrity in the audience!

Finally the night came. I bought and borrowed cushions and placed them in rows on the floor of the gallery. Then I put lots of candles around the room, started the pre-show music of some wailing Bulgarian choir and waited. Soon the little room was packed. When I say 'packed', I mean about fifty people showed up, but in a space that small that meant standing room only. To indicate the start of the show, Lorne walked into the performance area and played halting esoteric jazz on her clarinet. Nicky wandered slowly around the room lighting the candles. It didn't say comedy, it didn't even say show. If I had been sitting in the audience that night my heart would have been sinking fast. In alternating Danish and English Mother Teresa was introduced, and in I walked, draped head to toe in Irish linen tea-towels.

By the end of the show I had learnt two things: it was forty-five minutes long and people really seemed to like my Mother Teresa.

I was giddy with excitement. Fifty people, mostly fairly good friends admittedly, liked my show. Emma Freud interviewed me and told me to ring her. A woman called Judith Dimant who worked for a venue called the Pleasance in Edinburgh came up to me and told me how much she liked the show. People bought me drinks. The handsome friend of a friend slept with me. The accolades were pouring in.

I did the show twice more above the pub. True, there were slightly fewer people and laughs on both occasions, but they were still successes, and friends who had witnessed my failed drama career looked relieved. I had found the thing I was good at, and as sure as awkwardness follows sex, my career would, I was sure, take off. I seemed to be right. I had hardly taken off my tea-towels and started wondering what to do next when I got a call from Judith Dimant. There had been a cancellation for the midnight show in the cabaret bar at the Pleasance. Did I want to do two weeks at the Edinburgh Festival? I ironed my tea-towels and packed my bag. I was taking the show on the road.

8

A Little Something off the Fringe

AUGUST 1991: I EMERGED FROM Waverley Station. The city of Edinburgh loomed above and around me with an imposing, confident grandeur that struck me as out of place in a city in the UK. It had the air of a small European principality: the festival had arrived and old women with newly washed and set hairdos in see-through plastic rain hoods gave way to shiny-haired boys and girls who had leaflets for hands. I had never been tempted to go to the festival as a punter, finding the whole idea of it too daunting, but now I was here for a reason.

I had no idea how lucky I was with my accommodation. While all the other first-timers were shacked up four or five to a room or in campsites outside the city, I swanned around in an enormous, beautiful flat which belonged to the family of a woman I had worked with at Melange. Zebra-skin rugs, pictures in silver frames sitting on a baby grand piano – I might have had the good grace to feel guilty except that I knew that come the end of the festival all the shiny-haired kids would return to leafy loveliness and utility rooms, while I would be creeping into a fire-charred lift designed to accommodate coffins.

I also didn't realise how lucky I was to be fast-tracked straight into one of the premier venues on the fringe. It was still hard to get audiences and reviews, of course, but at least I stood a better chance than most other first-timers. I did twelve nights. The show started at midnight and somehow I managed to make it last for an hour. The audience seemed to be mostly made up of people who worked at the venue and a handful of pissed people who couldn't get into anything else.

Every night I came off stage and went into the dressing room where the next show's comedians would be waiting. It was a late-night line-up of stand-up comics compèred by a greasy-haired, baby-lipped man called Mark Lamarr. I would pack my tea-towels up, and they would ignore me and share private jokes. They made me feel like I was back on the rugby field in Bandon Grammar School, and yet this time I knew deep down that it was different. I might not have been ready for the first eleven, but I could at least play the game. I knew that I had a perfect right to be there.

On about the third or fourth day I had a review. It was a good one. That night I came off stage and the comics spoke to me. At the time I thought they couldn't be bothered to talk to me until the review gave me some sort of credibility. For years after that I couldn't like Mark Lamarr. Then, when I became a stand-up comic myself, I understood. Despite all the bravado and the pissing in sinks, the balance between doing well or badly on stage is so unpredictable and so spurious that no one wants to jeopardise their chances. Before the review, to have spoken to me would have been to have touched potential failure. Each night they must have heard the thinly populated applause and then seen me appear at the door like some linen-draped comedy albatross. Now I can appreciate Mark as one of the best and most conscientious comics working in Britain today – oh, yes, and as a nice person too.

That year in Edinburgh I met Simon Fanshawe. As far as I knew he was the gay one with glasses off *That's Life* and a former winner of the Perrier award for best comic on the fringe. We had lunch one day and I remember being so impressed when someone came into the café and asked him for his autograph. I had no idea at the time what a huge debt of gratitude any gay comic in Britain owes him. Whenever articles are written about gay comedy, they always seem to go straight from Larry Grayson to Julian Clary and me. There are two people that Julian and I owe our careers to and they are Simon Fanshawe and Kenny Everett; Simon for being the first openly gay comic on the circuit, and Kenny for charging at the borders of good taste without stopping to apply for a visa.

I bumped into Simon again in a gay club a couple of nights later, and as we were chatting he told me he ran a comedy festival in Brighton called Laughing Gas and he offered me a one-night gig at the Ship Hotel. I was delighted. Then, by an enormous stroke of bad luck – and who could have seen this coming in a million years? – I got a part in a play. I had so far hidden my burgeoning comedy career from my agent Barry Brown – I was terrified that he might start demanding ten percent of the very little money I had managed to earn – so when I got the call to say that I'd been cast, I couldn't tell him that it clashed with my big night at the Brighton Comedy Festival. The play was a musical written and directed by Tim Luscombe, called *Eurovision*. Later it would be produced by Andrew Lloyd Webber and become one of the biggest flops ever seen in the West

End, but at the time it was a huge cult success at the Drill Hall, a fringe venue in London. To begin with I tried to get Tim to write me out of it for the one night, but he sucked his teeth and told me that he felt that was impossible. In the end we compromised. I would be written out of the second half and I would miss the curtain call.

I'd planned that particular evening like a military campaign. Nicola and my actor friend Darren got to Brighton early to set up the props on the stage. As the audience for *Eurovision* were still applauding the end of the first act, I was sprinting out into the street where Stephan was waiting in his little Peugeot, the engine running. Driving faster than someone delivering a replacement kidney, he pointed the car south and put his foot to the floor. Not many people can tell you this with first-hand experience, but I can assure you that getting changed into a nun's habit made of tea-towels in the front of a small French car travelling at speed is not an easy thing to do. This was long before everyone had a mobile phone, so the good people of Brighton simply believed I was going to show up. As we hit more roadworks and heavy traffic, I wasn't quite so sure.

Finally we arrived in Brighton. Dressed in white, holding my small black handbag, and with my tea-towel flapping around my head, I ran down the sea front towards the Ship Hotel. A burly man in a suit at the door stopped me.

'Are you Mother Teresa?'

Panting and wiping off sweat with my very handy towel, I assured him that I was.

'Follow me.'

We raced through corridors and kitchens. I could hear Bulgarian music wailing, I could smell candles, I was on.

A Little Something off the Fringe

The show went down better than it had ever done. I played with the audience and made jokes with local references. The laughs sounded genuine, and not just charitable and kind. I went back to *Eurovision* the next night convinced once and for all that this comedy thing wasn't just something I was doing while waiting for better acting jobs to come along. It was what I wanted to do for ever.

The next year I headed back to the Edinburgh Festival for the whole three and a half weeks. This time I was in a much smaller venue in the Pleasance called the Attic. Each night I felt like a comedy version of Anne Frank, except more people found her.

One night the stage manager came into the dressing room.

'Do you mind if there are some people in wheelchairs in the audience?'

'Of course not,' I assured her, though I did silently wonder about fire regulations. They might find some burly men to carry them up five flights of stairs, but if tongues of flame started licking around them, these people were going to be toast on wheels. I decided that very early on I would make some jokey references to them to show that they were up for a laugh and that the rest of the audience could relax. Not a problem.

Once on stage I looked over to the three wheelchairs, which seemed to be taking up about half the room. Before I could say anything, one of the disabled people let out a weird, high-pitched moan which sounded a little like whale music. This was accompanied by a rather startling head roll. This was not a group of friends out for a laugh, this was a severely handicapped group, and if the whale sounds and rolling eyes were any indication, I didn't think I'd be engaging them in any sort of witty audience banter. As the show went on I strained to interpret each new outbreak of marine music, but it was impossible. They were so random. Sometimes I thought it might be a laugh, occasionally a heckle, but mostly I felt they were cries from the heart: 'Who the fuck thought it was a good idea to drag us up five flights of stairs to see this fool? We were promised a possible miracle cure!'

It's true that there had been quite a few misunderstandings surrounding my alter ego. The idea of a show about Mother Teresa may not have been immediately obvious, but it shocked me how many people got the wrong end of the stick. Hotel receptionists would look confused when I showed up after doing a gig at some arts festival or other. 'Oh, we were expecting Mother Teresa.' Now I'm sure the lady was all for humility, but I really doubt that the world's foremost living saint would be booking herself into the Travel Inn while in Bristol.

On another occasion, I was delighted to get a call from a researcher at BBC Scotland. She worked on a show that was hosted by an Irish singer called Dana. It was a religious programme, and they told me they were very keen to do something about the show.

'Does Dana have a good sense of humour?' I asked.

'Oh yes, it could be a very light-hearted piece.'

'Great.'

I was amazed that this Dana woman was evidently so open-minded and had such a dry, deadpan sense of humour. What a fun and ground-breaking religious programme this must be?

A letter arrived from the researcher a few days later and alarm bells started to go off in my head. This wasn't deadpan, it was serious. They thought they'd be interviewing the real Mother Teresa. Someone with, I presume, a university degree and who had been employed by the BBC had been flicking through the programme for the Edinburgh fringe and had seriously thought that Mother Teresa was abandoning the poor of Calcutta for nearly three weeks to appear in a sixty-seater attic. I wrote the researcher a letter on behalf of Mother Teresa apologising that she was unable to write it herself but she was very busy, what with trips to the launderette and watching *Countdown*. The penny must have dropped. Almost by return of post I got a brief note sadly informing me that the programme was now overbooked and there would be no time for the interview with Mother Teresa. It will be a lifelong regret to me that my Mother Teresa never got to meet Dana and her great sense of humour.

Some work did come out of doing the show. I began doing a 'thought for the day' on Craig Charles's breakfast show on London's Kiss FM, and lovely Simon Fanshawe had me on his Radio 5 show. But it was becoming clear that while my live performances worked fairly well, it was a very niche audience and it wasn't clear to anyone, including myself, what else I could do with my show.

Back in London I met a producer called David Johnson. He became my comedy agent. David is a great big, lovable bear of man and I couldn't imagine being in Edinburgh with any other promoter now. David has a fairly unique approach to promoting his shows. He settles into the Assembly Rooms bar and tells everyone he speaks to that they must go and see his clients' shows. I know that on the surface this doesn't sound like very effective marketing, but that is to underestimate the vast numbers of people David knows and the sheer man-hours he puts into this endeavour. He and his then business partner Mark Goucher, an immaculately groomed man, a Cher to David's Sonny, worked out of a tiny basement office just off Tottenham Court Road.

And work they did. Venues were booked, posters made, gigs booked. Sadly, they needed me to make money for them to make money, and while they never lost faith in me, they certainly lost money while promoting me. Happily, some of their other ventures like the Reduced Shakespeare Company, *Trainspotting* and 'Puppetry of the Penis' subsidised their little debt-spinner. Doubtless it was through some sort of desire to widen my appeal that David and Mark encouraged me to drop the tea-towels and write something more accessible.

Because the Edinburgh fringe programme goes to press months before the actual festival, year after year I would have to come up with a performance title and then set about trying to write a show that in some way related to it. My first outing post Mother Teresa was the tastefully named 'Karen Carpenter's Bar and Grill'. This was more like the show I had originally intended to write: a series of monologues loosely tied together by a story, albeit a hastily thrown-together one. To be fair it didn't really work. There were a few funny ideas, like a fly-on-the-wall documentary about a closet heterosexual, a weird sequence where Karen Carpenter was abducted by aliens who travelled the universe in a giant Fray Bentos steak and kidney pie tin, and a few jokes that I'm ashamed to admit I still use today.

It wasn't until the next year, in 1994, that I finally bit the bullet and wrote a show featuring me as myself. At last I was the one standing there talking to the audience, and I really liked it. The show was called 'Charlie's Angels Go to Hell', and it was based around my travels in America and my time at the hippy commune. The idea was that Charlie's Angels were my moral guardians and came to my rescue when I found myself in any situation that was out of my depth. I don't remember any individual bits of it as being particularly funny, but as a whole it worked. It was my biggest success in Edinburgh to date. Good reviews, sold-out shows – it made me feel legitimate.

There is an odd, insular thing that happens during the festival, where it's easy to forget about the outside world. If it's important in Edinburgh, then it's important everywhere else. I can only assume that that is what David and Mark were thinking when we decided to transfer my little hit show from Edinburgh into the West End. True, it was only the Arts Theatre, a smallish venue by anybody's standards, but it was still the West End. Although we all probably sensed impending doom, it wasn't the sort of offer you can turn down, so the posters were printed and the invitations for the opening night sent out.

On my way to the theatre I stopped at a phone box and rang my parents in Bandon just to make sure that they were there – I didn't want them showing up and surprising me, because what would have seemed like a nice idea would have gone horribly wrong. They still didn't know that I was gay and, as I have stressed in the preface to this book, there are still things I think they'd rather not know about my life.

The lights came down at the end of opening night and the crowd erupted. I was in shock. I walked around the party afterwards numb with happiness. My little show was a West End smash. The next night I walked out to an auditorium about a quarter full – obviously word had not reached the world at large yet about my amazing hit show. The music started and I performed my strange opening dance number. I came to a stop, panting slightly at the front of the stage. Just before I began to speak I heard a man in the audience say very loudly 'Daft queen', and apart from a few coughs that was the last I heard from the audience that night. Not a titter.

The show dragged on for three weeks, and the responses I received most nights were somewhere in between the ones I got on the opening night and those on the second night, but ticket sales never really picked up and finally David and Mark broke the welcome bad news to me – my run had reached the finishing tape. Oddly, because the reviews had been all right, most people didn't know what a disaster it had been. The posters looked good, I had got a lot of publicity from doing the show, so apart from having to do the actual performances, it had been very good for my career.

Thanks to Simon Fanshawe's ex-producer Will Saunders, I was regularly doing interviews on *Loose Ends* by now – not celebrities, just people I think Ned couldn't be bothered to talk to. The female judo champion was given to me when the show went to Hull ('Not the first time I've been tossed by someone wearing big pyjamas'), and in Taunton I got Mr Sheppy the cider maker ('Mmm, tastes familiar. Is it Cox?'). I loved doing the show and really enjoyed all the people who worked on it. Sitting in the pub after the show with Ned was a real treat as he told us endless stories of theatrical luminaries behaving badly.

Once *Loose Ends* went live to South Africa, and in case of a technical disaster Emma Freud and I were called into the London studio on standby. If anything went wrong we were to introduce some pre-produced clips of old shows to fill the airtime. The show began, and Emma and I sipped our coffee and listened politely. I think it was while a South African poet and M P was telling an anecdote about singing in parliament that we grew a little restless. Emma, pregnant at the time, decided to show me some breathing exercises. Soon we were both on our backs recarpeting our pelvic floors. In the distance I could just hear one of Ned's guests saying something about how the world had become much smaller when suddenly South Africa seemed to have fallen off the edge of the earth and Radio 4 listeners could just hear Emma and I panting and groaning as we got up from the floor. A puzzled nation assured itself, 'No, it's Graham Norton, they can't be fucking!'

The other positive consequence that came out of 'Charlie's Angels' was a meeting with Helen Chown. She had done the P R for the show, but once it was over she started working with a man called John Keyes who ran the Paramount Comedy Company. They asked me if I wanted to do some stand-up gigs. I had always resisted doing pure stand-up, but between 'Charlie's Angels' and bits of the 'Karen Carpenter' show I thought I probably had enough material. Also, despite having to pay no rent, I knew I didn't have enough money. The other reason I decided to give it a whirl was that John and Helen got me the gigs – I didn't have to phone round the promoters themselves and risk rejection or, perhaps worse, open spots.

My first gig was at the Comedy Box, a small comedy club above a pub in Bristol. I got the train down and I have never really known nerves like it. I tried to act nonchalant about the whole thing because I didn't want the promoter or the other acts to know that this was my first proper gig. I waited in the big, empty pub kitchen that smelt of wet facecloth. I could hear the other acts going well and seriously wondered what sort of giant mistake I had made. I looked at the industrial size deep freeze and considered climbing into it. Too late. I was on. Now, I'm sure I was awful, but people did laugh and I did some OK ad-libs and generally felt like I had got away with it and fooled at least some of the people most of the time. I went back to the candlewick bedspread on the skinny single bed of the bed and breakfast and felt like a comedy king. I was a working stand-up!

The next morning I got a message to ring Helen. There had been a cancellation in Ireland. Could I fly out that day to do one night in Sligo followed by a gig in Galway? Could I? I was a working stand-up, that's what we did. I headed straight to Stansted and flew off to Knock airport. I was very excited, not just by the thought of the gigs but also of actually seeing Knock airport for the first time. At first glance it may just look like another bungalow though with a driveway long enough to accommodate a jumbo jet, but its very existence is as miraculous as any Virgin appearing on the gable wall of a house. A man called Bishop Horan – well, he was a bishop, that wasn't just some nickname – had constantly argued that Knock needed an international airport to service all the planeloads of pilgrims from around the world.

'What pilgrims from around the world? We haven't seen any,' was the response of many.

'Well, of course you haven't. They can't get here until the airport is built,' replied the wily Bishop.

Undeterred by the lack of government funding, he set about raising the money through charity. Years of fund-raising finally paid off. He turned the first sod of turf and the bulldozers moved in and soon Knock had a runway that could cope with the world's largest aircraft and a terminal building that looked like yet another bungalow. The effect is that flying in you feel like you are approaching someone's house up a really big driveway. It was only when the bishop died that they discovered that his fund-raising hadn't quite been up to the job and in fact the airfield of dreams was built on huge debts. I rather admire Bishop Horan. His dream was so strong that he couldn't let the mere absence of money stop it from happening. He died a happy man, and just in time.

I was doing the gig with a man from Newcastle whom I'd never heard of before. I had been sold to the Irish promoters as a headline act. Well, I supposed I did appear regularly on the BBC, was a veteran of the Edinburgh Festival and had delighted West End audiences with my solo show. The poor fools must have felt lucky to get me.

Night one was Sligo. The function room at the back of the small hotel was transformed into a comedy club. The man from Newcastle struggled through his act, and then it was time for me. Somehow I managed to get away with it once more. I think I spent most of my time on stage just talking to a loud group of women near the front who had taken an irrational liking to me.

Night two was in Galway. This was the big time – a city – and we were playing its premier nightclub, and what's more this was a big gala anniversary night for the club. A couple of the lads had ironed their shirts and quite a few of the ladies were wearing tights. It was probably just the crossing of their legs, but the atmosphere did seem really charged.

Newcastle Man kicked things off and he went down much better than the night before, but he still wasn't great. I charged on to the stage after I was introduced thinking this was going to be an easy ride, and was met with the sort of look a piece of meat might get if it fell from the ceiling in a vegetarian restaurant. I started my unpolished act. They polished off their interval drinks. I was talking about the hair on my shoulders. They were just talking. Slowly the volume of the audience threatened to outdo that of the microphone. I was in deep trouble and had no idea how to get out of it. A couple of lads started to heckle, but even that wasn't fun. I knew they hated me, but they didn't know how to make me stop. I hated them and didn't know how to get away. There was an increasing number of people trying out a pretty straightforward heckle of 'Fuck off!' Didn't they realise that I was the last act? If I left there was nothing else.

I tried to reason with them. In a very understanding but slightly threatening voice, I announced, 'Look, if you all want me to fuck off, I will.' This was the news they'd been waiting to hear. At first there was a random cacophony of 'fuck off's, but that gradually grew into a loud bass chant. 'Fuck off! Fuck off!' This made the second night of the West End show look like a flower-throwing ovation. Although dying on stage is awful, the thing I learnt that night was that it isn't as bad when it happens to you as it is when you are watching it happen to someone else. It's hard to explain, but trust me, it's true. The other thing I found out that night was that they still had to pay you even when you bombed.

I liked my new job.

9

Love Is in
the Airfare

STAND-UP IS A VERY ODD job. Twenty minutes' work can make all the difference between a good day and a bad one. The contrast is so extreme that those twenty minutes contain all the pressures and tensions of most twelve-hour days in any other job. The good thing about that stress is that friendships with other comics develop in dressing rooms with a hothouse intensity. People you've only met a handful of times you consider really good friends. Only they understand what you've been through and so a weird special bond develops.

The other part of the job consists of spending hours in other people's cars travelling to and from gigs up and down the country. Every comic has a list of people they dread making a journey with: the ones that smell, the ones that analyse their own act for the entire trip, and let's not forget the standard bore.

But on the whole it was fun and I was enjoying myself and no longer feeling like I was drifting. I had got much better at stand-up over quite a short space of time, though I was never a great or even a very good club comic. I hated being the closing act because I was never a sure thing. Far better to put me second on the bill or, my favourite of all, as compère. But I can't have been that bad because I found

I was making some money. It started coming in just in time.

A knock came to the door in Cockroach Towers one day. I looked through the spyhole and saw a stern woman with a clipboard. I guessed the chances of her being involved in some gang-war vendetta were fairly slim, so I unlocked the door. She was from the council and she told me in no uncertain terms that I shouldn't be living in the flat. She explained that the block was going to be torn down and that the council had no responsibility to rehouse me. I, of course, informed her that I would be going to the Citizens Advice Bureau and fighting her to the highest court in the land.

After she left I looked around at the buckled floors, the bare wires, the cockroach corpses and wondered why on earth I would fight for the right to stay in this place. I should be thanking the woman who, after five long years, was kicking me out of this hell in the skies.

Over the next few months I did as many gigs as I could and finally scraped together enough money to put down a deposit in order to rent a flat. I found a small one-bedroom place near Columbia Road flower market in the East End. When I say small, I really am not exaggerating. They had created a one-bedroom flat from a room that would have been described as 'a bit cramped' in the property section of the *Toy Town Gazette*. The hallway looked like a mini Studio 54, while the bathroom and kitchen both looked like ads for Flash cleaning powder *circa* 1972 – Avocado and Donkey Brown respectively – but for ninety pounds a week I could live alone and in Zone 1.

My friend Nicola helped me move, but I'm ashamed to admit that I left most of my belongings behind. I just shut the door on my bed, desk, sofa, clothes and books. I did this mostly because there was no room for any of this stuff in my new doll's house, but also because I wanted a new start. I often drive home via Queensbridge Road now, and while the lady with the clipboard was right about their plans to knock down the Holly Street estate, there is one lone tower block still standing and it's the one we lived in for all that time. It has been totally refurbished and I believe it is used as accommodation for the elderly. Finally Grange Court has come full circle – it's 'like an hotel'.

So this was my life. I lived in my retro shoebox, did the occasional bit of work on the radio, and travelled around the country doing gigs. It wasn't exactly what anyone would call a career, but it was the closest I'd got to one so far. Of course, as soon as one part of your life seems to be going all right it's time to focus on how rubbish the rest of your life is. After gigs I would come home and literally stare at the empty bed. I am a frighteningly self-reliant creature, but some nights I did yearn to have someone else lying there beside me. It wasn't about sex, just that basic need we all have to be held. Somehow, seven years of being single had gone by since Ashley had broken my heart. I was beginning to wonder if it would ever be fixed.

A couple of friends called Stuart and Steve, whom I had met when I did some corporate events for the travel industry, had invited me to dinner one night. Normally I might have looked forward to it, but I was tired and a bit grumpy that day. The previous night I had done a gig in Chester with Jo Caufield and Rob Hitchmough. It was in a wine bar and restaurant, which was fine except that nobody seemed to notice the start of the show because they were too busy eating their microwaved lasagne and chicken Kiev. Food was served throughout, and frankly there are only so many jokes you can make about *Hollyoaks* to distract from the comings and goings of garlic mushrooms. Afterwards, on the way home in the car, Jo and I bitched on about this stupid idea of serving food while Rob was a little non-committal. It was only when I did the gig he ran in the Aztec comedy club in South London that I understood why. There they didn't just serve food, they served food that made noise! Sizzling platters of fajitas and Southern chicken could arrive at any moment to ruin a punchline. It's one thing being heckled by punters, but when the food starts talking over you . . .

We'd got back very late from Chester and I'd crawled into my tiny bed. The day of Stuart and Steve's dinner party I just wandered around in a daze, dreading the night ahead. What made it worse was that they had also invited some American friend of Stuart's. I was assured that he was a lot of fun and ran this crazy tour in LA called Graveline, where he would drive tourists around in the back of a hearse and show them where famous people had died. He sounded ghastly.

I showed up with my bottle of wine and newly brushed teeth wondering how early I could leave without seeming rude. Stuart and Steve gave me a drink and showed me into the living room. I glanced at the people dotted around the room with their gins and vodkas and pressed jeans, but there was no sign of the dreaded American. I was introduced to everyone and when we got to the only sexy man in the room Stuart said, 'And remember I told you about my friend Scott from LA?' This was Scott? He was cute and sexy! Why had I thought he wouldn't be? I've no idea, but here he was, tall and broad, masculine and funny, with beautiful eyes and a great smile. I knew he would never be interested in me, but still he was something good to look at over dinner.

Towards the end of the meal people started talking about going out. Where was there to go? We were near Islington and someone remembered that on Sunday nights there was a club called Popstarz which played good eighties pop music. Having had a few drinks I was no longer tired or grumpy. I was up for going if everyone else was.

The club was crowded and soon the whole dinner party group had lost each other, all the better to find new people, I thought. Suddenly, Scott was by my side.

'Are you drunk?' he asked.

I thought about it.

'No.'

His eyes lit up and he smiled at me. 'Would you like to be?' he asked.

I didn't hesitate. 'Yes!'

Shots were consumed, arms touched, eyes met, courage grew, and finally – hurrah for alcohol – we kissed. We never saw the others again that night, we just drifted around the club kissing and dancing like the happiest drunks are prone to do. We weaved out into the street where passion led us down an alley. At first it was very sexy, hands and tongues and trousers all over the place, but suddenly we heard someone's footsteps and were instantly transported back to the reality of the smell of piss and old kebabs. Giggling and zipping ourselves up, we stumbled back on to the street. He was staying with Stuart and Steve and he had to go back because they would be waiting up to let him in. We kissed some more, exchanged numbers and arranged to meet the next night.

The next day my friend James Holmes rang to see if I wanted to meet up for a drink. I explained why I couldn't.

'I have a date tonight and I'm actually looking forward to it!'

I'm aware that there hasn't been much dating in this book so far and very little sex. Given what a slag I've been over the years, I'm not sure why. I suppose that if you are trying to tell the story of your life, people whose names you can't remember and that you only slept with because you were drunk don't seem that important. True, I'll never forget the man who wet the bed and then locked my clothes in his washing machine so that I was trapped there for hours, nor can I erase the memory of going home with some man only to discover that he was so hairy that going to bed with him made me feel like Sigourney Weaver in *Gorillas in the Mist*. The bendy cocks, the tiny cocks, really all the cocks cease to be interesting by the time the light of dawn shines through the bedroom windows and the effects of the vat of lager you drank have worn off.

James knew that usually if I agreed to a date it was only because I couldn't think of any way to get out of it. What made this one so remarkable was that I couldn't wait to see Scott again. I tidied my miniature palace – just in case – and headed off to the bar where we'd agreed to meet. I got there on time and sat trying not to get too drunk too soon. I flicked through the free papers you find in gay bars and fought the temptation to look at my watch too often. Scott was late. The large wet towel of shame that comes with being stood up had just started to wrap itself around me when suddenly there he was! Smiling and apologetic, he told me that he had got lost. We chatted and laughed and gossiped all evening. It was that total rarity in the world of dating – we were *both* having a good time! That night Scott ended up with me in my monk's cot and there were no interruptions.

Love Is in the Airfare

Scott was only in London for a few days before visiting his cousin in Paris and from there heading back to his life in LA. The whole thing had that heady intensity of a holiday romance, where you throw yourself into a passionate relationship completely because you know you won't have to reap the consequences. On the Friday morning we said goodbye at my flat. He asked me to get a Eurostar ticket and come with him to Paris for the weekend, but I had to say no. I had rent to pay now and simply couldn't afford it. I watched him through my window walking away. He turned and waved and I realised I might never see him again. Before he had even walked out of view I had picked up the phone to ring Eurostar. They had a ticket for later that day. Fuck the rent, the ticket was mine!

I left a message for Scott with Stuart, asking him to call me. He rang and we arranged to meet in a bar I knew in the Marais. This weekend was going to be perfect.

I had never been on Eurostar before, and that night I learnt a valuable lesson. A high-speed rail link between London and Paris is a great idea, but it is only good if it works. We were delayed for three hours. I sat looking out at a Kent hedge and it dawned on me that in all my romantic spontaneity I had failed to get a phone number or address for Scott in Paris. He would be sitting in a bar assuming that I had got cold feet and wasn't coming. My friend Helen, who was still living in Paris with her French husband, was away that weekend so she couldn't help. I tried directory enquiries to get a number for the bar but they couldn't find it. It became clear that there was nothing I could do except wait for the train to inch its way forward towards Paris.

I got to Paris and did the only thing I could think of,

which was head to our meeting place, even though by now I was so late that there was no way that Scott would still be waiting. I got the metro, and when I got to the Marais I ran off in the direction I thought the bar was in. It turned out I didn't know the area as well as I thought. In the past I had always had Stephan and tankards of red wine inside me to help me and sharpen my senses. I turned corner after corner, each street looking as familiar as the last, but none of them was the one I was looking for. I stopped to gather my thoughts for a minute. I was feeling fairly hopeless at this stage, but at the same time I knew there was nothing to do but carry on searching. I chose a street and headed down it. Had I seen that shop before? Was that the same blue building I'd walked past five minutes ago? And suddenly, there was Scott right in front of me . . . Scott! I had literally bumped into him. We hugged and kissed and beamed at each other. What in the cold light of day might have been described as 'a happy coincidence' in that dark street in that foreign city in the dead of night seemed like a miracle of cosmic proportions. We were in Paris and we were officially in love.

The rest of the weekend was one romantic cliché after another. Laughing, drinking, talking, fucking, it was like one of those cheap romantic videos they make for karaoke machines. I often wonder what would have happened to Scott and me if there hadn't been any room on the Eurostar or if our meeting had all gone smoothly and we hadn't shared our date with destiny when we met in the street. I don't believe in love at first sight, and yet there has to be that moment when you are hanging above the abyss of love and you decide to let go and plummet out of control towards total madness. By the time I was sitting on the train heading back to London I was looking in the papers to check on airfares to Los Angeles. There is no better feeling than falling in love; it's just when you land that it hurts.

Things couldn't be better. I was in love, and also on the career front things had suddenly dramatically improved. At the previous Edinburgh in 1995, two women had come into my life: Melanie Coupland and Anna Wilkes. They ran a talent management company that was part of the production company TalkBack, which was owned by Mel Smith and Griff Rhys Jones. After my show one night they were waiting to speak to me. I knew that TalkBack Management were supposed to be very good and that they represented people I really admired like John Hegley, Sally Philips and Angus Deayton. Melanie is dark while Anna is fair, and as they sat on either side of me having a drink I tried to work out what they wanted. Could they really be offering to represent me? I can only imagine how unconvincing my 'I'll have to think about it' was. True, John and Helen had got me gigs and David and Mark had produced my shows, but TalkBack Management were the gateway to the next level and to super shiny telly . . .

So now I had every angle covered: I had a boyfriend and a top showbiz agent. Except that I appeared to be living alone and not earning any money. Scott sent me some cash to put towards an airfare and Nicola offered me some to cover the rent, but I still couldn't see how I could swing a trip to LA to be with the man of my dreams. Then, as has happened so often in my life in times of trouble, religion came to my aid.

Father Ted was written by Graham Linehan and Arthur

Matthews and they were represented by TalkBack Management. The second series of *Father Ted* was being cast, and Melanie and Anna asked the boys if there was anything in it for their new Irish client. 'No' was the instant response, but Melanie and Anna persisted and eventually got me an audition for the part of Father Noel Furlong. I thought I was totally wrong for the part because I was too young and too Protestant, but I went along anyway.

The good thing about auditioning for Father Noel was that he spoke in long speeches. It was just showing off without the actual acting stuff of dialogue or reactions. The director and producer laughed quite a bit and I knew that it had gone well, but I assumed that I hadn't got the part when I didn't hear anything for a few weeks. Graham told me later that after my audition they had said, 'Well, that was funny, but now we had better find someone who is right for it,' but they had never got around to auditioning anyone else.

Being in *Father Ted* is the only cool job I've ever had. In retrospect I feel so proud and lucky to have been part of what is undoubtedly a classic sitcom, but at the time it was mostly a promise of money to come that meant I could go ahead and plan my trip to LA. The episode of *Father Ted* that I was in would rehearse and film in early January, so just after Christmas I flew into the sunny arms of Scott and California. Again we had a perfect time together. Even his dog liked me. I had no idea how we could make this long-distance relationship work, but I did know that I didn't want to let this man go.

Back in London I found myself in a rundown hotel behind Tottenham Court Road rehearsing *Father Ted*. It was quite daunting walking into this tight-knit group. Dermot Morgan,

Ardal O'Hanlon, Pauline McLynn and Frank Kelly had already filmed one whole series and had just got back from filming all the location scenes for series two in the west of Ireland. When I walked in, all the talk was about Ardal's hair. He had got it cut for his wedding but now it no longer matched the scenes they had already filmed. Through the gritted teeth of fixed smiles the production team agreed to get a wig made.

I loved the rehearsals and was made to feel incredibly welcome. If this had been my experience of acting when I had first left drama school, I'm sure I would have stuck with it for longer. This was fun. Ardal, Dermot, Pauline and Frank took their jobs seriously, but they had a laugh about everything else. Of course I suppose we could afford to relax and have a good time because it was a great script, so there wasn't that terrible anxiety about whether an audience would like it or not.

The episode was called 'Hell' and was about Ted and Dougal going on holiday but then discovering that the caravan they had been promised was double-booked with a tragic youth group led by the terrifying Father Noel. It seems an awful thing to say, given that I'm in it, but 'Hell' is still my favourite episode of *Father Ted*.

On the third day of rehearsals, I got a call from Melanie at TalkBack. I had a meeting with a production company called Rapido about co-hosting a game show called *Carnal Knowledge*. The main host was going to be a woman called Maria McErlane. As far as I'm concerned, Maria is up there with champagne and masturbation in terms of things that make life worth living. She is wise and funny in equal measure, and for my fortieth birthday she gave me a card that said, 'It's not homophobia, everyone hates you.' I had first met her in Edinburgh, and although we had got on I hadn't expected her to remember me, but when *Carnal Knowledge* was commissioned as a late-night series for ITV it was Maria who suggested me. A short meeting with her and Peter Stuart and Mark Ford from Rapido who would be making the show, and the job was mine.

The next morning I walked back into rehearsals for *Father Ted* and told them that I would be making twenty-six episodes of a new game show. It seemed incredible that the change in my fortunes could be so sudden and so complete. It didn't matter how little I was going to get paid for *Carnal Knowledge*, any amount multiplied by twenty-six was going to be a fortune for me.

I got back to work, but unfortunately I'm one of those people who gets worse the more they rehearse. By the time we did the final run-through in front of the suits from Channel 4, my performance had gone in a rather worrying direction. The suits huddled and discussed what they had seen. Declan Lowney the director and Lissa Evans the producer approached me. They wondered if I could possibly make Father Noel 'less frightening'. This was their polite way of telling me to stop playing him as a particularly predatory paedophile. I got the message.

When we got to the studio everything changed. The sets did half the acting for us, and bizarrely they had shipped the old battered caravan they had used for the location shots over to London to be used for the interior. Cameras were stuck through the windows as Dermot, Ardal, my youth group and I piled in as if we were in some sort of *Blue Peter* challenge. Luckily we didn't have to shoot the scenes too many times because I don't think the caravan would have made it. After the final particularly violent dancing scene, we discovered that we had bent the whole thing so out of shape that the door no longer opened. The taping stopped as we all clambered out of one of the windows.

When Melanie told me that Arthur and Graham were going to write me into another episode of the series I was thrilled. That episode was set on a plane and, rather like the caravan, they brought a whole plane into the studio. We sat in rows, faces pressed into cameramen's bums while the audience sat in rows staring at the outside of the plane. I didn't have much to do, but I just loved being a part of the *Father Ted* family, if only as a distant relative.

If filming *Ted* had shown me how much fun work could be, making *Carnal Knowledge* showed how much work work could be. Twenty-six hours of television filmed over nine days, one hundred and four contestants telling us every tawdry detail of their sex life . . . each night I crawled home exhausted and with the sort of pounding headache you'd accept if you'd been trying to find a cure for cancer all day, but not if you'd been asking people to draw their favourite sexual position. The worst shows were the ones we did first thing in the morning. An audience that had been picked up from shop doorways stared at contestants being forced to down a couple of bottles of beer. This was our warm-up. Then Maria and myself would come bounding out with our shiny clothes and dull eyes.

In the end we banned doggie-style from the 'draw your favourite sexual position' round because we both ran out of things to say about it. I wasn't sure whether straight people were really that fond of doing it from behind or whether it was just easy to draw. Despite the paltry prizes on offer, some of the contestants took it all horribly seriously. One night, as Maria and I walked out of the studios to find our taxis, we saw a contestant and her boyfriend's mother having a full-blown fist-fight in the car park. Apparently the mother felt her son had been 'let down', while the girl screamed at her mother-in-law that she was a 'filthy cow'. For a moment we toyed with the idea of stepping in to try and diffuse the situation, but only for a moment. We drove off as they fought on.

Carnal Knowledge brought me three things: a great friend in Maria, a fair amount of money, and my first taste of fame. Because the show was on in the middle of the night, our fan base was quite quirky: taxi drivers, students and the bouncers of the lap-dancing club near my flat to be precise. Mainstream we weren't, but I quite enjoyed my limited notoriety.

The new money meant that I could afford to have a birthday party for my thirty-third birthday and Scott could fly over to be there and meet all my friends. I invited everyone I knew to the upstairs room of a gay bar in Soho called the Yard. I don't think I had attempted to have a party since the one I had imagined I was having back at university. I remember Scott and I sitting on the tube as we headed into town, both so nervous – him because he thought there were going to be so many people there, me because I thought there was going to be nobody there. In the event it all went well, and although I realised that Jesus had achieved a little bit more than I had by the time he died aged thirty-three, I still felt pretty good. I had lots of great friends, a man I loved and, for the first time in my life, some money in the bank.

Scott and I desperately wanted to be together, but it seemed mad for me to go to California to start all over again just as my career was beginning to inch forward after so many years of trying. Equally, Scott loved his job driving his hearse around LA. He was a self-styled 'death hag', and working for Graveline Tours was his dream job. However, all this changed dramatically when Scott went back to California.

I was sitting on my miniature sofa watching my normal-sized TV which took up half my living room when the phone rang. I picked it up as I headed for the loo and pressed the answer button. It was Scott. He sounded traumatised. I sat on the toilet and began to get on with things in London.

'Are you all right?' I asked.

A short pause and then, 'I've been sacked.'

'What?'

He had come back to his apartment in Los Angeles to find his boss had pulled the plug on Graveline and left Scott a curt note. The note didn't explain anything, it just said, cryptically, that he'd thought he could trust Scott. I for one knew that he could trust Scott. I had been witness to how he had devoted his life to this other man's company and kept it afloat against all the odds. Scott tried to find out what had happened, but his boss wouldn't take his calls and didn't reply to his emails. He would have stalked the boss to get an explanation, but he lived in Kansas. Scott poured his heart out, and while I felt sorry for him I couldn't help but think, as I reached for the toilet roll, that this was good news. Now Scott would have no reason to stay in California, he could come and live with me.

The loss of his job really hit Scott badly. A combination of his love of the business and the injustice of his dismissal meant it was almost like a bereavement for him. I tried to talk him through it as best as I could from a distance while drip-feeding all the reasons he should come to Britain. I would probably be earning enough for two if we were careful, he could maybe set up a similar tour of London, and, well, fuck all the other reasons, we could be together. Apparently this was an offer that he could refuse, and he vowed to find a new job in LA.

With two episodes of *Father Ted* and endless *Carnal Knowledge* episodes under my belt, I felt like a television veteran. I started to have meetings with more and more production companies about shows that never saw the light of day. Meanwhile, in a poorly lit part of the TV forest, a sad little plant was just about poking its head above ground. Channel Five was coming and they needed programmes.

Stand by for a complicated series of connections that end with me getting a job. Lee Hurst had just become a big star thanks to *They Think It's All Over* which was made by TalkBack productions. TalkBack also represented Lee at the time. Lee had a format for a comedy panel game which he had pitched to Anglia TV. Anglia was owned by United News and Media, who also owned a big chunk of the fledgling Channel Five. They needed big names and so wanted Lee's show, but Lee wanted to be a panellist and not a host, so the hunt was on to find the man for the job. Melanie was privy to all of this and got me a meeting with the executive producer Graham Stuart, who was head of entertainment at United. Graham Stuart has played a major role in my life, but I can truly say that our first meeting was very forgettable, so much so that I have. All I know for sure is that he didn't hate me and I got the job.

The new show was called *Bring Me the Head of Light Entertainment* and was going to be filmed in Anglia's own studios in Norwich. Every Monday a group of comedians would gather in Liverpool Street station and get on the train together. For some reason I was quickly cast in the role of Mother, so that I would have everyone's tickets and make sure we were all on the train and that everyone had their coats and bags when we got off at the other end.

The programme was one of those panel games like *Never Mind the Buzzcocks* or *They Think It's All Over*, where the panellists are expected to do vast amounts of homework. The minute we arrived in Norwich, the teams were locked in their dressing rooms to sweat blood over new jokes for the two shows we would record in the evening. I was the host – I went to the pub. The director Jim Brown, the producer John Naigh Smith, the writer Ian Pattinson and myself would walk through the streets of Norwich, coats flapping in the breeze, until we reached a lovely little pub on the river. Lunch was ordered – 'Just a spritzer, I'm working' – and then we would read through the script and laugh out loud, annoying showbiz laughs while travelling salesmen glared at us with their mouths full of cheese and pickle.

The shows usually went quite well, in part because they were funny, but I also think the Norfolk audience probably helped. The only other show that was filmed in Norwich at the time was the Vanessa Feltz show, so ours must have seemed like *Monty Python's Flying Circus* in comparison. For the first few Mondays we all stayed in a small hotel which is still the only one I've ever stayed in where if you asked for a single room, that is precisely what you got. The beds were strange, narrow little pallets draped in brushed nylon that were too narrow to even have a wank on. Later in the series, Lee, because he was the star of the show, was able to ask for a minibus to bring us back to London. That epic weekly journey became part of the strange ritual. I always sat in the front drinking white wine I'd stolen from the green room, while the comics in the back trashed every other comic on the circuit. I usually fell asleep before we hit the M11.

More money. I don't mean to sound obsessed by cash, but bear in mind that I had never really earned any before and I was now thirty-three years old. Also the money was being put to good use. I sent some to Scott to help him out, and in London, after searching for the perfect place, I found a smart two-bedroom flat near Brick Lane. It had a shower and quite a big fridge that I hoped an American might like.

Bring Me the Head of Light Entertainment was a moderate success on Channel Five, but Melanie was very excited because the Channel 'liked' me. I think the idea was that the Channel would build its own new talent. 'New talent' is TV speak for 'cheap talent'. Established stars cost a lot of money and they didn't have that.

As part of the whole 'a face of Channel Five' thing, I had been a guest on their new five-nights-a-week chat show hosted by Jack Docherty. It was filmed in the Whitehall Theatre just off Trafalgar Square in front of a live audience, and I loved being a guest. Then one night, as I was on my way to do a gig, my phone rang. I held it away from my ear. It was Melanie and she was excited. I had been asked to guest-host *The Jack Docherty Show* for a week. Did I want to do it?

I didn't even pretend to think about it. 'Yes!'

10

Talking with Strangers

E VERYTHING SEEMED TO BE HAPPENING at once. Scott had finally decided that he could bear to leave the city where he had no job or money and move to London. We planned that I would go to California and help him pack everything he owned into a truck, drive across America to Chicago, where it would be left in storage with friends, and then he would come back to the UK with me. The only problem was that I couldn't do it right now because I was busy. There was the guest-hosting of Jack's show, and then I was doing yet another show at the Edinburgh Festival. I promised that I would come after that. It would give him time to get organised. He agreed. Neither of us noticed that compared with when we had first met, I had been getting busier and busier. We just knew we had enough money for the airfare and the job I loved was going really well. Scott's job was just gone.

I remember arriving at the Whitehall Theatre to guest-host my first show. I went through the stage door and climbed the endless concrete stairs to the star dressing room which was in effect Jack's home. I was already putting my tooth-brush, toothpaste, razor and shaving cream on Jack's sink when I found a card. It was addressed to me. 'Dear Graham, I hope you have a great week but remember the following.

Please feel free to be a) hilarious, b) attractive, c) charming, but on no account should you be d) BETTER THAN ME. Lots of love, Jack.'

My first guest that night was Uri Geller. I introduced him by saying, 'Channel Five were worried that with me hosting, the show might be too gay, so I'm sorry to say that my first guest is a big bender.' The show went well, and over the week it got better and better. We found a truly awful pop video of a new girl band from South London called Vanilla. They had obviously saved their dinner money for a week to come up with the budget for the filming, and the song, 'No Way, No Way', was just as bad. Each night I showed another bit of the video. I gave them nicknames like the Spice Girls, and on the Friday night show, the brave ladies actually showed up and performed the song. It could have been an awful moment of television because we were just laughing at them, but somehow it managed to be funny and sweet. Every now and again I will bump into someone who asks me about Vanilla, and I regret to inform the public that the band have since split up. I did meet two of them in a shop recently, and no, they weren't working in it. They were on their lunch break.

When the week was over I felt robbed. I had found my dream job but it was someone else's. The executive producer had been Graham Stuart again, and he saw how much I had enjoyed doing it. He suggested we put together a proposal for my own chat show on Channel 4. I nodded. 'Hmm, yeah, that's a great idea.' I felt like a child being promised something nice for my birthday just to stop me being jealous as I watched the other kid opening his presents.

Off to Edinburgh. Over the last few years my shows had

changed a lot. Now they were pure stand-up, but each year I tried to include something quirky and odd. The last show I had done was *Graham Norton and his Amazing Hostess Trolley*. The title was somewhat misleading since there wasn't actually a hostess trolley in it. I put out a story that my hostess trolley had gone missing during the journey from London to Edinburgh. A local radio station even put out an appeal for someone who could lend me one. The truth was that I had never had one and never wanted one because I would have had to drag it up and down the stairs from the dressing room to the stage every night, and that wasn't my idea of show business.

In that same show I had a section called 'Raffle Chat Show'. I got the names of people who had paid by credit card from the box office and then I just randomly introduced them as my guests. I asked them a list of simple questions about their relationships and sex lives, a bit like those questionnaires that celebrities sometimes do in the back of glossy magazines. It was quite a risky thing to do but it usually turned out to be pretty funny, or at least interesting.

One night I called out a man's name and a hand went up. All eyes in the tiny auditorium turned to him. He looked ill, very ill. He was obviously a person with AIDS and he was clearly dying. I hesitated for a moment. I wasn't even sure if he could walk to the stage, nor whether he wanted to. Equally I didn't want the audience to feel uncomfortable. I think I asked him in a fairly straightforward way if he wanted to play. He did. He came to the stage and sat beside me. The audience was very quiet and the atmosphere was still. None of us knew where this might go. The man was lovely and as he answered my trite questions about love and sex, I could feel the crowd warm to him. I found out that he was in a relationship and that they lived together in Clapham. He was completely open and honest, and my silly questionnaire took on an awful seriousness because of what love and sex had done to him. I had reached the final question, and I looked at my sheet of paper in horror.

'If you could shag anyone in the world, but it was the last person you could ever shag, who would it be?' I read out.

To anyone else in that room the question would have been a cue for some jokey answer about Brad Pitt or Pamela Anderson, but for this man it had an appalling relevance and reality. He looked down for a moment and then looked up with a small smile before answering, 'My first boyfriend in Australia.'

I can't explain what happened in that moment. I don't know why it wasn't awkward, macabre or even mawkish, but it wasn't. It was just a man telling a group of strangers who the love of his life was, and this was a man who knew because his was nearly over. I don't think there was a person in that audience that night who didn't ask themselves the same question. I know I did, and the answer was 'Syd'.

About a year ago a woman came up to me at a corporate gig I was doing and told me that she had been in the audience that night and just wanted to tell me how moved she had been by it. As we stood there talking about the show, drunk men from the sales department jostling us, we both had to wipe away a stray tear.

Normally my little Festival gimmicks didn't take me to such unexpected places. I read from school diaries, I phoned out to have pizza delivered, and then when the guy arrived I'd make him act out the start of a porn scene with a woman in the audience. Probably what was most successful was when I rang people who had put their numbers in gay personal ads. If you aren't familiar with gay personal ads, let me assure you that they are really quite different from the heterosexual variety. There isn't much in them about pina coladas and walks in the rain.

I would read out a selection of truly vile ones and the audience would choose which one I called. Sometimes we just got an answering machine, but usually, because the show was quite late, I managed to get through to an actual person. I still love that moment when the stranger's voice suddenly comes through the speakers and a wave of embarrassment, guilt and glee sweeps through the audience. Everyone holds their breath. 'Hello.' Then a simple 'What do you look like?' leading to a physical description so detailed that a police artist could put together an identikit of their cock. In the bar after the show I always got people coming up to me asking, 'Was that phone call real?' They couldn't believe what had just happened. It wasn't as if the calls were particularly pornographic or even that funny, but because I have done so many phone calls since and on television, it's hard to describe how shocking and exciting they were back then.

Graham Stuart came to see the show and afterwards was full of excitement. We could use the telephone idea in the chat show that he was preparing to pitch to Channel 4. 'Yes, that's right – whatever.' Standing in a suspicious puddle in an alley outside the Assembly Rooms, I was finding it hard to take his offer seriously.

Every year at the Edinburgh Festival a strange fever sweeps through all the comics. Almost before anyone gets to Scotland they begin to talk about who is going to be nominated for the Perrier Prize, and then, as the days turn to weeks, the talk becomes an obsession. Sometimes it is described as the comedy Oscar, but I think of it more as the comedy Booker or Turner Prize – the people involved and the media think it is wildly important while the vast majority of the population couldn't give a shit. I knew that quite a few Perrier judges had been to see my show, but I didn't think too much about it. In past years I had got sucked into the nominations speculation and then been terribly let down when I wasn't. This year I didn't care. I really and truly didn't care. I couldn't have cared less. The list of nominations was announced and I was on it. All right, I cared a bit.

I honestly didn't think I was going to win, which is just as well because I didn't. The announcement was made at midnight after all the nominated acts had finished their shows. We all crammed into an old German beer tent, and the announcement was made. 'And the winner is . . .' And that was the moment when I hated myself. I knew that there was less chance of me winning than of the Irish basketball team carrying off the Olympic gold, and yet in that little pause after 'winner is' some awful tiny self-deluded part of my brain couldn't help but pipe up, 'It could be me!'

The winners were the League of Gentlemen. 'Hurrah! Well done!' I cheered and clapped as loudly as everyone else. On a deeply shallow level, though, I really didn't mind. Firstly because the League of Gentlemen were brilliant, and secondly because the trophy for the runners up was much prettier than the winner's gold bottle of Perrier.

Back in London I did a few more weeks standing in for Jack Docherty. Although I still enjoyed it, the atmosphere had changed. The series producer I really respected had gone, and some days I felt quite exposed. Also, because Channel Five wasn't really taking off as people had hoped, it was becoming increasingly difficult to get guests for the show. This was when I really grew to rely on Graham Stuart. He wasn't supposed to be working on this show in a very hands-on way, but each lunchtime he left United and came over to the show to go through the script and the interviews with me. He had worked on a vast number of chat shows over the years and his suggestions usually made a lot of sense. I began to wonder if the idea of us putting together our own show for Channel 4 wasn't that far-fetched after all.

I had never been so busy. A new series of *Bring Me the Head of Light Entertainment* was in the pipeline, and as well as guest-hosting *The Jack Docherty Show* I was appearing on lots of other comedy panel shows and doing more and more live gigs. It was around this time that if my name was mentioned in the paper, it was tagged with the word 'ubiquitous'. Although it went against all my instincts, I began to turn down jobs. I remembered what had happened to Tony Slattery when he'd seemed to be on TV all the time, and I was determined not to have it happen to me. There are all sorts of ways to wreck your career – one is to say yes to too many jobs, and another is to say yes to the wrong job. Although I'd never thought of myself as very ambitious or the sort of person who had a career plan, I liked my new life and I was going to try to keep it going for as long as possible.

I finally took a break and headed out to California for the long cross-country trek with Scott. For me the idea of Scott coming to Britain was very straightforward. I wanted him to be with me, end of story. Of course, for Scott it was a very different thing. He was leaving everything and everyone he knew to come to a country full of strangers, bad weather, poor service and the sort of vehement anti-American feeling that you only become truly aware of when you are living with an American. Worst of all, he was leaving his dog behind. Seeing Scott saying goodbye to Osso is one of the main reasons why I have never got a dog.

For some reason he wanted to bring his small grey wreck of a car all the way to Chicago with us. We pulled away from the kerb slowly in a huge truck packed full of all of his belongings, with his car on a trailer behind it. Like a couple of very dull circus performers we steered our caravan of love towards the desert.

Given that I had already crossed America by road nearly twenty years earlier, I don't know why its huge size took me so much by surprise. We thought we would give ourselves an easy first day, so we eased ourselves off the coast and across towards Las Vegas, which according to the map was very near. Hours later in the dead of night we were still rumbling along in the desert. Then in the distance there appeared to be a beam of light shining up into the night sky. The nearer we got the brighter and bolder it seemed. Like Jesus in reverse, we followed the star to find the gold, and if the wise men were fat, old and badly dressed, there were way more than three of them. I love Las Vegas. It is such a pointless, amazing place. Jaw-droppingly awful, but undeniably impressive. Paris full of friendly Americans, Venice with extra slot machines, New York with a roller-coaster subway – why would anyone go anywhere else? We managed to park our mighty convoy, and almost before we had booked into our hotel we were shoving coins into slots.

The next morning, poorer but sadly not wiser, we headed out to do a quick bit of sightseeing before we headed on. Scott had very specific tourist's demands. If it had something to do with a dead celebrity then it was on the itinerary. Las Vegas had the Liberace museum. Whatever you think it is going to be like, that's not the way it is. The collection is housed in a little shopping centre in the suburbs. The other businesses in the centre hint at the different kinds of visitors the museum gets – there's a shop selling religious artefacts and a gay bar called Good Times. I'm sure Liberace would have enjoyed the irony. On the day we went, most other people seemed to have missed a few newspaper stories. A talcum powder cloud of old ladies gathered around the till in the gift shop. 'Tell me, dear, how did he die?' They trundled back towards their bus muttering about how dangerous a bad cold can be.

Back on the road stretching endlessly into the distance, splitting the empty world into two, we stopped to see a large asteroid crater: we stood behind a small rail with other dead-eyed travellers staring into what appeared to be a large hole in the ground. We followed signs to see a petrified forest. If you haven't been in a petrified forest, let me tell you that the most common wildlife to be found in one is the bored tourist. Then we took a sharp right, drove for two hours, saw Billy the Kid's grave, and then drove two hours back to where we'd turned off.

Most nights were spent in low-price motels watching TV, but there were a few evenings where the end of our driving day coincided with our arrival in a big town. Amarillo in northern Texas was one of them. We had a shower and then checked out our gay guide to America. Sure enough there was a gay bar. We probably should have guessed that it wasn't going to be very busy, given that we were able to park our massive truck-and-car combo right outside. Inside it was a typical provincial gay crowd, which is to say that the place wasn't a gay bar at all. It was just a place for all the people in town who didn't fit in anywhere else.

We sat at the bar and ordered our beers. The woman next to us started to talk. I guessed the drink she was spilling over my jeans wasn't the first one that she had enjoyed that evening.

'Where are you from?'

I told her.

'I'm going to visit there soon,' she said.

'Really? When?'

'Not sure. Just got a few things to sort out.'

She then went on to tell us what those few things were: her mother had disowned her when she ran off and married the local drug dealer. He turned out to be abusive so she left him and was now trying to piece her life back together. Things, however, were now going great. She had finally reconciled with her sister, in fact tonight was really special because her sister had asked her to watch her kids.

'Oh, and weren't you able to?' I asked.

She looked at me with a puzzled face, then glanced at her unsteady drink.

'Oh, I see. No, no, they're out in the car.'

'The car?'

'Yeah, just outside. Do you want to come out there and share a joint?'

We politely declined. One of life's great mysteries had

been solved: I now knew where they found the guests for the Jerry Springer show.

Oklahoma was memorable, but again not for any good reason. The bomb in the federal building had blown the heart out of the city. Although not directly related to a celebrity, death on that scale meant that the site was on Scott's 'to see' list. A high chain-link fence covered in dead flowers, rain-soaked teddies and curl-cornered photos marked out the enormous death plot. In another time and place it could have been an eclectic art installation, but here it was just an enormous improvised monument to what stupidity and fear can achieve. I don't know how I expected to feel, but it made me horribly uncomfortable and awkward, as if I had intruded upon a moment of private grief. Scott took his photos while I hovered by the truck. We drove on.

Finally the mammoth trek was over, the things in storage and Scott finally parted with his car, which he gave to a friend. It was time for our new life together in London.

During our trip we had addressed all the pitfalls, dangers and risks of living together and talked endlessly about them. Moving somewhere just to be with someone was never a good idea. One person supporting the other often causes problems. Scott wasn't going to be able to work and I was really his only friend in the UK. I reassured him and stroked his arm. This was going to be different. Our love would be enough.

The first thing we had to do was get Scott a work permit. I'm sure if we had been clever or if I had thrown money at the right sort of lawyer this wouldn't have been too difficult, but being naïve, full of love and badly advised we joined the Stonewall Immigration Group. I don't mean to suggest that there is anything wrong with Stonewall, which is a political organisation that lobbies Parliament for equal rights for gay men and lesbians, but when we joined there was no legislation in place that recognised same-sex partners so we became just another test case trying to change the law.

We went to a meeting to get some advice and the name of a lawyer who would take our case. When we walked into the room I was struck by the number of older men sitting beside very beautiful Brazilian and Asian men. Bastards! I glanced at Scott and, much as I loved him, I admit that for a split second I did feel slightly short-changed.

We were told that we would have to put together a lengthy application to the Home Office. This was not simply a matter of filling out forms, it also required a folder of evidence of our relationship, photographs, airplane tickets, that sort of thing; and also, most embarrassingly, letters from mutual friends bearing testament to our love. The thought of asking people like Nicola, Helen and Maria to describe what a lovely couple we made made me feel slightly sick.

Scott immediately contacted his family and the letters started to pour in. I couldn't ask mine because unbelievably the subject of my sexuality had still not been raised. The way I thought about it was that if I had been my parents' neighbours' son they would have known, so if they really didn't want to know that I was gay by now, it was their choice.

I was doing a TV show in Dublin so I thought I would take the opportunity to bring Scott over to Ireland to meet my parents. This wasn't intended to be some gay rite of passage; I just thought it would be nice for him to meet them and see where I had grown up. As we stepped from the train in Cork I was surprised to see my sister Paula, rather than my father, waiting for us. Sure enough, on the drive back to Bandon my obviously embarrassed sister tried as casually as she could to drop into conversation a message from my mother. 'She told me to tell you that you're not to upset your father.' Now I'm not sure what my mother thought was going to happen – did she think Scott was going to turn up in an A-line dress and some size twelve high heels? – but the message was clear.

In any event, the meeting was fine. Then a few months later I made my usual weekly phone call to my mother. She answered, sounding a bit distant.

'Are you all right?' I asked.

'Well, no, no, I'm not,' she replied.

'What's wrong?'

'I just think it would have been nice if you had told your family certain things before you announced them on television,' she said curtly.

'What?'

It turned out that as part of some show I had made with Rapido for Channel 4 I had done some joke about being Irish and gay. I had made similar jokes before on other shows, but this was obviously the first one that that she had seen.

'But you told me not to tell you!'

'I did not!'

'You said I wasn't to upset my father.'

'Well, I didn't want you to.'

'And was he?'

'Well, no. It turns out he had guessed.'

'And you knew?'

'Yes.'

'So what's upsetting you?'

'I just think it's such a lonely life.'

This was of course the parental cliché, but it goes to the very heart of why parents are upset to find out their child is gay. It's not about homophobia, it's just their worry that you won't be happy. I assured her that I wasn't lonely and that I was very happy, and that was the end of the only conversation I have ever had with my mother about my sexuality.

I don't really know how Scott filled his time, but I seemed to be away a great deal, either at gigs or sitting on a minibus coming back from Norwich in the middle of the night. The good thing was that yet again I was earning even more than I had been and the extra expense of the new flat and my live-in lover weren't causing any financial strain. Given that Scott hadn't grown up in a wealthy family and hadn't been earning very much in LA, he took to money like a duck to bottled water. It wasn't long before he was filling his time by looking for a bigger place for us to live. Of course I didn't say anything – God forbid I should rock the boat – but I did feel that the love nest I had spent so much time finding and working for in order to pay the rent had been rejected.

A phone call out of the blue. I hardly needed to pick up the receiver Melanie was so excited. I had been nominated for a comedy award. How thrilling! What for?

'Best Newcomer for *The Jack Docherty Show*.'

'Who am I up against?'

'Phil Kay and, well, this is the slightly awkward bit . . . Jack Docherty.'

It took a moment or two for the news and its significance

to sink in. Melanie went on to explain that I should have been nominated for *Bring Me the Head of Light Entertainment* but someone at Channel Five had ticked the wrong box. Oh well, it was thrilling to be nominated, even if there was no way I could win.

The big night arrived and tragically I can still remember what I was wearing. Although shiny, it was almost tasteful for me – a sort of glittering Nehru jacket affair and some trousers that were so tight my legs looked like satin sausages. Scott and I got to our table in Studio One of London Studios and joined Jack Docherty and his wife, various other producers from his show and Graham Stuart. All night people were trying to tip-toe around me and the very obvious fact that Jack was going to win, but every now and again someone would come up to the table and just see Jack. 'It's in the bag, mate, it's in the—' Then they caught sight of me smiling in my shiny blouse. I really didn't care. It was the Perrier award all over again: I was genuinely thrilled to be nominated and required nothing more.

Finally it was time for the award for Best Newcomer. Jack and I laughed and wished each other luck. Jonathan Ross introduced Kathy Burke, and the two of them cracked a few jokes before she opened the envelope. My back was to Jack as I looked at the stage. Cameras were trained on us both, and just before Kathy announced the name I heard one cameraman whisper to the other, 'I'll cover Jack to the stage.' Of course I knew I hadn't won, but I couldn't help but be disappointed to find out in such an offhand way even before it was official. I fixed my grin and refocused on the stage.

'Oh!' cried Kathy. 'It's my favourite Irish homosexual!'

What? But I'm the only . . . and then I heard it – my

name. The rest was a blur. I think I kissed Scott, maybe shook hands with Graham, but mostly stumbled to the stage as quickly as I could before someone changed their mind or Kathy revealed that she was only joking. I blurted out a few thank yous – the people at TalkBack, David Johnson and Mark Goucher, probably my parents – but then I just dried up, clutched my award and walked off.

I was no more than a couple of seconds backstage when it dawned on me. I had forgotten to thank anyone who worked on the show, Jack himself or my great supporters at Channel Five. I felt like such a complete selfish bastard, but, but . . . there is no but. It was unforgivable. I was taken backstage to the press room for photographs with Kathy and the award. In between the flashes I just kept telling everyone, 'I forgot to thank all the people I worked with.' 'They'll be all right, don't worry,' I was told repeatedly.

One of the production assistants led me around the back of the set and, in a commercial break, ushered me back to the table. Jack was full of smiles and shook my hand. The others weren't quite so good at hiding their displeasure – there were a few 'well done's through rigid smiles. I apologised again for my sin of omission, but everyone assured me that it was all right and of course they understood.

In terms of my professional life, this was the best thing that had ever happened to me and in lots of personal ways I suppose it was too. I might not have been bred for disappointment exactly, but nor had I ever won anything before – not even a raffle. But sitting at a table with Jack and all the people who worked with him day after day slightly put a lid on my euphoria. Even then, however, I was so full of a Good Thing happening to me that somehow I hadn't fully taken on board that mostly what had happened that night was a Bad Thing. It was only later that Scott told me what it had been like at the table after I had been whisked backstage. Apparently everyone around the table had gone very quiet. I'm sure certain things were left unsaid about me at the time to save Scott's feelings, but he said it was a fairly horrendous experience. The only bright spots had been when Dale Winton and Barbara Windsor (and I will always appreciate them for doing this) came over to congratulate Scott.

The party afterwards didn't feel very festive. I had a prize, but the awkwardness of how I had won it married to how badly I had handled my acceptance of it meant that the usual air punching and champagne popping just felt very out of place. I couldn't help but feel like the bad guy. Scott and I slipped away fairly early. Just as I was saying goodnight to Graham Stuart, a man came up and congratulated me. After he walked off I asked Graham, 'Who was that?' A beaming Graham replied, 'Kevin Lygo, Head of Entertainment at Channel 4.'

We didn't go straight home. Instead we stopped for a last couple of drinks at the White Swan, the East End gay bar that gained a certain notoriety when Michael Barrymore used the stage there for coming out. We stood at the bar in our finery drinking pints, and a few people who had been watching the award show on TV came over to offer their congratulations. It was like taking off a tight pair of shoes. The stress of the award show melted away and we were just another couple getting drunk.

11

So Time

CHANNEL 4'S OFFICES ON HORSEFERRY Road in London make you feel important. I strode through the revolving doors and announced myself to the bright-eyed receptionist sitting in her tower of glass and televisions. 'I have an appointment.' It felt as if the very least the meeting could be about was the merger of huge international companies or peace in the Middle East. I signed in, was issued a security pass and was then whisked away in a glass pod lift to a higher floor. Then I started talking about a show that had a few celebrity guests and maybe a member of the audience telling a story about wanking.

Graham and I had meetings with a commissioning editor called Graham K. Smith. All three of us had grown up not knowing anyone else called Graham, so we all found a childish pleasure in being in an All Graham Gang. We talked about the show in very vague terms. Essentially it would be a chat show and maybe I would do some talking with the audience or make a phone call. It was my stand-up show from Edinburgh with a few celebrities thrown in to make it seem like a television programme.

Eventually we met with Kevin Lygo, the man who had shaken my hand at the Comedy Awards. Kevin is very rare amongst television executives in that he is both funny and genuinely seems to know what he is talking about. I know that doesn't sound like much to ask from someone who has risen to the top of their profession, but you would be surprised. Most people who are in control of the programmes we watch seem to take great intellectual pride in not actually watching any television. Kevin and Lorraine Heggessy, who runs BBC 1, are happy exceptions to that rule.

All these meetings at 4 went very well, but Graham and I always left feeling slightly frustrated because no one was actually telling us that the show was definitely going to be commissioned. We kept playing around with the format, and I remember the day when Graham Stuart came up with the idea of using the Internet as well as the phone. I had never turned on a computer at the time, and although I smiled and nodded (boat be still!), I was thinking that it sounded really dull. I decided not to worry because it was beginning to look like the programme would never see the light of day.

In the middle of all this media cock-teasing, Scott had found us a new house to rent. It was further east in Bow and it was enormous. Arranged over four floors it meant we could have a study each. Scott was desperate to get a computer and try out the World Wide Web. God, what did everyone see in this Internet thing? Didn't they realise it was going to be like laser discs all over again? I reluctantly agreed to his demands and a computer arrived and was installed in his study. Almost instantly I became an Internet widow. Scott spent more and more time in his study with the computer and less and less time with me. I can't blame him, because I was so rarely there and when I was, all I wanted to do was drink wine and watch TV. I had brought this man to Britain with promises of endless love and attention, but once he'd arrived I was always out. It must have been hell for him because thanks to our application to the Home Office for his residency he had had to give up his passport. He was in effect trapped in Britain, unable to work. Of course it's relatively easy to be sympathetic in retrospect. At the time, knowing all the extenuating circumstances didn't make it any easier to live in a house with a big grumpy American sitting at his computer all day. Occasionally we still had fun and I told myself that we were just going through a bad phase, but sometimes as I sat alone flicking through the channels I wondered if the good times had been the phase.

Scott desperately wanted to get involved in the show we were planning, but although I was more than happy to discuss it with him at home, it just seemed eggy to bring him into an office full of television professionals. I suppose this was partly because I felt like such a fraud myself, and also because I was aware that it just wasn't the done thing. I told myself that I was protecting Scott and our relationship from the stresses of working together, and besides, why would he want to be my Debbie Magee?

Having spent months in non-committal committee meetings, suddenly we got the call. Channel 4 wanted to do a pilot and, should that go well, a series of six shows that would go out at 10.30 p.m. on Friday nights. After the initial celebrations had died down, we thought about the challenge we had to face. We had always imagined this show as a fairly low-key chat show that might play on a Wednesday or Thursday night, but they were asking us to take over from the slot that *Eurotrash* had been so successful in. Patently that post-pub Friday-night audience would need a little more than some Irish poof bantering with Simon Callow about his latest stage triumph. Kevin Lygo was obviously slightly nervous about his decision because he kept telling us, 'This is an entertainment show – not a chat show!' Thrilled as we were to be making any show, this did strike us as slightly odd, given that all we had ever pitched to them was a chat show.

Because nobody told me that I wasn't supposed to, I showed up for every pre-production meeting that was arranged. I've since learnt that this is not the norm. All the technical types with long hair and big bunches of keys would really prefer never to meet the presenter of a show, and if they have to then at least let it be after all the truly important work is over. People walked in for meetings about the set design or the graphics and were slightly taken aback to see me sat at the table with a cup of coffee and lots of pictures I'd ripped out of magazines. I'm sure if you talked to these people they might speak about me in terms of being a control freak, and I suppose they're right, but the way I look at it is that I'm the one fronting the show, so if it is a disaster I'd prefer it to be my fault.

A great deal of time was spent talking about what to call this new programme. The Channel and Graham Stuart would have been perfectly happy with a straightforward *The Graham Norton Show*, but I had a very strong gut feeling that my name shouldn't be in the title. For some reason I had decided that it would be unlucky, and I also had that weird thing where although I wanted to jump up and down waving my arms and shouting 'look at me!', I didn't want people to think that was all I was doing. I wanted to call it after a bar in Los Angeles called the Frolic Room, but when

I suggested this at a meeting the expression on the faces of the other people told me that I might as well have just let off a big fart. More suggestions please. *The Lock-In*? Too negative. *Last Orders*? Someone else had already used it. At one meeting, the writer Jez Stephenson was joking around because when I had guest-hosted *The Jack Docherty Show*, it had been called *Not The Jack Docherty Show*. 'Why don't we call it *The Very Graham Norton Show*?' he asked. *Completely Graham Norton*? *So Graham Norton*? We laughed and moved the conversation on to something else.

Finally I realised that I was not going to convince Graham or Channel 4 of any title that didn't include my name, and people seemed to actually like *So Graham Norton*. It was decided. I now realise that if I was going to lose any fight about my own show then this was the one to lose. Ever after, if there was any dispute about anything about the show, I could use my trump card – 'It's supposed to be *So Graham Norton*, and I don't think that's very me.' I'm sure there were times when the Channel 4 executives deeply regretted the day they inadvertently gave me such power.

We worked out of offices on Oxford Street that had previously been occupied by some sort of bucket-shop travel agent. It became clear that they had shut down and vacated the building quite suddenly given the number of times someone would poke their head around the door looking for their tickets to Uganda.

Graham Stuart and I put together a small team of people, some of whom still work with me today. The worry was that we had yet to find a producer. Graham couldn't do it full time because he was looking after other projects at United, and we weren't having much luck. I suppose it was always going to be hard to find a talented, successful producer who had the time and the inclination to risk their reputation on an untried performer doing a totally new show in the relatively low-profile summer season. We worked on confirming all the elements of the show, not really mentioning to Channel 4 that with weeks to go there was still no one to produce it.

Being the host of a show after guest-hosting someone else's or being just a guest on various panel games took quite a lot of getting used to. I didn't feel any different, but it was clear from the outset that I was the boss. The first meeting I had with the team was very strange. I was introduced to them all and that was fine, but then as the meeting went on I noticed that if I spoke everyone shut up and turned to look at me. If I made the slightest little joke they all laughed . . . for just a little too long. I'm sure this still happens in meetings now, but what worries me is that I've just stopped noticing. I remember being really upset when someone on the team organised a barbecue one weekend and I wasn't invited. It felt like a punch in the stomach, but then I realised that this was the way it was going to be from now on. I was the boss, and who invites their boss to a party? They wanted to have fun, and I imagined them all standing around eating their burnt raw sausages having a great time ripping the shit out of me. There is still an invisible, unavoidable glass wall between me and the people I work with, and anyone who pretends it doesn't exist is an idiot. Of course I am extremely close to some of the team, but no matter how drunk we get, our work relationship continues to hang around us like the smell of dog shit stuck to someone's shoe.

Finally Peter Kessler, the man who had produced *The Mrs Merton Show*, was persuaded to come on board as producer.

Looking back, he had an awful job. He was joining the process really late so that most of the big decisions had already been made, and he was sharing an office with me, and I had tasted control and it had affected me the way the taste of human blood can send a shark into a killing frenzy. I really enjoyed his company, but we continually clashed, which involved, it has to be said, deeply unprofessional behaviour from me.

Making a pilot show is a horrible experience. The Channel wants to see exactly what the show will be like, but it is impossible to make it the same as a show that is going to be transmitted precisely because it isn't going to be. The atmosphere in the audience is invariably oddly low-key because they know they can't sit at home looking for their own face in the crowd – 'Oh, doesn't my jumper look red?' – but the hardest part is getting guests. Who would want to be on the pilot for a show hosted by someone they don't know? We were very lucky to get Davina McCall. She looked great and told a very funny story about when she was hosting *God's Gift* and one of the male contestants stripped down to a thong, and thinking he was indeed God's gift turned around to wiggle his arse at the girls only to reveal a little piece of poo waving hello to the pretty ladies.

Our second guest was slightly less successful. He was a famous American psychic, but sadly he is only a celebrity in America, and even sadder on so many levels he seems to have stopped being a psychic everywhere. Scott knew him from LA (dead celebrity circles) and swore blind that he did have amazing powers, but nothing was in evidence that night in London Studios. He approached the audience.

'You're planning to move house.'

'No.'

'Mmm, well, you will move house.'

Or:

'You're planning to change careers. What do you do now?'

'Nothing. I'm unemployed.'

And so it went on. There was one moment of excitement when he correctly identified a man as a lawyer, but later we found out that the guy worked for Channel 4 and they had met in the green room.

Anyone who saw the pilot and then the first few episodes would have noticed one big difference. In the pilot I – yes, it was all down to me! – decided that instead of a house band I would have a woman called Lorraine Bowen. She is still on the cabaret circuit and if you get the chance to go and see her, you must, she is brilliant. She plays a tiny Yamaha organ that she balances on an ironing board and she sings inspired little ditties about things like making apple crumble. I love her. Her job was to introduce the guests with specially written songs. I thought she did a great job and gave the show a really odd feel. I suppose I was still back in my Mother Teresa mindest of making sure that if something wasn't funny at least it was mad in a Sarah Bright-man kind of way.

The pilot was edited and given to Channel 4 to watch. They had lots of problems with the whole thing. They didn't like the lighting, they wanted the set to be changed – but in terms of content the only thing they didn't like was lovely, brilliant Lorraine. Maybe I should have fought harder for her – Scott certainly thought so – but the pilot hadn't gone that well and I wasn't feeling overly confident about the whole thing. I felt if I gave in to the Channel on this one issue they might leave us alone to get on with the show. Lorraine was out and I felt like a shit. The good news, though, was that our compromises and changes had worked and Channel 4 gave the go-ahead for a first series.

Ben Devlin was the associate producer on the show, and he took over the role of guest booking quite early on. There are many jobs in television, some more glamorous than others, but guest booking is just below picking up the shit from Wendy Richards's dog. I'm not quite sure how Ben managed it, but for our very first show we had the dream line-up of Ivana Trump, Kathy Burke, Sooty, Sweep and a special guest appearance by Gordon the Gopher. The day before, we heard that Ivana wouldn't stay for the whole show – in fact, more than that, we found out that Ivana was only doing the show on her way from Waterloo, where she was arriving on the Eurostar, to a restaurant she was having dinner in. It did sort of help to put everything in perspective: for me, the biggest night in my life; for her, a mere pit stop for make-up and hair.

It was around that time that I had my first, and I'm happy to report, last panic attack, or what I believe to have been one. I woke up and lay in bed not wanting to wake Scott, and I was filled with the feeling of panic (you can see why I might have thought it was a panic attack). Somehow it was related to the new show and all the pressures it was putting on me or, more accurately, all the pressure I was putting on myself. I lay there twitching and listening to the warm rhythm of Scott's breathing and literally thought to myself, 'I don't want to feel like this. Nothing is worth this.' As calmly as I could, I worked through what the worst-case scenario could possibly be, and as far as I could work out that would be ending up back working in a restaurant, and as bad as that was it had never made me wake up feeling like this. I resolved to never feel like that again, and miraculously I never have. If you suffer from panic attacks I'm sure you found that little tale unbearably twee and smug, but for me, having waited for success for such a long time, it was a strangely liberating thought to embrace failure and realise that it wasn't the end of the world.

Nowadays I am universally nice to all my guests because I want to keep them happy, and also from a practical point of view I need so many of them, but in that first show I was quite tough on Ivana Trump. She had various business projects on the go and I asked her if she felt a new casino was really what Bosnia needed right now, and then I went on to be rude about her daughter's name, Ivanka. Looking back, I was one. Kathy Burke was hilarious, but because we had packed our forty-minute show with so much puppet business her interview was edited down to almost nothing. Lessons were learnt.

I watched the first show go out sitting beside Scott. Almost before it was over the phone rang. It was my agent Melanie – you may have gathered by now that very few other people call me. She had watched the show at TalkBack with some man who produced Griff Rhys Jones and Mel Smith's show. She handed the phone over to him and after briefly congratulating me, he started to criticise the way it had been edited. I had to agree because I had thought the same myself, but nevertheless, having someone tear your first TV show apart isn't quite what you want while your theme music is still ringing in your ears. It would be another few months before I fully realised the significance of that phone call.

That first series was full of highs and lows. Guests like Lorraine Kelly and Stephen Fry were brilliant, but other people proved difficult. Kylie Minogue seemed incapable of telling one of her own anecdotes. At the time I thought it was because I was gay and so not flirting with her properly, but I've since seen her do it on other shows. She smiles and laughs, but never really engages with the interviewer. I guess she is just happier when she is singing, as am I.

David Blaine was a fairly disastrous guest. At the time very few people in Britain had heard of him, but my producer Peter was a real magic buff and Channel 4 had just bought his first *Street Magic* special. We booked him. Given what we had seen him do on his TV show, he did turn out to be a disappointment.

'Can you do the levitation for us?'

'In the studio in front of the audience? No.'

Later in the day I was in a lift with him when he decided to thrill me with his levitation spectacular. It was like some dreary fifth former in the dinner queue, trying to impress his friends. In the end, all he felt able to do for us on the show were some card tricks. Fine. What he hadn't bargained for was a British audience. We have been brought up with Paul Daniels and the like, so when David asked someone 'Is that your card?' he got a simple, unexcited 'Yes'. After all, it would have been a pretty piss-poor trick if it hadn't been your card. David, however, was used to the good people of some of New York's less affluent neighbourhoods, who had never seen a card trick before, screaming and calling him the devil before they ran off into the night. Barbara from Maida Vale was never going to do that. David started to lose his confidence, dropping cards on the floor and fluffing his patter. The audience became restless. They had never heard of this American magician and now they knew why. From that night forth I haven't been able to bear the man or the power his self-fuelled hype has over a mindless media. Pulling a rabbit out of a hat is a magic trick, not eating is a diet.

There was one night in that first series when the show seemed to really hit its stride and show us how fantastic it could be when it worked. We were in our third week, and the guests were, perhaps, my favourite combination ever – Grace Jones and Judith Chalmers.

I already knew that I should be careful with the unique Miss Jones. The night before, Scott and I had met with her briefly in the Met bar to talk about the show. As expected, she kept us waiting for quite a long time, so Scott and I had a few cocktails. I had never been in the Met bar before, and given all the stories I had read about celebrity customers and raucous excess I was slightly disappointed to find it a bit like a posh youth club. Finally Grace appeared and we were ushered to a booth. We talked briefly about the format of the show, and I did general gushing. We were all a bit distracted by two skinny kids with long hair dancing in front of us.

'Is that a boy or a girl?' boomed Grace.

In fairness I couldn't tell.

'Maybe it's an hermaphrodite' she concluded.

Scott asked Grace if she had heard the rumours about the famous Hollywood actress who was supposed to be one.

Now, this is the moment where it all went a bit wrong.

Grace said, 'I don't think so,' and then continued, 'People say it about me all the time.'

I don't know why, but for some reason Scott didn't hear

the second bit of what she had said and he blithely leaned over to her and said apropos of the actress; 'Well, there's no smoke without fire.'

Too late for me to interject and explain to Grace that he wasn't in fact referring to her. The globe-like eyes rolled back in her head, she pulled her neck to its full extent and glared at a clueless Scott. 'Bull. Shit,' she snarled with the sort of menace that could have cured severe constipation. We left shortly after that.

The next night she prowled on set determined to make an impact, in turns flirting with me and then trying to strangle me. Slowly she calmed down and simply began to enjoy herself. By the time I called a man in New York who cleaned apartments in the nude, both the audience and myself felt as if anything could happen. It was like the best nights at the Edinburgh Festival. He refused to believe that it was really Grace Jones talking down the phone to him until finally she started singing the chorus of 'La Vie En Rose'. Now, I've always been a fan of Grace Jones, even before I saw her on the back of a truck all those years before in San Francisco, but I'd always assumed that her singing voice was somehow created by the record producers. That was stupid of me. Her deep, pure voice sent a shiver through me. I have goosebumps just thinking about it. There was also the undeniable thrill of thinking about how much my life had changed since I had stood at the side of the street in a huge crowd trying to catch a glimpse of her. Now she was singing in my ear.

I just assumed that the second half of the show would be an anticlimax, but I was so wrong. Judith trotted down the stairs in a bright pink suit and proceeded to tell the nation that she didn't wear knickers. Then, in a surreal moment she and Grace started chatting about the pros and cons of wearing thongs. I just sat back and listened to them and thought to myself, 'I like my show.'

The other thing that made the whole night really special for me was that my parents were there. They had never seen me do anything, and to begin with their presence made me more nervous and self-conscious, but soon I had to forget about them and just get on with it. Occasionally I would glance over to where they were sitting, and I could see them laughing. Without doubt that must have been one of the coolest feelings in the world. After the show I felt we had a new-found respect for each other. It was as if for the first time in my life I felt like an adult around my parents, and they saw me as one.

In the green room my mother made a beeline for Judith Chalmers and they chatted on like old friends. Meanwhile, in another corner of the room, Grace Jones, who before the show had requested Cristal champagne and platters of sushi, was tucking into sausage rolls and glasses of fairly rough red wine. I turned to my father.

'Would you like to meet Grace Jones?'

He thought about it for a moment and glanced over to where she was standing by the buffet.

'No.'

Enough said.

12

Who Put the Good in Goodbye?

THE PHONE RANG AND IT wasn't Melanie. My mother went through her normal report of life in Bandon. Guttering had been power-hosed, lunches had been digested, traffic lights had been fixed. I listened in my usual slightly distracted manner as I paced around the kitchen, but I could tell that something was wrong. Finally she talked herself out of all other available news and had to tell me why she had really called.

'Your father has been diagnosed with Parkinson's disease.' Of course I didn't know much about it, apart from the fact that it was degenerative, so for some weird reason I failed to understand the seriousness of the news. I simply thought that somewhere down the line in years to come my father might develop a bit of a shake. I failed to see that it was the end of the world.

What I did understand was that my mother was very upset, so I decided to go home for a visit. Walking in and seeing my father made me realise what an idiot I had been on the phone. Although my father was still walking and driving, it was clear that this disease had him in its grip. There was a lot of talk about medication and how it hadn't started to work yet but that when it did he would get some of his strength back and of course exercise would help and how the husband of a friend of a friend had it and he was doing very well. A forced brightness filled the house while my father sat quietly with God knows what thoughts in his head.

I have no idea how I would react if I was given the news that I had something like Parkinson's disease, but I like to think that I would fight it and continue to find a quality of life. It seemed my father decided quite early on that it was a fight he couldn't win and so he declined with an alarming speed. I went back to work in London, but my mother kept me updated with his progress, or lack of it. He had been forced to give up driving and so my mother, in her mid-sixties, had taken driving lessons and passed her test first time. I was so proud of her and so scared for her at the same time. For a while things seemed to settle down, and we hoped that somehow it had got as bad as it would get for the moment. Perhaps the medication was starting to work?

Scott tried to help and encouraged me to talk about it, but I didn't want to. Somehow seeing what my father was going through made me feel even more isolated from Scott. Things between us had gone from good to indifferent, and now they seemed almost permanently bad. There seemed to be no sign of Scott getting his passport back and no news about our application. Scott had a lot to be angry and resentful about. It didn't help that professionally I seemed to be doing better and better.

A new series of So had been commissioned along with a Christmas special. But who would produce it? Peter had decided to leave the world of light entertainment and make documentaries. We were back on the hunt, and although I now had a moderate hit on my hands, the word was out that

Who Put the Good in Goodbye?

I was 'difficult' because I wanted to be involved in all aspects of the show. Graham Stuart arranged for a lunch with a man called Jon Magnusson. I knew that the name was familiar but I thought it was just because I'd heard people talking about him. He had started in radio, and then done a lot of work with Mel Smith and Griff Rhys Jones before moving on to work with Rory Bremner. Tall and Scottish and with an impressive CV, he was instantly intimidating to me. During lunch he reminded me when I had heard his name for the first time. He had been the man on the phone when Melanie called after the first show. I warmed to him. He had obviously watched quite a few of the shows and I agreed with nearly all of his criticisms. We decided to give each other a go, and nearly four hundred shows later we are still working together.

News from Ireland wasn't good. My father had some infection and had been taken into hospital. I headed home. If I had got a shock the last time I had seen my dad, it was nothing compared to what I found this time. Parkinson's wasn't winning this fight on points – it was a knock-out. Pale, paperlike skin covered his wasted body. His mouth had become small and thin and his eyes seemed huge and frightened. I stood at the window pretending to study the view as I surreptitiously wiped away tears. This was my father. The man who had let me win races in the back garden in Waterford. He was the man who could lift anything, open anything, fix anything. Now he lay on a bed like a baby bird that had fallen from a nest. My mother, my sister and myself sat around the bed trying to chat. It was unbearable and it was going to get worse.

Parkinson's disease is especially cruel. It doesn't even do

you the favour of killing you. It just moves in and with an awful efficiency simply packs up your quality of life. It was clear that things had reached the stage where it was no longer possible for my mother to care for him at home. While I went back to London to run up and down stairs in a shiny suit, my mother and sister started to look for a nursing home for my father.

The second series was an even bigger success than the first had been. Jon and I quickly stopped being nervous of each other and began to really enjoy working together. A viewer sent us a Doggy Phone and it slowly became part of the furniture. Phone calls to Miles O'Keefe, the actor who had played Tarzan opposite Bo Derek's Jane, turned into a weekly feature and our guest booking moved up a notch with people like Joan Collins and Roger Moore coming on the show. That was also the series when the world first saw a little old lady in the audience called Betty.

I was thrilled when the letter arrived. 'Perhaps you remember me?' Of course I remembered Betty. For three years at drama school she had made me coffee, and now she wanted to get tickets to see the show. I arranged for her to come along and invited a bunch of friends from Central along too because we all remembered Betty really fondly. After the show I brought her into the green room and showed her the group from school. She looked at them.

'Hello. Where's Rufus Sewell? Is Saskia Wickham here?'

It turned out that Betty, as well as being a sweet little old lady from North London, was also obsessed by fame. She had volumes of photo albums of herself with famous people dating back years, and now that she had found her way to my show where she had access to at least two celebrities a week, there was no going back. Week after week I would see her beaming face in the audience, and I was genuinely pleased to see her. I started to do little jokes about her in the warm-up, and then the director started using shots of her laughing after a particularly rude joke.

The first time we actually used her in the show was on St Patrick's Day. The guests were Carrie Fisher and Terry Wogan, and at the end of the show we were doing an item called 'Lucky O'Dip', which was essentially people from the audience pulling various items out of a sawdust-filled barrel. We had found an amazing vibrator that was in the shape of a tongue. The label proudly proclaimed that it was designed for women by women and when it was fully charged it went at a frightening lick. We thought it would be funny to see Betty pulling this out of the barrel, and sure enough it was. We liked the prop so much we got more in and gave them to various other guests, including Joan Collins, but forever after it was simply called Betty's Tongue.

Over the years she has become more and more a part of the show. We've dressed her in a tutu, she has French-kissed strangers and even attended the MTV awards in Barcelona. Recently I was walking down a street in New York, and I could tell that a policeman on the other side of the street was looking at me. There are so many weird laws in the city that I immediately thought I must be doing something wrong, but just as I drew level to him, this big New York cop shouted 'How's Betty?' This woman who for her whole life had been fascinated by fame had now in some quirk of fate ended up becoming famous herself.

Each week my mother would talk to me on the phone and tell me what she thought of the show and the guests.

She taped them and then brought them to the nursing home to show my father. By now their lives had taken on a grim new routine. My father lived in a nursing home in Macroom, and each day my mother drove the thirty miles there and back through twisting country roads to spend time with him. I went home as often as I could, but it couldn't be often enough. I saw the terrible toll it was all taking on my mother, but it seemed as if there was no alternative.

Writing about this now it seems incredible that I was able to keep going with the show, but at the time it seemed like life was just going on. There were bits of it that were good and bits of it that were bad. Scott and I were by now going to couple counselling. Why anyone goes to it is a mystery to me. If things have reached that stage, why not just admit that the relationship is over? Week after week I sat there not really saying very much while Scott moaned to the poor woman about me. I suppose he enjoyed it and I guess I owed him that much. I just wondered when it would end. When would the clever lady eventually tell us that it was officially hopeless and we should call it a day? Given that she was being paid by the hour, I guessed that would be never.

More shows were commissioned and then the Channel asked if we would like to do a live show to usher in the millennium. This seemed like a great honour, but more than that it solved the terrible problem of what to do on New Year's Eve. I told Scott the good news. Apparently it wasn't. Very reasonably he had imagined spending the night with family or at the very least just with me. The poor man was essentially going out with a junkie except that my drug of choice was work. For the umpteenth time in our relationship I chose work over him, but I told myself that since things were going so badly between us anyway, why would he want to spend time with me?

I had never done live television before and I'm not really in a rush to do it again. The good thing about working that night was just being in the centre of town. I stood on the roof of London Studios on the bank of the Thames and stared across the capital. This was quite simply a London I didn't recognise. The city was transformed into one huge, good-humoured party and I was pleased and proud to be a part of it.

The show we did was more or less what people might have expected. We had a live link to a sex club in Amsterdam, some members of the audience ran naked across Westminster Bridge, and of course we had a celebrity presence in the shape of Raquel Welch via satellite from Los Angeles. I chatted to her a bit throughout the show, but just after midnight when I went back to her to say thank you and goodnight, her face said it all. She glowered into the camera and said, 'I hope in the new year your level of taste improves.' The audience hissed. We'd been having a great time, and some woman from Hollywood was trying to piss on our parade. It wasn't professional and I'm not proud, but it was the first thing that came into my mind, so I said it: 'Grumpy old bitch.' The screen went blank. Later we discovered that she had misunderstood an item in the show because she could only hear it, and that was what had upset her so much. We had played a game called 'drunks say the funniest things' where drunk people had described a celebrity and we had to guess who it was. At some point someone in the audience mentioned Raquel Welch's name, and somehow our long-distance diva had got it into her head that we were saying that she had slept with the drunk person. Still, it's curious that over the years not one person has ever come up to me and said, 'Oh, you got Raquel so wrong. She's really a lovely person.' Not one.

The climax of the evening was when a lovely lady named Helga started our fireworks for us by firing a ping-pong ball out of herself and hitting a target. In rehearsals we reassured her that so long as she managed to fire the ball, then it really didn't matter about hitting the target because the fireworks would go off no matter what. Being the professional that she was, that ping-pong ball hit the target every time. It makes me proud to think that in years to come, when archivists are going through how the arrival of the new millennium was marked by TV stations around the globe, there on Channel 4 will be Helga with her legs in the air and feathers in her hair, firing out ping-pong balls.

A few months later we recreated the moment to mark the end of series three. Always conscious of taste and decency, we positioned Helga carefully so that her back was to the audience. Unfortunately we forgot that this meant the celebrity guests would get quite an eyeful. It was too late to do anything about it, and Joan Collins and Richard Wilson sat there and were able to enjoy the full depth of Helga's talent.

Months went by, viewing figures went up and we even began to win some awards. The Comedy Awards acknowledged the show and we got a BAFTA nomination.

One Friday I was just leaving the Ivy where I had been having lunch with Kevin Lygo when my mobile phone rang. It was my sister Paula. I should come home. My father wasn't dead, but the doctor had made it clear that the end was going to be sooner rather than later. I hung up. Walking down Long Acre towards Covent Garden, I called my travel agent and organised my flight for later that day. Then I went into a men's shop and bought a plain black suit. The shop assistants joked with me about the show and all the outrageous things that we had done on it. I laughed and signed autographs as they packed up the suit I would wear to my father's funeral.

It was dark when we got to the nursing home. We crept into my father's room and the three of us gathered around the bed in the gloom. We sat and listened to him breathing. Every time he exhaled, we waited to see if there was going to be another breath. Occasionally his face flickered, but he seemed calm and peaceful. We stayed there by his side till late into the night, but eventually we decided to go home, get some sleep and come back in the morning. We each in turn held his hand and kissed his cool cheek goodnight.

The next morning as we were having breakfast, the phone rang. I happened to be nearest to it and so I answered it.

'Is that Graham?'

'Yes . . .'

It was the matron from the nursing home. I expected her to ask to speak to my mother, but she carried on.

'Your father passed away a few minutes ago.'

'OK. We'll be there soon.'

My sister and mother were standing close to me looking at my face for news. I had no idea what to say or how to say it. I opened my mouth.

'That's it. He's gone.'

As long as I live I never want to hear again the sound my mother made at that moment. A cry that made everything so clear. She hadn't lost her husband, or the father of her children. She had lost her lover. She was no longer some grey-haired lady standing in her pristine kitchen, she was the embodiment of pure grief. She might have been seventeen hearing that her boyfriend had been killed in a motorcycle accident.

We sat in the car outside the nursing home for a while until we finally felt ready to venture inside. I don't know what I expected to feel when I saw my father's body lying there. I suppose I thought he would simply look the same as he had when we had left him the night before but without the slow unsteady breathing. But this was different. I'm so glad I did get to see my father's body because it made it so clear to me that he was gone. The body on the bed looked like my father – but it wasn't him. I'm sure you know by now that I'm not a very religious person, but there was no doubt that my father's spirit had left this body that had failed him so badly.

The local rector arrived, and along with a few of the nurses we stood by the bed and said prayers. Obviously we were crying, but oddly what moved me most was seeing that the nurses too had tears streaming down their faces. It said so much about my father that even without his stories and sparkle, his profound sweetness had touched these strangers. Sad as we all were to have lost this man, some of the tears felt good too. He was free. Much as we would miss him, there was no one in that room who could have wished him alive again to continue having to deal with his disease.

Whenever people I knew had a death in the family I was always faintly embarrassed and gave them a wide berth, assuming that they would want to be left alone. In a small town in Ireland that isn't an option. Almost as soon as we got back from the nursing home the doorbell started to ring. Neighbours who had heard the news came to pay their respects. They brought cakes, they brought bottles of whiskey, but mostly they brought their memories of my father. Far from being intrusive or insensitive, as I thought such visits would be, they were wonderfully comforting. We realised that all we wanted to do was talk about the man who had left the room. Nearly every visit ended up with us all laughing at something my father had done or one of his stories being retold. That sense of community and support brought me a whole new respect and affection for Ireland. All the things that I had thought were there to hold me back I now found were there to hold me up.

The funeral was perfect. A hot sunny day in May and a church full of people from all over the country. I knew my father was well liked, but to see the people all standing in rows with their heads bowed made it so real. Afterwards we stood and people walked by, pausing to shake our hands. 'Sorry for your loss', 'Sorry for your loss'. The words start to lose all meaning and yet they meant so much. All the rituals of death came together and made perfect sense. Of course not everything was perfect. The choir sang one hymn to the wrong tune – my mother quite liked that because it gave her something to criticise – and then the editor of the local paper asked me if I would consider doing an interview just as the hearse drove off taking my father to the crematorium. That took my breath away.

Back at the house we had the happiest, biggest party I can ever remember having there. I topped up glasses and chatted to people I hadn't seen for years, and all the talk was of my father. A small army of ladies fell easily into separate troops of buttering and slicing and then later washing and drying.

After everyone was gone it was just Rhoda, Paula and Graham. I'm sure my father left many legacies, but the one that means most to me is how much closer I've become to my mother and sister. We had never been distant, but somehow sharing that time of raw grief helped us open ourselves up and see to the very core of each other.

Later that same week I stood on the stage at the Grosvenor House and held a BAFTA. I held it up and, looking into the camera, thought about my mother sitting in her bungalow watching the television.

'I'd like to dedicate this to Billy Walker,' I said.

13

Housekeeping

SCOTT AND I FINALLY SPLIT up. I think my father's death made me realise that life is too short to waste time in a situation that is making you unhappy.

Trying to describe why a relationship fails is in itself doomed to failure. Oh, sometimes a used condom found under the sofa might do it, or an argument that ends up with pieces of furniture in the street could help finish one off, but for the most part it is an endless accumulation of little things. The bold facts were that Scott and I were madly in love at the beginning and then I was too busy for him, but this must have happened to other couples who have survived such things. There is no denying that the fact that I was busy on television did nothing to help. I hate to describe myself as a celebrity, but as far as Scott was concerned I was one, and going out with a celebrity was hell. The moment you leave your front door with your famous friend it ceases to be about you, and the awful truth is that it isn't anything to do with self-esteem or paranoia – it actually isn't about you.

Scott was always cast as bad cop whenever we went out for a drink or a meal. The one who got rid of the person who was chatting to me while I smiled and nodded. Usually I was pleased, but sometimes Scott did his job with such zeal that even I was a little embarrassed. Who could blame him? I lost count of the number of times people just started speaking to me without saying excuse me and stood with their back to Scott. If they did speak to him it was usually because they wanted to speak to me. Again, he wasn't being oversensitive – that was what was happening.

Now when I date people it is funny to see how quickly they become disenchanted with what at first must have been the main attraction – going out with someone off the telly. Somehow they think that some of the attention will rub off on them, but unless you can get your tits out at premieres it really doesn't.

What was doubly hard on Scott was that when he met me I wasn't well known at all. The fame thing happened very quickly, and even I found it hard to deal with, but at least it was happening to me.

I suppose that was why I hated the counselling so much, because it was very hard to defend myself; but also I just kept asking myself, why would he want to stay in a relationship that was making him so unhappy? Surely he would leave me?

Scott had finally been granted his residency and was given his passport back. The first thing he wanted to do was go back to visit his family. This was fine by me. I had bought a house, but I was having the bathrooms redone so I was renting a flat in Soho. No Scott plus apartment slap in the heart of London's gay village equalled big fun as far as I was concerned. By then, I really didn't care any more. This sounds harsh, but the relationship had gone so wrong that I didn't have it in me to be nice. Nor could I be sensitive to his needs. How Scott continued to put up with me is a mystery.

Housekeeping

When he got back and started making noises about more counselling, I told him that I didn't want to go back to the same one. He agreed that she'd been useless and he began to search for someone better. Now, I don't quite know how I got the wrong end of the stick, but I thought when he came up with the name of some new counsellor that we were just going to go for one big last hurrah session where we would finally split up but in a controlled environment. I practically skipped to the man's door. When he asked me how I saw the relationship, I began with a breezy, 'Well, it's over.' I could tell at once from the expression on Scott's face that in fact that wasn't what he'd been expecting to hear. Even the counsellor looked slightly surprised. However, it was done. I had said it and there was no going back. Scott and Graham were no more.

I am still genuinely fond of Scott, and I know that at one time I was deeply in love with him, but in the last couple of months it had been hell. The day he moved out was very awkward and uncomfortable. He handed me the keys and headed off to his new flat about half a mile away. I shut the door, and for the first time in five and a half years felt truly alone. I knew that in time I would miss him, but in that moment it was like a great weight being lifted.

I had no intention of dating anyone very soon, but happily the gay world provides for all sorts of loose definitions of what exactly dating might be.

Most Wednesday nights a few of the gay men who worked on the show and I would end up at the White Swan for what is called 'Amateur strip night'. Like most things, this sounds a lot sexier than it actually is. Before I went I always imagined it as full of hunky regular guys stripping in front

237

of other people because it turned them on or because . . . well, I'd never thought too long about why they would do it. In fact, nobody thinks too long about why they do it, which is the problem. Some of them think they might have a chance as a professional stripper – they're wrong: think of the first round of *Pop Idol* auditions without pants – but the vast majority do it because they are drunk beyond reason or shame and think that the £10 you get for entering will do nicely for a few more drinks and the night bus home.

A lot of the people who go are regulars, and we normally ended up standing at the same place in the bar and having a drunken laugh at the expense of the poor unfortunates on stage. There was one guy I thought was very cute who was often there, and I kept chatting to him. One night I guess we had both had one drink too many and started kissing. He ended up coming back to my house. We had a few more drinks and finally stumbled up the stairs to the bedroom and the bliss that was sure to follow.

I woke up and blinked at the world like an albino piglet with an eye disease. I seemed to be alone. I looked around the house, but sure enough the man was gone. In the kitchen, as I stood staring at the kettle trying to remember how it worked, I found a note.

'Dear Graham, thanks for last night. I've never had someone fall asleep on me before. Call me.'

The shame of it all. I can't pretend this was the first or indeed last time that this has happened to me. Drink has a way of making me take some quite snap and final decisions. 'I want to fuck him, no, wait, I'd prefer to pass out.' I felt so sorry for this poor man lying there with me, head rolled back and drool trickling on to the pillow, and yet there was the small 'call me' at the end of the note. Embarrassed and frustrated because I hadn't got what I had wanted, I phoned him. He was charming and understanding. We arranged to meet in a club on the Sunday night.

When I saw him again I was fairly sober and pleased to see that he was as cute as I'd thought he was when I was out of my mind. We were chatting, but he kept looking at his watch.

'Anything wrong?' I asked.

'No, sorry. It's just that at midnight it'll be my birthday.'

'Really! How old will you be?'

Now, I hadn't really thought very much about his age. I'd assumed he was late twenties, early thirties. He finished his Smirnoff ice.

'Twenty.'

It was as if scales fell from my eyes. Of course he was! How could I have been so blind? I was looking into the face of a child. *Going* to be twenty? Only drink had stopped me from having sex with an actual teenager! Later, drink also meant that I did have sex with an actual twenty-year-old.

Since Scott I have found myself with many inappropriate sleeping partners – guys who I know are too good-looking or young for me, but then again it's not as if I have pursued them. I suppose the problem is that a mature, sensible man would never be impressed enough to sleep with someone just because they were on TV.

Another reason I think I ended up having sex with younger, cuter guys is because I was feeling much more confident about my body than ever before. Around the end of series two I was finding it quite hard to look at myself on screen. If I hadn't been working on television I probably would have been happy enough. I was in my late thirties and in a stable relationship, the perfect time to let yourself go, but TV is the cruellest mirror on earth. At home you can tuck your shirt in just so, check yourself in the bathroom from a certain angle and leave the house thinking that that is how you look all day. The camera catches you from every angle – the folds of flesh under your ears, the pouches of flab draping over your waistband, the weird lumps of fat sticking out of the back of your suit jacket. It is completely unforgiving. I decided to do something about it.

I developed my own fairly eccentric diet plan where I could only eat things that were green or white. To begin with this meant a fairly strict regime of fish with peas, spinach or a little rice. Over time I included chicken without skin and potatoes without butter. The clever thing about my diet was that you could drink as much as you liked, but only things you could see through. So no more lager or red wine, but endless white wine, vodka, gin and champagne. As unscientific as this was, it began to work.

In addition to thinking about what I ate, I also began my hate/hate relationship with the gym. I began working out in late 1999, and I still find it just as hard to make myself go now. Although I feel great afterwards, there is something so monumentally futile about working out in itself. You run, but you are going nowhere. You lift heavy things, but everything ends up where it started. You work out, but you still end up as old and fat as the people who didn't bother. I'm by no means skinny, but as I climb fifty flights of imaginary stairs or run for three miles towards a CNN newsreader or some MTV video, I try to imagine what sort of life I would have to lead to maintain my weight without going to the gym: tiny salads and not a drink in sight. In the end it makes more sense for me to be miserable for an hour three or four times a week than to be deeply unhappy all the time. It has to be said that occasionally the alternative of eating anything I want and spending my savings on rent boys seems very tempting indeed.

After Scott left, I started going back to Ireland more and more. If I hadn't spent enough time with my father, I wasn't going to make the same mistake with my mother. Every time I said I was coming home, my mother would threaten that we'd spread my father's ashes. This was a task that none of us wanted to do and, what's more, we had no idea where to do it. There was the beach at Dunworley where we had spent our summers, but we all agreed that dumping your father into the ocean was more like throwing him out than spreading him. We needed land, and, while the garden was tempting, it did seem a bit lazy. It was decided that we would drive up to the small village in Wicklow where he grew up, and once we got there we would find a nice spot.

My sister drove the car, and just like the day of my father's funeral the weather was glorious. Carnew is a funny little place. The wide main street makes you think that once upon a time there were great plans for it but in the end nothing happened. A few shops and pubs line the grand thorough-fare, and then suddenly on one side of the street it all stops for a high wall. Carnew Castle. Across the road there is the church where my grandparents are buried, then the old school where my father went, and around the corner the house he was raised in. It seemed right to bring him home.

My mother had remembered a field that Dad had often talked about ploughing with horses when he was a boy. It is up a long hill out of the village and looks out over half the county. It sounded perfect, and we could all imagine my father spending eternity there. Now we just had to find it.

We found the road it was on fairly easily, but the actual field was slightly trickier. Presumably boundaries had changed over the years, so the exact spot where my father had followed the horses up and down was really just guess-work. Paula and I looked to Mum for a decision. After two or three runs up and down the hill, she convinced herself about the spot.

'Here! This is it, stop the car.'

Paula pulled into the side of the road and we all got out. There was a farmhouse with cars outside it about one hundred yards away. We tried not to look too suspicious as we took my father in his temporary plastic home out of the boot of the car.

We went up to the gate, but it really wasn't how I remembered gates being when I was growing up in the country. This thing was about six feet high. I climbed up and over and Paula passed Dad to me through the railings. My mother, not known for her agility, began the climb. Using some words I never thought I'd hear my mother say aloud, she slowly got herself to the top. Here she stalled. My sister helped her get one leg over and I was there to catch it. Like Annie Oakley astride a very thin metal horse, Rhoda was majestic and triumphant. Now we just needed to get the other leg over. After a couple of tentative attempts, the sudden realisation that she was six feet off the ground with nothing to hold on to hit her. She began to shriek, 'Get me down! Get me down!' With very little help from Paula or myself she quickly transformed into a monkey in a head-scarf and headed for firm ground. We paused to get our breath and then Paula noticed something. The huge, insurmountable gate wasn't actually locked.

Once in the field, we stood together, and the seriousness of what we were doing came back to us. We walked away from the gate till we found a place beneath a tree that had an uninterrupted panorama of the countryside. My mother said a prayer and then unscrewed the lid of the jar. Taking it in turns, we took handfuls of the ashes and scattered them into the wind. We said goodbye and all of us started to cry. Handful after handful we flung the ashes into the air, but there seemed to be no end to the man. Also, the slight breeze had become a bit stronger so that after each throw, we had to dodge the ashes coming back at us. From a distance we must have looked like three people dancing to unheard music in a field. Although we were all still crying, we had also started to laugh – even my mother. It's one of my happiest memories that day, the three of us dancing around in the sun and the wind, laughing and crying and releasing my father for ever.

We all knew that the first Christmas without Dad was going to be hard, especially for my mother, so I came up with a plan. She would spend Christmas with me in London and then we would head off to San Francisco for New Year. Because I couldn't drive at the time, trying to choose a place to visit was quite hard. We had to be able get around, but it couldn't be too hot or too cold and there had to be enough things to interest my mother. At the same time, I wasn't completely selfless – I wanted a bit of nightlife too. Previously I had taken my mother for long weekends to Seville,

Venice and Paris. These were no-expense-spared affairs and I really enjoyed being able to do it for her. I think Venice was her favourite, though I felt a little awkward. It was such a romantic city and all the other tourists seemed to be in couples, so when I walked into a restaurant with my mother I could sense people looking at us and silently thinking, 'Christ! *He*'s fucking *her*?' I never mentioned it to my mother.

I was really looking forward to seeing San Francisco again after so many years and I thought my mother would enjoy it too. My only worry was the hills. Visiting the city requires quite a bit of walking, and when people talk about the 'hills', in some cases words like 'mountain' or 'cliff' would perhaps be a little more accurate. In the event I needn't have worried about my mother. I had done something to my back trying to sleep on the plane, and I hobbled up the steep slopes while Rhoda the mountain goat scampered along beside me.

Since meeting Carrie Fisher on Ruby Wax's late-night round-table talk show, we had become good friends. She'd sent me hundreds of emails and we'd forwarded to each other all the filthiest, weirdest stuff that the web had to offer. Carrie lives in Los Angeles, but when she heard that I was visiting San Francisco she began trying to arrange for myself and my mother to visit George Lucas's Skywalker ranch. This was very sweet and kind of her, but of course it was hard to explain to her that my mother had never seen and barely heard of Star Wars, so for her this übertreat would really just be some strange day out. As it happens, Carrie's kindness was thwarted by the holiday season. It seemed no one was at the ranch. I told her not to worry about it, we were having a great time, and we were.

Alcatraz, the cable cars, Fisherman's Wharf, we did all

the touristy things. On New Year's Eve we went to see the wonderful singer Barbara Cook in concert. She has a beautiful voice and has been around for ever, appearing in countless Broadway shows and revues. In terms of gayness, taking your mother to see Barbara Cook in concert on New Year's Eve in San Francisco sort of takes you off the scale. My mother and I sat with a few hundred gay men beneath an almost visible cloud of cologne and waited for the concert to begin. The lights dimmed, out walked Barbara, much screaming and clapping, and then she opened her mouth to sing. Nothing. She couldn't remember the words to the song. Then it turned out that she couldn't remember the words to any songs. She apologised profusely. The audience did a lot of 'We love you, Barbara' shouting and the pianist gave her a pep talk. It was every performer's nightmare actually happening. Barbara somehow managed to get through the show with a great deal of charm, good grace and looking over the pianist's shoulder.

When we got back to the hotel there was a message from Carrie. 'You are going to get a call from my friend Sharon Stone inviting you to a brunch.' This information had barely sunk in when the next message began to play. 'Hello, this is Sharon Stone.' Sure enough she was inviting me and my mother to her house for a small New Year's Day brunch. I went next door to break the news to Rhoda. 'Oh. Well, you go.' I knew how she felt. I didn't particularly want to go either, but I explained that we could not go home and tell people that we had turned down the opportunity to go to Sharon Stone's house for brunch. And so that is how the next day I found myself looking at my mother in her purple woollen suit standing beside Robin Williams while he did improv about the recent election. The fixed grin on my mother's face seemed to suggest that he had not found a new fan in her. Perhaps sensing that he was losing his audience, he picked up someone's handbag and pretended to make it talk, and then improved off to delight some other brunchers. Sharon, truly a natural beauty, even up close, was charm personified and didn't even punch my mother when she told her that her new baby's name, Roan, wasn't really Irish, just a modern made-up one to sound Irish. I admired the view, the bagels, my feet, the nerve of the woman.

We spent most of the time chatting to what my mother called 'two very nice girls' but what anyone one else would have called a couple of bull dykes. We poked around the house as much as we dared. It was beautiful, lots of dark wood and a stunning view out towards Golden Gate Bridge. After a toilet trip that meant we saw a bit more of the house (leopard-skin Ralph Lauren towels slightly suspect), we made our excuses and left.

Back at the hotel my mother rang Paula to tell her all about it. 'The house was beautiful . . . she was very nice . . . a buffet, I would have done it differently . . . and as for that Robin Williams, well, he didn't exactly go' (and here my mother launched into her best Mork impression) '"Nanou, nanou" but he might as well have.' For once my mother and I were in complete agreement. It seems most people talk about Robin Williams in terms of being 'on great form' or 'always hilarious', but that day at brunch I just wanted to say to him, 'You've won an Oscar, relax, we all know you're funny.'

*

246

Shameless.

Mother and son in Venice.

Me and my dad.

Dame Elizabeth Taylor

Liza and David in happier times, 2003.

My favourite Christmas card ever.

The only wedding
photo I've ever had.

New Year's Eve, before the incident with Mo.

The invitation to my 40th birthday party.

Yes, I'm 40, and I'm fine about it!

My favourite teacher and good friend Niall, at my 40th.

Huggy Betty.

Patrick Sewart goes where
no man has been before …

Britney considers a
lesbian wedding.

Grace Jones
experiences fear
for the first time.

Even Doggy phone has to rehearse.

I wonder what guest I'm introducing here?

Graham Stuart, Melanie Coupland and Jon Magnusson –
the people without whom …

My very first award,
forgetting to thank
everyone.

Getting the International
Emmy from two of the
funniest women alive.

Despite all her rubbing she
couldn't get me hard.

New York. A new city, same terrible dress sense.

Back home the show was going from strength to strength. We were winning more awards and audience figures were growing all the time. Occasionally the press became a bit excited by something that happened. For some reason when we got Mo Mowlam to officiate at a dog wedding, the papers reacted like it was the end of civilisation as we knew it. I felt badly for Mo, because we hadn't wanted to embarrass her or make her look foolish, it was merely a way of involving the guest in a game where we laughed at little dogs in costumes. Many people wondered why Mo Mowlam had agreed to appear on the show; after all she was a government minister and this was one of the stupidest shows on TV. I'm fairly sure various people strongly advised her not to, but at the end of the day Mo likes having fun and she enjoys being popular. My show was both of those things. Politically it probably wasn't the wisest thing to do, but that is why people love her – she isn't very politic. Happily Mo doesn't blame me for the fall-out and she and her husband Jon have become good friends.

Another item on the show that provoked the wrath of the *Daily Mail* was a visit we made to a website that featured the Pipes of Pam. It was one of those fairly straightforward sex sites that offer live shows via webcam, but this one had the added delights of Pam, who was able to insert a penny whistle into what some people would call her tuppence and play a basic tune. Lulu was the guest and she looked on in fascination, horror and awe as Pam pulled down her panties and gave us a halting, but nonetheless beautiful, rendition of 'God Save the Queen'. There were complaints, quite a few complaints, in fact several hundred complaints. It was referred to the Broadcasting Complaints Commission. In the office we were like shame-faced schoolboys who'd been caught shoplifting porn mags. We did sort of feel that things had got out of hand and that perhaps we had pushed the boat out a bit far. But amazingly, when the Commission delivered its conclusion we were off the hook. It was a long, dull report full of legal jargon which essentially said, 'You were watching *So Graham Norton*, what did you expect?'

It must be so frustrating to the people who complain that all that really happens is that we sit around the office laughing at them. My favourite one was after we had featured a woman called Madame Pee Pee who did a show involving a brandy glass and bodily fluids. It sounds worse than it was. An irate woman called in and just shouted down the phone, 'For God's sake, what is this? I'm supposed to be taping it for the nuns!' It was only later that we remembered that Daniel O'Donnell was supposed to be the guest that night, but like any good Catholic he had pulled out at the last moment. The thought of groups of nuns and Irish housewives huddled by their television sets watching Madame Pee Pee gave us a warm feeling inside.

Unbelievably, while all of this was going on the BBC were having meetings with me asking me to join the corporation. Part of me was tempted, but I wasn't ready to quit Channel 4 so soon. They sent me a proposal detailing what shows they would want me to do and how much they would pay me. It was about the same amount of money as I was on at Channel 4. I politely declined and thought no more about it.

My producer Jon and I were off to Japan to make a travel documentary called *Ah-So Graham Norton* where I stayed with a Japanese family and generally experienced all the weird and wonderful things that Tokyo had to offer. One night we were filming in some obscure part of the city and trying to get something to eat. Eventually we found ourselves sitting around a large, smoking fire pit. Our eyes streamed and our stomachs growled. Small plates of raw food were brought. We cooked little pieces of chicken and vegetables. The more we cooked the hungrier we seemed to get. After what seemed like hours, we had all had about a mouthful of food each. A tray of giant prawns arrived. We put them on the fire. 'Oh my God!' We watched aghast as the prawns started to writhe around. Alive and not having a good time, they waved their little claws at us. It was late and we were tired and hungry. Even the vegetarians amongst us began to laugh.

Somewhere towards the end of what we were reluctantly calling our dinner, the production mobile phone rang and one of the crew went outside to answer it. They came back in and handed it to me.

'It's your agent, Melanie.'

I took the phone out into the street. Across the continents I could sense her breathless excitement.

'I've been trying to reach you all day!'

'I've been filming,' I said, hungry and slightly irritable, 'what's so urgent?'

'The BBC have come back with another offer.'

Now I was really annoyed. We had been through all of this, I didn't want to go.

'They are offering you five million pounds.' I nearly vomited badly cooked prawn.

I stood holding the phone not saying anything. Tokyo pushed by me and signs I couldn't read flashed above my head. Five million pounds! Obviously I was tempted, who wouldn't be? But then I thought about it more clearly. The money had changed, but the rest of the offer was exactly the same and it was an offer I had found very easy to turn down only a week before. I was already earning more money than I ever dreamt I would. I had no children, not even a dog to worry about it.

'No,' I said.

Melanie, sounding more serious than I had ever heard her, asked me if I was sure.

'Yes.'

I hung up the phone and walked back into the smoking fire pit. I was in shock. Was it possible that I, Graham Walker, from Bandon, Co. Cork, had just walked away from five million pounds?

It was, and it felt good.

14

Friends in Dry Places

I ADORE DOLLY PARTON. EVER since I was a little boy there has been something about her that has drawn me to her. Maybe it's the bright colours, maybe it's the music, maybe it's just a subconscious desire to breastfeed, I don't know, but I love Dolly.

From the very beginning of *So* I kept asking for the Queen of Country to be on my show. Time and again dates didn't work out, but then I would see her sitting beside other chat show hosts. I felt like a jilted lover. She was meant to be mine!

Normally I try not to get too personally involved in the booking of guests, but with Dolly it was different. I sent her letters, flowers and rare books about fairies (seriously). Such was my onslaught that the lovely woman took the time to send a personal note of thanks to me along with the promise that she would do her best to do the show. I clung on to the piece of paper which was really just a polite note telling me to fuck off and leave her alone, but to me it was as precious as a scrap of the Turin shroud.

We had a new booker on the show, a man from Ireland called Tony Jordan. We had worked together years before on *The Jack Docherty Show* and I had always been in awe of the dignified patience with which he daily suffered getting

253

shat on from a great height by publicists and agents whilst simultaneously enduring mountainloads of abuse from us. I really don't mean to belittle what he does in any way. As I've said before, it is by far the hardest job in the business and Tony is the best. Perhaps I didn't always think so, but when he brought me the news that he had booked Dolly Parton he was a god in my eyes.

The day before the show I was summoned to meet her in her hotel room. By now I had met a lot of celebrities and people I really admired, but I had never been this nervous before. I couldn't bear it if she didn't like me, and the sky would fall in if . . . if – it was too horrible to contemplate – if I didn't like her.

The record label PR man showed me up to her room and I was left alone to wait on an overstuffed sofa. Dolly would be out in a moment. I could hear voices that were getting nearer; soon there was just a door between us; then suddenly it was thrown open and she came dancing into the room singing 'He's going to marry me!', a lyric from the song 'Marry Me' that she was going to perform on the show. She twirled around the sofa and collapsed in a fit of giggles on the cushion beside me. Small, shiny and exquisite, she was like a Fabergé egg with tits. Although she is made up of so many elements that are fake and superficial, she exudes a genuine warmth and profound goodness. When you are with her you feel as if nothing bad could happen. Happy and relieved, I wallowed in my love for her.

Dolly was the first guest ever to sing on the show. She burst out of a giant wedding cake and sang 'Marry Me' while the audience went mad. Never had I felt less like I was working as we chatted and laughed – it felt like people just happened to be watching. At the end of the show she was obviously tired and headed back to the hotel to try and get some sleep before flying off to the Grammies the next day. She quickly said goodnight and walked off set. I suddenly had awful doubts – maybe she didn't like me.

The next few days were strangely flat, not just for me but for everyone in the office. It was as if we were all experiencing a sort of comedown from our Dolly high. The P R people from the record company called to thank us for the show and to tell us how much Dolly had enjoyed herself. They also mentioned the idea of me doing some sort of special with Dolly where I would go to Dollywood, her theme park in Tennessee, and she would show me around. It sounded like a pretty slim premise for a whole show, but we took it to Channel 4 and they bought it. I tried not to get too excited because the chances of Dolly having a break in schedule at the same time as me were pretty slim. I pushed it to the back of my mind.

A producer called Laura Parfitt had worked with me at *Loose Ends* and on various occasions had tried to get me to do something else with Radio 4. I did want to keep up my connection with it, because I saw Radio 4 as a sort of pension plan. If I just hung on, I too could be eighty and still play *Just a Minute*. However, because of TV commitments and a private fear of the posh and educated Radio 4 audience, I had never been able to accept one of Laura's offers. Finally she came up with a proposal that I found very hard to refuse. We would go to New York for about a week and make a series of programmes about the city in front of a live audience. Each show would be a themed exploration of an aspect of living there, be it death in the city, money, sex or politics.

I would interview a different panel of expert guests on each show and talk to the audience. That is more or less how Laura explained it to me. All I really heard was 'a week in New York'. Yes please!

Because of my TV schedule we wouldn't be able to record the shows until early September. Autumn in New York, what could be nicer? We had a wonderful time. The guests were great and the audience were so receptive that it suddenly made me think that maybe I could work in America. Each night after the show we headed into Soho or the Village and sat outside eating dinner and talking about how good life was. We finished recording the last show on 9 September 2001. The series was called *Graham Norton's Big Apple Crumble*.

It was never to be broadcast.

The day after we had finished the radio series I flew to Knoxville in Tennessee. Yes, Dolly had found some space in her schedule and our Christmas special from Dollywood was happening. I was thrilled. Although I had never heard of Knoxville before, it is in fact quite a big town, a city if you speak to the locals; however, we weren't staying there. We were heading for real Dolly Country, a place called Pigeon Forge, home of Dollywood and little else. To call it the middle of nowhere is to make it sound too central. It is really just a highway with a few fast-food joints and the occasional peculiar tourist attraction, like a full-sized concrete dinosaur or a shop selling nothing but Christmas ornaments all the year round.

The other thing about Pigeon Forge, which the same reader who is still using this as a travel book might well want to take note of, is that it is dry. That is to say, you cannot purchase any alcohol there. But of course, who needs drink or drugs when you are at home to the wondrous madness that is Dollywood? The place is enormous and is part folksy, homespun charm, part Hollywood camp and part fairly basic park rides. Only one woman's name could rightly sit on top of the gates. The Dolly Museum, the replica of the cottage she grew up in, the Dollywood gift shop, the piped Parton music that plays all over the park all day every day . . . yes, it's true, the place could make you hate a lesser woman. Somehow, though, Dolly makes you realise that she gets the joke, and also, in a very odd way, although the place is about her, she makes it seem as if it is actually all about the visitors and their enjoyment.

The second morning we were in Pigeon Forge I got up fairly early to go down and meet the film crew for a day's filming. Because it was off-season the park was closed that day and Dolly wouldn't be available for filming until the following morning, so it was a good opportunity to film lots of dull set-ups. I started the coffee pot and turned on the TV. There is a daytime show on American television called *Live with Regis and Kelly*, sort of like *This Morning* but with better soft furnishings; however, this particular morning it was late starting because the news was still on covering some stupid story about a light aircraft that had crashed into a building. How annoying. I had my shower.

When I came out of the shower I felt like Bobby Ewing in *Dallas*, except that surely this was the dream. In a few minutes the world had changed. A second plane had flown into the World Trade Center. Unbelievably the news anchor was telling me that they weren't little planes but full-sized commercial aircraft. I stared at the screen. Could the Twin

Towers be that big? I went downstairs to find the crew and a few other guests standing in the lobby in front of a large television. We all expressed our disbelief about what was happening. My mobile started to ring, people making sure that I wasn't still in New York. I reassured them and headed off to the Dollywood site.

There is something so special about being in a theme park when it isn't open to the public. We walked along the pretty winding roads till we found Dolly's apartment. She has never actually slept in it, but she does use it as a dressing room when she performs shows in the park. The decor suggests that the person who did it knew only two English words and they were 'pink' and 'frilly'. We worked steadily all morning filming various set-ups in the bedroom. One of the guys who worked in the park brought us some batteries we had asked for. He casually told us that a plane had crashed into the Pentagon and that another one might have hit the White House, he wasn't sure. He ambled off. No one said anything, but if we had we would have all just let out a long slow 'fuck'. We worked on but were desperate to know more. We pounced on the young man who delivered coffee. 'Some tower fell down, I think.' Well, he was obviously mentally subnormal, how could that be possible? By lunchtime Dolly was no longer singing throughout the park. Out of every speaker came news. We sat eating sandwiches listening to a large plastic rock under a bush. It told us the awful news in full.

America was under attack. We couldn't make any inter-national calls, all flights had been grounded, we were under siege. No one knew where it would end, but we did all feel fairly safe. On the list of terrorist targets we were pretty sure that Dolly Parton's theme park in Pigeon Forge ranked quite low. The other odd thing we learned was that we seemed more distressed and shocked by the news than any of the locals. One of our drivers had a cousin who lived in New York, but most people had never even visited the place. It was a real lesson in just how enormous a country the United States of America is. The feeling seemed to be that the good people in Tennessee, at any rate, had always known that New York was a dangerous place and that building things that tall was just an accident waiting to happen.

That night we had been planning to film at another of Pigeon Forge's attractions, Dolly's Dixieland Stampede, a cross between a rodeo and dinner theatre, but we assumed that the show would be cancelled. 'No Sir! We got nearly two thousand people coming to the show tonight!' And so on the very night of 11 September I was sitting in a huge arena with two thousand proud Americans. The lights dimmed and an announcer welcomed us and told us about the amazing dust-free sawdust that the arena was covered in. Out came the troop of performers on horses, and while they did their tricks a small army of waiters invaded the auditorium, dumping food in front of us like a blanket bombing. Bang, bang, a large brown thing landed on each plate. What was that? Bread perhaps? I stared closer into the darkness. No, that would be a whole chicken. Lovely as it looked I wondered how we were supposed to eat it. The audience looked at one another unsure of what to do, and that was the precise moment when the Master of Ceremonies, sitting on his big white horse, began to sing his haunting melody. I seem to recall that it was called 'Supper-time', but what is really etched on my mind for ever is the bit of the song that went, 'We don't need no forks or spoons, we just eat things like raccoons!' I don't know what the lyricist charged them for that little couplet, but it was worth every cent when you consider how much it must have saved them on cutlery and washing-up. Then, no sooner had we picked up our chickens than the show moved on to the chicken races. If anything is going to motivate a hen to run fast it must be the smell of cooking chicken. They repeated the trick when they served the next course of pork ribs and the pigs lined up at the starting flag. By the time the ostrich races started I felt very full.

The theme of the show was a contest between the North and the South, and the finale was a huge spectacular about one great nation united beneath one flag. The costumes and horses lit up and vast Stars and Stripes unfurled above the crowd. The people stood and clapped and cheered much as I imagine they did every night, but on that night their strident triumphalism seemed almost touching. These people had such faith in their great country, but as they cheered and clapped their greasy hands, their President was in a bunker. I do love America, but sometimes it can seem like an overgrown baby.

The next day we were filming with Dolly and the park was open. Men and women with the sorts of thighs you don't see anywhere else in the world waddled around in shorts. Lots of people wore small American flags on their lapels, but that was the only way you might have guessed that not everything was completely normal. The planes seemed to have stopped crashing into things; although we couldn't leave Pigeon Forge we just got on with our filming, hoping that planes would be flying again by the time we were ready to head home. We settled into our surreal world and went a bit native. New York did seem very far away, and because we were at the park all day we didn't get the constant reminders of what had happened there: a grotesque smoking wormhole in the Big Apple.

One of Dolly's ideas for the show was that we should sing a duet. This was very nice of her, but there was one slight problem: I can't sing. Some people say this in mock modesty, but I truly cannot. Even when I'm by myself in the bathroom belting out show tunes I am aware that in terms of listening pleasure it's up there with cats having sex – my singing voice is like an aural fart. Dolly wouldn't be told. 'It'll be cute!' Jon, who not only knew that I couldn't sing but is also an accomplished musician in his own right, packed me off to singing lessons. It was decided that we would crucify 'Islands in the Stream'. My singing teacher, Pepe, was obviously the person you turned to in an emergency; her other clients included the man from the Halifax commercials and the Spice Girls.

We were doing a very short version of the song, really just two verses and a couple of choruses, but I seemed to go to endless lessons. Eventually I ended up in a recording studio in London with Pepe and Dolly's half of the recording. I bravely droned my way through it and we sent it back to her people. Word reached us that Dolly thought I sounded like Mick Jagger. I'm guessing from that comment that she was never much of a Rolling Stones fan.

The plan was to film the video for the song in the water park called Dolly's Splash Country, which she had just opened opposite Dollywood. She and I would be in rubber rings floating down one of those long, gentle water rides that they have in many parks. All the people who worked there kept asking us with incredulous looks on their faces, 'Dolly is going in the water?' It was as if someone was suggesting that Linda McCartney was going to eat a pork chop. We knew that this whole part of the show was Dolly's idea, but even we began to doubt that it would happen.

On the day of the shoot we arrived at the park and got set up. I went off to the men's toilets and got changed into my borrowed wetsuit. I emerged looking like a cheap hot-water bottle with legs. Dolly drove up and came over to greet us. I loved filming with her because in all the waiting around I got to chat with her about all sorts of things. She is an incredibly wise and generous woman. The people of Pigeon Forge hold her in huge esteem, not just because she is a local girl done good, but because she is a local girl who has done so much good for the people of the area. Obviously her theme parks provide much-needed employment, but she is also involved in an extraordinary educational project. Every child who is born in the county gets a free book every month for the first four years of their life, and she started a reward scheme that saw the state's lowest graduation rate become the highest. In addition to all that she funds a mobile kids' library that goes to all the remote areas that don't have access to bookshops or libraries. She told me that there are kids in Pigeon Forge who don't even know that she's a singer; as far as they are concerned she is just 'the book lady' who happens to have her own pair of fleshy bookends.

It was very clear that none of those children was at the park that day. From the reaction of the people standing by the water you might have thought that the least Dolly was going to do was walk on it. She went off to a dressing room to get ready. We couldn't imagine what she would look like ready for a swim. A short while later she returned. Her regular wig had been replaced by a loose, wet-look one and she wore a custom-made wet suit that hugged every nook and cranny of the Parton package. Jessica Rabbit would have looked flat-chested in comparison. On her feet she wore a pair of extremely high-heeled mules. Just as she reached the water's edge she slipped off the shoes and I noticed that she was still on tiptoe. I can't be sure, but I think that after years and years of wearing six-inch heels, the muscles in her legs have shortened so that she can now no longer stand with both feet flat on the ground. We clambered into our rubber rings and, holding hands, set sail. The music blared out of a big ghetto blaster and as we lip-synched to it I could sense the excited crowd thinking, 'Christ, it doesn't take much to become a famous singer in Europe!' Sadly, of course, they were right.

By the time we finished filming the first few commercial flights had begun to take off. The staff at Knoxville airport behaved as if it was the number-one terrorist target in the world. Luggage was all unpacked; everything was X-rayed and X-rayed again. They had thought of everything except that after we got through all the security and into the departure area there was a cheery restaurant with a large steak knife at every place setting. People were still learning.

I hadn't imagined that I would be back in New York anytime soon after that September, but *So* was nominated for an International Emmy so a happy band of us headed off to what was left of Manhattan. We weren't staying near ground zero, but somehow I could feel the city had changed. People were truly grateful that tourists were there, strangers chatted, and everyone wanted to tell you where they'd been on 11 September. Trendy shops had uncool signs in their windows saying things like 'Dare to love New York'. Who could help loving this city that received such a huge punch to the stomach and yet was still going on with the show?

The International Emmys are not quite the same as the regular Emmys – they are less like the Oscars and rather more like the Heating and Plumbing Awards held in the bland function room of some hotel. When it came time for our category, Joanna Lumley and Jennifer Saunders came to the stage. To say that they were the most famous people there is to suggest that there was somebody else famous at the event. That would be wrong. They read out the nominees: a German comedy programme, the Channel 4 sitcom *Spaced*, the Miss China pageant and us. We were the winners. Truly the makers of the Miss China show were robbed. They had staged something only slightly less ambitious than the Second World War, whereas we had a man hanging in a home-made sling being serenaded by Elton John. Still, I was delighted when they called out the name of our show. Graham Stuart and I went up to collect it and then posed backstage with Joanna and Jennifer for photographs. I had an Emmy.

Because I had the show to do I was flying back on Concorde. Now, I know one should never speak ill of the dead, but why all the fuss? Despite the special places to check in and wait for the departure, once on board it was like the shuttle flight to Glasgow. My Emmy award was too big to put in my luggage and I didn't want to check it in because I thought I would never see it again. Security stared at its very sharp wings, but because it is such an iconic thing in

America I don't think they could imagine it being used for evil purposes. In the end the captain had to come and examine it and give it the all-clear. I gave him a reassuring look that I hoped said, 'I promise not to stick these sharp bits into your neck and let you bleed to death while I aim your plane for the Houses of Parliament.' He must have heard me, the Emmy was on.

You could sort of tell that the plane was full of really rich people. Before take-off a nice steward came up to each passenger.

'Once we are in the air, would Sir like some champagne?'

Now, given how much the tickets for this plane cost, the correct response is, I believe, 'Yes, please, and could you serve it in a bucket?'

He asked the lady sitting behind me, and she enquired, 'Are you still serving the Tattinger '88?'

The steward beamed. 'Yes, madam.'

A cold voice responded, 'No, thank you.' Now that's too rich.

That Christmas both my sister and mother were coming to stay with me. I supposed we would do all the normal things like watching TV and eating and drinking too much, but I didn't quite know how to entertain them on New Year's Eve. Happily Mo Mowlam came to the rescue. She and her husband Jon were going to see George Melly playing at Ronnie Scott's jazz club in Soho. Would we like to join them? It was a perfect idea. Mum would like the music, and though she would never admit it, I knew she would get a kick out of meeting Mo Mowlam. There had been some disappointment the year before when she'd got home to find that many of her friends didn't actually know who Sharon

Stone was; Mo would be a much stronger hand to play at the bridge club.

On the night I ordered a taxi and we picked Mo and Jon up as they didn't live far away. We headed for Chinatown for dinner and then walked the few streets to Ronnie Scott's. The evening couldn't have gone better. The atmosphere was fantastic, the music was great and even my mother hit the dance floor. There was none of that usual New Year's Eve pressure of wondering, 'Is this fun? Am I at the right party?' We knew that the answer to both those questions was 'Yes'.

The one cloud that hangs over every New Year's Eve if you go out is the worry about how you are going to get home. This year, despite the great time we had all just enjoyed, it was to be no different. We stood huddled outside the door of the club and finally someone managed to procure us a taxi. It turned out to be a minicab, but what the hell, we could all pile in. Jon, who was the largest in the group, sat in front while Paula, Mo, Mum and I squashed into the back. We were all wearing our coats, it was hot, the journey was taking for ever and then I heard an odd sound. We had all been wearing little cardboard party hats, and out of the corner of my eye I could see that Paula was being sick into hers. Poor thing. I wondered if anyone else had noticed – certainly nobody mentioned it. First stop was Mo and Jon's house. The car stopped and out they got. As I said goodnight to them I could see that all down the side of Mo Mowlam's outfit there was a long stream of my sister's vomit.

Once you have vomited on someone I don't believe there are any set rules of etiquette. I apologised on Paula's behalf, but Mo assured me that it was all right and headed off into the night. My sister was still being really ill and we got home as quickly as we could. I tipped the driver so much he probably bought a new car. Poor Paula was mortified. Terrible to vomit on anyone, but somehow worse when it is the nice lady who brought about peace in Northern Ireland. You could understand how Mo managed to do that because she did a very sweet thing the next day. Rather than wait for my sister to make her obligatory grovelling apology phone call, she rang us first thing in the morning to see if Paula was all right. If ever someone vomits on me, I hope I have the grace and good humour to do the same.

Once Paula and Mother went back to Ireland I had about a week before *So* started up again. I fancied a bit of sunshine and my friend Tim Lord phoned me from Cape Town encouraging me to go out there and see him. With a slight 'nothing to lose' attitude, I managed to get a flight and a room in a hotel. I was off to South Africa.

At the time I didn't know Tim as well as I do now. He is a successful lawyer and I first met him through Simon Fanshawe. He'd invited me to a dinner party and, classy person that I am, after coffee I had sex with another of the guests. Not in front of people, but it's still not the done thing, I find. Since then we had seen each other now and again, but this idea of taking a holiday together was quite rash.

The flight to Cape Town is a long one – eleven hours – but it is overnight and there is only a two-hour time difference, so when you arrive you are tired, but at least you know why – you didn't sleep very well. It's a lot better than jet lag. I had been to South Africa once before when I went to do some gigs in Johannesburg, but I'm guessing I wasn't that impressed by the place because I noticed that trip hasn't managed to make it into this book. When I was in Jo'burg everyone was very rude about Cape Town. 'The people are horrible, everything is really expensive, you wouldn't like it.' Of course when I actually arrived, I realised why they told me such tales. They must barely be able to live with their jealousy. Cape Town is as close to paradise as I have found on earth. Not in a tropical beach kind of way, though they do have great beaches, nor in a glitzy South of France fashion, even if they do have some brilliant restaurants and bars. It is just an atmosphere. The people couldn't be nicer, the weather more beautiful, the setting around the slopes of Table Mountain more spectacular. It all conspires to turn a fairly ordinary small city into a truly special place. Maybe they put something in the water, but from the moment I got off the plane I was in love with it.

I was only staying for five days, and on about day three I had just finished a boozy lunch with Tim (I haven't even mentioned the delicious wine!). We started walking back to the car. Obviously I had drunk most of the wine because Tim was driving. I weaved past an estate agent's and was drawn to a photograph of a beautiful white house that reminded me of something you might see in the Hollywood hills.

'Look at that!' I said to Tim.

Because he was a good deal more sober than I was, he converted the price into pounds. It was cheap – really cheap.

'Will I buy it?' I asked, full of booze and bravado.

Tim was delighted. 'Yes!'

Luckily for me the estate agent's was shut, so we decided that first thing the next day we would come back. I thought that I would go along with this ridiculous plan until I sobered up, but when I woke in the morning it still seemed like a good idea.

I went into the estate agent's with Tim. My show isn't broadcast in South Africa, so as far as the charming lady behind the desk was concerned we were just a couple of poofs wanting to have a nose around some gorgeous houses. She couldn't have been nicer. She was called Louise and she drove us to the house in the picture. Now, as a shopper I do have a fatal flaw. If I try on a pair of trousers, for instance, so long as I can physically get into them, I somehow feel like I have made a commitment to them and buying them is the honourable thing to do. If I put them back on the hanger it would be like teasing them. Sadly I have discovered I'm a bit like that with real estate. I walked into this house and immediately felt like it was mine. I pretended to do sensible things like ask about the hot water and how old it was, but all I really wanted to do was yell 'Sold!' and start buying furniture. I held out for a few minutes, but because time was short I simply told Louise that I'd like to buy it. Now, estate agents in Britain don't have a great reputation, but this lovely woman refused to let me buy it until I'd looked at other houses on the ocean side of the mountain. Reluctantly, I agreed.

The other side of the mountain was terrifying. The houses looked like they had been built by porn barons and the other estate agents showing us around them looked like they had got some sort of bulk discount on their botox. After a long afternoon of pretending to be interested in gold taps and marble stairs, I rang Louise.

'I've looked. Now will you please let me buy my house?'
She did.

That was nearly four years ago, and Louise and her husband Craig are now friends. What I didn't know at the time was that I was her first sale. In the end, houses are just bricks and sinks and bits of wire and pipe and I completely understand people who see them as nothing more than that, but perhaps because of my slightly gypsy childhood I find that I respond to them in a very emotional way. Because they are real estate and therefore 'an investment' I somehow get away with buying them, but in reality to me they are just a huge indulgence, way beyond clothes or hotels, and yet like a combination of both.

I hated leaving, but I would be back in a couple of months to get the keys and discover if I really did love Cape Town or if I'd just made quite an expensive mistake.

15

And So Endeth

C APITALISM, BAD. TRADE, WICKED. SHOPS, evil. Rainbow-coloured home-knitted jumpers filed across Waterloo Bridge making their way to Oxford Street for the 2002 May Day protest. I, on the other hand, was on my way to have lunch with the Channel 4 boss Michael Jackson at the Royal Festival Hall on the south bank of the Thames. Helicopters throbbed overhead, and as I watched six policemen on motorbikes chapcroning one man with a beard pedalling his three-wheeler over the bridge, I couldn't help but think that the police had perhaps overestimated the threat of this particular group. Unless the smell of wet wool was considered a chemical weapon, I felt fairly safe walking along the banks of the river.

Lunches with executives are always a bit weird. They feel that they have to invite you and you feel that you have to go. Sometimes the small talk can dwindle to tiny talk by the time coffee and a blessed bill and release arrive. Michael Jackson, however, is almost the opposite of this. His penchant is for big talk. Most of the time I could sort of keep up, but sometimes the French film or American architect he mentioned were just too obscure and I just had to nod and smile like one of those plastic dogs people sometimes put in the back window of their car.

The lunch didn't begin well. Michael asked me if I'd like some wine. Using my Concorde mantra, I, of course, said, 'Yes please,' and then stopped myself from blurting out the 'in a bucket' bit. Having asked if I preferred white or red – 'White, please' – he perused the Bible-like tome that was the wine list. Finally he chose one. We looked at the helicopters flying over the capital. The wine arrived. It was red. A flustered Mr Jackson went back to the list while the gleeful waiter pointed out wines that were white. I have never been more interested in helicopters in my life.

Finally food and wine had arrived and we were talking about Channel 4, and since my contract was going to be up for renewal quite soon, what I'd like to do next. I really didn't know what to say. I was still really enjoying *So*, but my worry was that I thought that the public would start to get bored of it after another series. He seemed to agree and then, almost casually, he mentioned the idea of going five nights a week. My eyes lit up. Ever since filling in for Jack at Channel Five this had been my dream.

I knew that Graham and Jon back at the office would be as excited as I was. For anyone doing a chat show this was the Holy Grail. It had never worked in Britain, but we believed that we could make a success of it, or at least have an amazing time trying. Talks began between Channel 4 and SO Television, the production company that I had started with Jon and Graham. Meetings followed about how many weeks a year we would do it for and what time in the evening it would be shown. In order for it to work I felt it had to be on for as many weeks as possible and always on at the same time. The idea was to make it a part of the TV landscape rather than anything special. In America the five-nights-a-week talk show succeeds because of its inevitability. Very few people would watch it every night, but most people would dip into it once or twice a week. It was decided that we would start later that year, during the summer. We began production on our last ever series of *So*.

Since I had come back from South Africa I had become closer and closer to Tim until finally, very drunk, we rolled around some bar in Soho and decided we would give dating a whirl. Poor Tim. I think he thought that going out with the guy off TV would somehow be cool, but of course all his smart lawyer friends were just faintly embarrassed rather than impressed when he showed up with the ridiculous poof from Channel 4 on his arm. I suspected that I wasn't exactly the love of his life when on Valentine's Day he took me to the media brothel that is the club Soho House and then over dinner confided that he thought we made 'a very plausible couple'. Just what I'd always wanted to be.

'Who's coming to dinner?'

'Tim and Graham.'

'Oh, they are so plausible!'

I had gone back into the dating game full of good intentions, but after a few weeks we decided to go back to being friends, which is what we still are.

It was also after getting back from South Africa that I discovered one of the great loves of my life – driving! Up until that moment, whenever someone had suggested that I learn how to drive I had always pooh-poohed the idea. I had lived all my adult life in London where a car really never seemed like a necessity and I quite liked feeling a little bit eccentric – 'Oh, I couldn't possibly drive! I'd kill myself!' In order to fully enjoy my new house in Cape Town, however,

I realised that I would have to get behind the wheel. I rang a central London driving school and was booked in with a saint called Howell. It sounds stupid to call a driving instructor 'inspirational', but he really was. He made me believe I could drive. He was the human equivalent of that feather Dumbo had to have in order to fly.

As anyone who has learnt how to drive will know, the first lesson is a huge shock to the system. Somehow I thought day one would be a lot of chatting in the car, but no. Within minutes I was driving down a road – a public road. Although Howell had dual controls, a perverse part of my brain couldn't help but think, 'If I really wanted to kill someone in this thing I could!' Howell did his best, though at times it was difficult. Reversing around a corner for the first time was never going to be easy, but somehow I think that having a crowd of schoolboys all waving in the windows shouting variations of the 'Hello, Graham, you big poofter!' theme really didn't help. I learnt in an automatic, because I can't understand why anyone could be bothered with a manual. It's like walking across the room to change channels after they invented the remote control. Technology is our friend, let's use it.

Finally Howell declared that I was ready for my test. At the time I still vaguely believed that I got nervous before I did a show, but on my way to west London on the morning of the exam I was suddenly reminded of what real nerves felt like. I was terrified. Happily, I think my examiner was equally terrified to be trapped in a small car with a renowned homosexual, because I passed.

I love driving, but a bit like the way I am with sex, much as I enjoy it I can't pretend that I'm very good at it. I try to tell myself that I will get better with experience, but in truth I have as much chance of parallel parking now as I did the day I took the test. I drive quite fast, using the brake as if I were trying to shake the head off a crash test-dummy. On the upside, so far, apart from the walls of multistorey car parks and the occasional parked car, I haven't hit anything – well, apart from one woman who crashed into me, but because I was a new nervous driver I decided that it must be my fault. She happily agreed.

I started driving into work every day. Plans were under way for the five-nights-a-week show, which we had decided to call *V Graham Norton*. We were incredibly excited, but we made the decision not to announce to the media that it was to be the last ever series of *So* just in case *V Graham Norton* was a disaster and we wanted to go back to it. As the countdown began to the last ever show, we became unexpectedly emotional. Getting a show is a huge stroke of luck, but having a hit show is a miracle. I was doing what I had always said I wouldn't – I was walking away from a hit.

I was going to have three guests on the final show: Cilla Black, Cybill Shepherd and Orlando Bloom. Cilla was very concerned about coming on the show and was the only guest ever to come into the office during the week to have a meeting about the content. When she left she seemed happy about everything. I'm not sure why she was so worried, and as it turned out I wasn't the one she should have been concerned about. The night before the show I went to the Dorchester and had a drink with Cybill Shepherd in her room. She was very funny and up, and I thought she would make a great guest. Annoyingly I didn't get extra time to spend with Orlando Bloom. Sigh.

Cilla was going to be guest one, and although nothing was said, I think Cybill was a bit miffed by this. I have long been a fan of Cilla, but somehow she didn't really work on the show. I think she fell into that trap that happens to some guests of being so worried about what's going to happen that they forget that they are just there to relax and enjoy themselves. She seemed a bit stiff and was being very proper. Somehow I thought she would be a real laugh and a little bit racy, and actually I've seen this first-hand many times since, but on the show there wasn't a hint of that. I can't be sure, but I'm guessing that Cybill Shepherd was watching this on a monitor in the green room and thinking to herself, 'Right, I'll show them who should have been guest one.'

I introduced her, and on came a woman who seemed to have had a personality transplant since the night before. The woman I had met was funny and bright, but this woman was like a wild creature unleashed. She sat down and immediately started talking about sex. I believe one of the first stories that came out of her mouth was about teaching Elvis Presley how to go down on her. I could see that Cilla was taking an instant and profound dislike to the woman.

Cybill then went on to mention something about being in a sandwich.

Cilla asked, 'What's a sandwich?'

Cybill turned to her. 'Two guys at once. You don't know what a sandwich is?'

'Well, no,' responded Cilla, 'I'm not easy like you.'

I may have blurted out the word 'Catfight'. I had never had this on the show before, where two guests so obviously loathed each other.

Cybill told us that Elvis was doing drugs when he had gone out with her.

Cilla remarked, 'Doing drugs as long ago as that?'

Cybill glared but just said, 'Yes.'

Poor Orlando Bloom wandered wide-eyed out into the middle of this, and immediately Cybill turned all her attention to him. I feared for his safety, and the look in his eyes said that he did too. She grabbed the Orlando Bloom action doll from *Lord of the Rings* out of my hands and started rubbing it between her breasts while staring at Orlando. He giggled nervously, and to be honest I wouldn't have been that surprised if he had burst into tears.

Finally the show was over, and although it had been a very strange one we were all quite pleased because we knew it would make good television. Afterwards I spoke to Cybill, and she was restored to the nice funny lady I'd met the previous evening. The person on the show had just been some sort of showbiz creation. Up in the star dressing room, Cilla sat with her entourage drinking champagne, asking everyone in turn, 'Did you know what a sandwich was?'

I always tend to get a bit out of control at the wrap parties at the end of each series. At one such event, after several glasses of absinthe, I failed to recognise Jon or Graham. That's drunk. At the party for our final *So*, I did quite well pacing myself, though I do remember at one point being sucked into a drunken rant of 'I'm so proud, I'm so proud', saying it to everyone and crying. I obviously managed to dry my tears because I ended up going home with a very cute young man who I had never seen before, but who said he was a friend of one of the stagehands. We got back to my house in Bow, and as we were staggering from the taxi to my front door, he grabbed my arm and out of the blue said, 'I've never had gay sex before. It better be good!' Luckily for him we were both too drunk for him to find out.

I had six weeks before the start of *V Graham Norton*. After heading back to Cape Town to pick up the keys for my new house (yes, I still loved it!), I was off to America. Although I had turned down the BBC, by some odd quirk of good fortune BBC America had decided to buy *So*. I was delighted because working in the States on projects like the ill-fated radio series and the Dolly documentary had made me realise just how much I loved the place. If I could find a way of working there more, then I could spend more time in the place. It was as simple as that.

I was being flown to LA in order to promote *So* to the great American press, and my Internet sister Carrie Fisher kindly insisted that I stay with her. She has a beautiful old sprawling house in Beverly Hills with a sweet little guest cottage. Although Carrie is a true friend, at that point I still couldn't quite get over that I was staying at Princess Leia's house and Debbie Reynolds was living next door. Who's that on the tennis court? Oh, it's Matthew Perry from *Friends*.

One night there was a party. It was Carrie's daughter's birthday and a host of people had been invited to celebrate. The director Penny Marshall was there, Al Pacino, Beverly D'Angelo and of course the Hollywood royalty that is Debbie Reynolds. I lurked in dark corners drinking white wine, occasionally talking to the other people who didn't seem to know anyone. There was cake, there was singing, it was an ordinary party except that it was in Hollywood. People started to leave, but of course I couldn't because I was staying. Oh, and there was still wine left. Eventually even

Carrie had gone to bed and that was when I found myself alone with Debbie and a bottle of Chardonnay.

We sat by the fire and she chatted to me as if we had been friends for ever. She told me tales about old Hollywood, Elizabeth Taylor, the studio system . . . It was like I was in a dream: me sitting with Debbie Reynolds. She has an amazing memory and is a wonderful storyteller, but I'm ashamed to say that my old friend, drink, was about to play its usual cruel trick on me: the wine had greater power than the Queen of Hollywood and I fell asleep. I'm not sure how long I was gone for, but when I woke up, I am happy to report that Ms Reynolds was still talking. Apparently she hadn't noticed that she had temporarily lost her audience.

The reaction of the American press to the show was very positive and I began to notice that sometimes it was Americans in the street and not British expats who were coming up to me to say hello and that they liked the show. BBC America was advertising the programme quite heavily, and it seemed to be getting a cult audience. Because of this I was approached by a production company to see if I wanted to do stand-up in New York. Given that I hadn't been very good at stand-up in Britain, I was a bit reluctant to try it in America, but they reassured me that it would be in a theatre space and I could do a full-length show in the same way I had in Edinburgh for so many years. I said yes.

I was only doing the show in New York for three weeks, so I'm not really sure why I felt the need to buy a house there. I was sitting at home in Bow when the post arrived. Amongst the offers of free credit cards was a catalogue from Sotheby's. I wondered why they had sent it to me – looking at the front cover, it seemed to be about a sale of Impressionist art. I hardly felt like their target audience. While I had my morning coffee I casually flicked through it, and there at the back were some advertisements for Sotheby's real estate. A picture of a house in New York caught my eye. It was a small carriage house in a private mews and it just looked like paradise. I took the picture into work and left it on my desk like a property version of a pin-up. Simply looking at it made me happy. Jon saw it.

'Are you going to buy that?' he asked.

'No,' I answered a bit too quickly.

'You can afford it. If I had your money that's exactly what I'd do.'

The seed had been planted. I suppose I could just about afford it, and . . . and, well, I wanted it. Again I tried to dress it up as an investment, blah, blah, blah, but really it was just shopping with a capital S. I flew to New York to see it, which meant that the various estate agents smelt cash. I was driven around town in limousines and shown amazing lofts and apartments, but in the end, like in Cape Town, I just wanted the one in the picture.

It turned out it belonged to Claudia Schiffer and she had just had it gut-renovated. Part of the deal was that I would buy all the furniture she had just put in it. It wasn't exactly what I would have chosen, but it meant I could move right in. When I came to do my stand-up a few months later I didn't need a hotel, I had my own little house in the heart of Manhattan, right by the entrance to the mid-town tunnel where twenty years before I had been driven in a bus, blinking at the brilliance of the city.

Claudia had moved out but I did find quite a few of her personal effects lying around – mostly make-up and toil-

etries. Every night in the stand-up show I gave away a different item that had belonged to Claudia Schiffer. Someone
on the last night walked away with the supermodel's lady-
shave. I'm sure to this day they think I was making it up
and don't realise the value of the DNA on those little blades.

As in my gigs in Edinburgh, part of the show involved a
random phone call, but I found that the personal ads in the
New York gay magazines didn't tend to have home phone
numbers and if they did they were always connected to an
answering machine. I didn't know what to do. One night I
was in a mid-town bar called Stellas. This sounds hopelessly
naïve of me, but I just thought it was frequented by a very
mixed friendly crowd. It took me about an hour to figure
what the combination of elderly gay gentlemen, attractive
Puerto Rican boys and a cash machine in the bar might
mean. One of the boys came over to me and started to talk.
His name was Sammy and he was very funny. On a whim
I explained what I was doing in New York, and while he
was very sexy I didn't really want to sleep with him, but
would he be in the following night for me to call him from
the show? I said I'd pay him. This all sounds very straightforward and almost logical in the retelling, but always remember
that when I am telling any story that involves a bar and boys,
it is a given that I was pissed out of my mind.

The next morning I found his number and even
remembered why he had given it to me. That night, I
explained to the audience who Sammy was and how we had
met and that I was going to phone him. I half expected him
not to be there, but he was. Sammy was a natural. He told
a very funny story about going back with some guy who on
the way to his hotel kept saying, 'I hope my friend likes you.'

Sammy just assumed it was going to be a Cybill sandwich, but so long as they were paying, who cared? Once inside the room he saw a miniature picket fence set up on the carpet and there inside the makeshift pen was the guy's 'friend'. A small hen. Not just any hen, however. This was showbiz poultry. The hen had appeared in *Babe: Pig in the City*, and the man was looking after it for its owner. Perhaps it was in the city for a round of auditions? While he sucked Sammy's penis he had to keep shuffling around the floor on his knees to make sure that the chicken was looking at him at all times. Never had a hen seemed so uninterested in a cock.

Night after night I phoned Sammy and he was brilliant. He always began with a new topical joke and then told his chicken story, and if that went really well, I'd encourage him to tell another story about pissing in a bottle for some man who wanted to drink it. Every couple of nights I'd go and find him in whatever bar he happened to be in, often working as a go-go dancer, and I would shove dollars of thanks down his pants. It was the perfect arrangement. Sammy knew that I had a show in Britain, but he didn't really know what it was. As far as he was concerned I was just some guy who phoned him up and then gave him money. I knew that later on I would simply be the subject of another story along with the chicken guy.

One night, BBC America, along with *Vanity Fair*, had a party for me at the Whiskey Bar in the basement of the Times Square W Hotel. I was asked whom I would like to invite. I immediately said Sammy, partly because I felt I owed him that much and partly because I knew what a kick he would get out of it.

And So Endeth

The Whiskey Bar of the W Hotel is exactly how you'd imagine it to be: dark and stylish and populated by stylish people in dark clothes. Models and actors-in-waiting handed around trays of tiny canapés and glasses of champagne. BBC America had set up a huge screen which was showing clips from my TV show on a loop. The *Vanity Fair* people, who, if their laugh-free reaction was anything to go by, had, I think, hated the show, came up to me one by one to offer me a pale, damp hand of congratulations.

'Oh,' they simpered, 'where's Sammy?'

'Over there. Do you want to meet him?'

I'm guessing none of them really did but they had no real choice. I loved watching the malnourished media stick insects trying to make conversation with a hustler who had been sucked off in front of a chicken.

At one point I glanced over at Sammy and he was staring at the screen. Of course I don't know for certain what was going through his head, but I imagine that he must have been thinking, 'All this fuss over Graham and all he's doing is talking. I can talk. I'm funny.' There is no doubt that Sammy could do what I do standing on his head, and suddenly I thought about the life choices he had made and the ones I had. What if that day in San Francisco twenty years earlier had gone differently? What if I hadn't said, 'Stop'? Perhaps it was a very patronising thing to think, but I began to feel badly for letting Sammy have this glimpse through the 'what if' window. He had been perfectly happy before I came into his life, and now I could tell I had subtly made him dissatisfied with his lot.

Eventually Sammy and I did sleep together. I didn't pay, but I'm fairly sure it was a thank-you bonus shag for all the money I'd given for the phone calls. Certainly he treated me as a client. It was odd to be in bed with someone who was totally there for you. It's one of those things that sounds like it should be great, but actually it's not. You know that they can't really be that into you, and so it's hard to enjoy their insincere attentions. Maybe it feels all right if you're paying because then at least you know why they're being the way they are.

Back in London a small army of people were preparing to go five nights a week for *V Graham Norton*. Vast offices had been rented near to the studios on the South Bank, and an enormous portrait of me dressed as Napoleon that had been done for the Comedy Awards one year covered a whole wall in reception. Graham Stuart thought it was funny, and the money he had paid for it went to Comic Relief, so I couldn't really complain. Jon was now a sort of überproducer, overseeing everything while three new producers took over responsibility for the day-to-day running of the shows. Beneath them were a couple of associate producers and beneath them three or four researchers and then various runners and production co-ordinators. The first time I walked in and saw the acres of desks was very daunting. All these people working all day every day just so I could sit on a chair and talk. Surely we should at least be trying to find a cure for some serious disease? As I peered across the rows of heads staring at computer screens, I did feel a bit like the tubby tyrant Mr Bonaparte. Was five nights a week going to be my Russian winter?

Most new shows are plagued by all sorts of teething problems, but because this was really just a broken-up version of the old programme we sort of hit the ground running. I loved my new life doing a show every night of the week. I was still driving into work every day so that I couldn't drink after the show, I went to the gym three mornings a week – I felt great.

Originally the plan had been to have a diverse mix of guests because there was no way of having celebrities every night. I imagined having authors and journalists sharing the limelight with the more obvious guest line-up, but we quickly found that it was possible to have someone the audience was pleased to see every night. Obviously some nights were less starry than others, but I can say hand on heart that I never brought someone down those stairs that I was embarrassed by. Even when bookings fell through on the day, I still said no to suggestions of guests that I felt weren't good enough. My standard line to the poor beleaguered Tony on those bleak days was, 'I'd rather interview the cushion on the chair.'

Because we were on right after the huge Channel 4 hit *Big Brother*, often my monologue at the top of the show would be about what had just happened on the reality TV programme. It was a particularly strong year in the house that year of 2002, and it was easy to make fun of the various people on the show. Jade emerged early on as the biggest personality, and much has been made by journalists about how I was horrible and then nice about her. It is at times like that when I pity journalists most, when they have to dream up some hidden agenda behind something that was very straightforward. At the beginning of *Big Brother* I found her wildly annoying, but then, as the weeks went by, I became fond of her. I had done the unthinkable for a journalist – I had changed my mind.

The night before the end of *Big Brother* we did one of my very favourite shows. Dustin Hoffman was the guest, and although I was by now very comfortable meeting big female stars, I was quietly dreading him: somehow it made sense that as a gay man I should get along with all the divas, but in my head Dustin Hoffman was a deeply serious actor who would loathe my silly little show. I couldn't have been more wrong. Dustin wandered into make-up and immediately started talking to me about the show. He knew it well because his kids watched it all the time on BBC America; in fact he had agreed to come on in order to please them. He was wildly complimentary to me and then gave me some advice about not playing the monologue straight down the camera too much. I often say that I will go to my grave a failed actor rather than a successful anything else, and here I was getting performance notes from a man who is without doubt one of the greatest living actors on the planet.

When I introduced him he bounded on to the set more like a stand-up than some self-obsessed, classically trained actor. He told stories about celebrities, he kept referring to the audience, he said hello to various people he had met during the day. One of the items on the show involved us reuniting Dustin with a cab driver that he had made a fuss of at an awards show several years earlier. Dustin was genuinely delighted to see the guy again. I don't think I have ever seen a man who enjoyed his fame more. He doesn't revel in it like some half-baked diva, he just understands what profound but simple pleasure he can bring to people just by saying hello, signing an autograph, or posing for a photograph.

It has been interesting over the years to see how the various stars treat their fans. People like Neil Diamond, and especially Donny Osmond, couldn't be nicer to their fans whereas David Cassidy seemed downright rude and dismiss- ive of his. He resented his fans for loving his seventies persona because it meant he couldn't move on. What he wants to move on to I have no idea. The great new album that he wanted to plug was just a collection of cover versions of other people's hits, and yet he deeply resented being asked to perform his own songs. He very reluctantly agreed to perform 'I Think I Love You' on the show, and when he did he made fun of it. His fans looked on not understanding why their hero seemed to hate the very song that they loved him for. Donny Osmond understands that you've got to respect the treasured memories that every fan brings to each song. I have huge admiration and respect for him, which is odd because when I was a kid it was David Cassidy I thought about as I karate-chopped away.

The end of the Dustin Hoffman show was a sketch where he, Betty and myself played various characters from the *Big Brother* house. Johnny the fireman, who was from Newcastle, was going to be played by Dustin. As we all clambered into our costumes backstage I could hear Jon giving him a crash course in a Geordie accent. Like the professional he is, Dustin listened quietly and then went on and stole the show.

The next night I was down at the Big Brother house for the finale. The idea was that I would meet Jade and ask her to come on the show. Looking back I don't know what possessed me to do this, but at the time it seemed really important. The evening was pretty hideous to be honest, but I loved seeing first-hand the expression on Johnny's face when they showed him the clip of Dustin Hoffman playing him. Ten weeks before he had just been another Geordie fireman with an outgoing personality, and now a true Hollywood giant was pretending to be him. It was one of the most surreal bits of television I have ever seen.

The next week Jade was a guest on the show every night, and it was like an educational film on the perils of fame. On the Monday she was the sweet gormless girl we had got to know on *Big Brother*, but night after night she became more and more difficult and divaish. I don't blame her, I blame the PR people and agents she was surrounded by who were pumping her full of shit, but then I don't really blame them either because they were just doing their job. Celebrity, when it is based on a special skill or talent, is one thing, but the sort of fame reality TV stars achieve is so groundless that the only way it can exist is if it is constantly propped up by people telling you that you are worthy of the attention, that you do deserve your celebrity.

Watching people desperately trying to hang on to fame is always depressing, but when I watch someone like Jenny Bond lying in a coffin being trampled by rats in *I'm a Celebrity, Get Me Out of Here*, I realise that fame must have a strange hold over people. When someone asks me if I would ever do a show like that, my stock answer is, 'Never say never.' Perhaps being on telly is like a drug and if you aren't getting a regular fix you'll do anything, even eat a fish eyeball in public, in order to get your TV high. I'm pleased to report that while working in New York, as I am at the moment, I don't miss being famous at all. I thought I might, but when my mother visited recently and we went to tourist spots where British and Irish people knew me, I realised that life without the attention is much nicer. I know it is hard to then explain why I'm trying to be successful here in the

States. Having thought about it a great deal, I think it is all about the job, which I still adore. Carrie Fisher has a theory that people in the entertainment industry do their work for free and then get paid to deal with all the other shit that comes with being well known. True, we get paid very well, but as another wise American, Billy Crystal, says when he meets people who want to be rich and famous, it's best to try being rich first, as you'll probably find that it pushes most of your buttons.

Please forgive me if this all sounds like I'm moaning about my success – God forbid! I completely understand how fortunate I am to be in the position I am, and for the most part I really enjoy all my encounters with people who like the show. Please feel free to chat if you see me out and about. But perhaps have a little think about what you want to say before you come over. You'd be amazed at the number of people who ask for an autograph and then look puzzled and surprised when I ask them if they have a piece of paper or a pen. One family in Blackpool asked if they could have their photo taken with me. I happily obliged and we huddled together in a smiling group. It took some minutes before I worked out that none of them had a camera. When I pointed this out they all seemed slightly annoyed with me, as if I was the one who had forgotten to bring my camera out with me. The family stood there staring at me, like a fuzzy photograph, perfectly pleasant but not fully developed.

16
Stars and Gripes

F AMOUS FRIENDS. THOSE TWO WORDS make about as much sense to me as Fun Run or Japanese Banquet. Although I meet celebrities almost every day as part of my job, I have made actual 'friends' with practically none of them. That is not to say that I don't like them – many of them I am genuinely fond of and indeed would like to hang out with – but to put it in perspective I think I only have the phone numbers for about six celebrities. When I apply to get home insurance they invariably ring me back and ask if I'm 'the' Graham Norton? As if that wasn't embarrassing enough, they then go on to ask me if I will be having many celebrities around to my house? It always seems so pathetic when I say 'No', that I then go on to assure them that I do have friends, it's just they aren't well known. Part of me wants to discuss it. Is Ann Bryson, the woman from the cheese commercials, famous? And why do you want to know anyway? Are you afraid that someone will break into my house and steal Angus Deayton?

Occasionally I am invited to something special where I meet a whole bunch of celebrities. Carrie took me to a Christmas party at Joan Collins's where I ended up sitting on her bed next to Roger Moore and George Michael. I shared a taxi home with the Queen's personal piper. As I dropped him off at Buckingham Palace he turned and said, 'I'd ask you in, but I need to give them forty-eight hours' notice.' I've a funny feeling that had they found out that it was me, it would have taken a lot longer than forty-eight hours.

I went to the Beckhams' for a World Cup party. It was all very glamorous and when Victoria greeted me I bent down to admire the huge diamond she had hanging around her neck. Just then David came over to say hello. I stood up quickly and just blurted out, 'I'm so sorry. I was just staring at your wife's tits.' He smiled – oh, that smile! – and said in his girlish whisper, 'I don't mind.' It was lovely to watch the two of them together that day, obviously in love and with the world at their feet. Sadly, due to the show's monologue jokes, I think it'll take even longer to get my next invitation to Beckingham Palace than to the Buckingham one.

The best invitation I've ever got, though, arrived one night on the set of *V Graham Norton*. Liza Minnelli was my guest, and although shaky and nervous at first, she slowly thawed out and became the Liza we remembered from before all the weight gain and illness. She had just got engaged to the previously unknown David Gest. Rumours were rife about his sexuality and the nature of their relationship, but what could not be denied was that since she had met him, she had lost wheelbarrows of fat and was planning a return to performing. Liza had come on the show to promote her first series of concerts, which were to be held in the Albert Hall later that month. Like the professional she is, she worked in plugs for her shows over and over again during the interview. Because of this, when she took out an envelope and told me it contained a very special invitation I simply assumed that it would be free tickets to the Albert Hall. When I ripped open the paper I stared at the card inside. I read it and then read it again. It was an invitation to the most talked-about wedding since Charles and Diana's. On the show I made a great deal out of how thrilled I was to be invited and of course I would be going, but afterwards I kept asking people if they thought it was serious. A few days later one of David Gest's assistants called to ask where they should send all the details about the wedding. It was true! I was going to New York to see Liza, the living legend, get married to a boiled egg in sunglasses! I was genuinely thrilled.

There is no denying that it was a star-studded affair, but there is also no denying that tickets weren't that hard to come by. At the reception I shared a table with Carrie (my guest), Helena Christensen and her boyfriend (she had been the second guest on my show the night Liza invited me), Mel C/Sporty Spice and her date (she had moved tables in the VIP section of a night club to accommodate David and Liza after my show), and Martine McCutcheon, who was the only one at our table to have met the blushing bride more than once. She was a bridesmaid. Anthony Hopkins walked by. There was Mickey Rooney. Joan Collins. Is that Elaine Paige? Thank God Elaine could make it. Alan Cumming, Rosie O'Donnell and of course Elizabeth Taylor and Michael Jackson. It was like a very random fancy-dress party. At the reception I think I might have had a little too much to drink again, because at one point I thought it was a really good idea to lean across the table to Mel C and apologise for all the times in my monologues when I'd called her a fat lesbian. The fact that she didn't punch me makes me fairly certain that she isn't one.

I imagine that most people had probably come, like me, to enjoy the bizarre spectacle of the whole event. The church was full to the rafters, everybody craning around to see who was there. The big news was that Whitney Houston had let them down and that Natalie Cole was going to do the singing. Then word reached us that Liza was having to wait because Liz Taylor, who was the maid of honour, was late. Apparently Liz had forgotten her shoes and it was felt that slippers or tennis shoes would be disrespectful. Carrie reported all the latest developments to Tracey Ullman on her mobile phone and, while she got a few disapproving glances, most people were just jealous that they didn't have the nerve to do the same with their friends.

Suddenly it began. There was a strange sequined pudding – 'That's Liz!' – and a surprisingly tall man looking like the maître d' from some restaurant with a circus theme – 'Is that Michael?' – and then, front and centre, the happy couple. No videotape can properly convey the full horror of watching David Gest in the flesh trying to floss Liza's teeth with his tongue. Even in the gallery where we were sitting you could hear the strange slurping that sounded like water draining through a plughole that's partially clogged with soap and pubic hair. However, the biggest shock was that, despite everything, somewhere in the middle of all this I did believe there was a happy couple. I couldn't begin to explain how that relationship, no matter how briefly, functioned, but there was no denying that in that moment the living legend was happy, truly happy, and the boiled egg with sunglasses was the one making her that way.

A few weeks after the wedding I got a call from David Gest. Would I like to introduce Liza Minnelli at the Royal Albert Hall? Of course the very idea of doing it was terrifying, but I had to say yes. This was Liza's return to the stage and a bit of showbusiness history. How could I resist being the answer in a really hard Liza Minnelli trivia quiz?

On the opening night I had to go in early to do a soundcheck, and afterwards David told me to go and say hello to Liza. I knocked on her dressing-room door and a quiet voice asked me to come in. Liza was lying on a sofa at the end of the room and I had obviously woken her from a nap. She wasn't wearing any make-up and as she reached up to kiss me I looked into her huge liquid eyes and was shocked to see how beautiful she was. Many years had passed, but you could still see the scrubbed beauty of the woman who had won the Oscar for *Cabaret*.

Liza was nervous, but she wasn't the only one. There was a palpable tension in the audience as well as backstage. No one knew if she could do this. Everybody wanted it to be fantastic, but what if it wasn't? The lights dimmed, the audience yelped with excitement and then I was introduced. People didn't exactly sigh with disappointment but I'm sure they wanted to. I ran on quickly so that the applause lasted long enough for me to get to the centre of the stage.

'Yes, like a showbiz version of the Easter story, she's back!'

The crowd roared their approval and everything was all right. They knew that I was just another fan and I wasn't trying to make the evening about me.

The welcome Liza herself got was incredible: a solid wall of applause, approval and love. At first her voice was a little tentative, but you could almost see her feeding off the crowd's adoration until by the end of the show she was a genuine knockout. She got a spontaneous standing ovation and I slowly made my way backstage to add my congratulations. I stopped off at my dressing room first because I thought I'd wait until David and the VIP guests had paid their homage. About five minutes later I went around to Liza's door. There was no crowd of people outside. Odd. I knocked.

'Come in, come in!'

I walked in to find Liza Minnelli all alone sitting at her dressing table, still sweating and wiping the make-up from her eyes. She looked up at me like a child who had just performed in its first nativity play.

'Oh, baby! Did I do OK?'

'Yes! Yes, it was brilliant. Simply amazing. Really special.'

'Really?'

She had just surfed the unconditional wave of love in a sold-out Albert Hall and suddenly I was having to prop her up single-handed. For a second I had a glimpse into how difficult it must be to be Liza Minnelli and what a hard job it must be to be part of her life. No one can compete with that audience, and yet that's the love everything else must be judged by.

I have seen many big divas respond to an audience over the years – Shirley Bassey, Cher, Dolly, Mariah Carey, Diana Ross – and it never ceases to amaze me how the applause almost literally pumps life into them. Beforehand some of them can be difficult or demanding and get a bad press because of it, but these performers are loved unconditionally by so many people that I suppose it's only surprising that they don't behave worse.

Dolly, as I've already said, is pure joy and I've never met anyone with a bad word to say about her. Shirley was a real coup for us to get and it wasn't that easy. We had booked her a couple of years before but then unfortunately she sat down to watch an episode of the show. Elton John was the guest and because he is so funny and rude the show was even more outrageous than normal. At one point I gave him a sort of dildo space hopper which was made to look like a football with a big cock sticking out of it. Somewhere in London an elderly lady swathed in taffeta looked on aghast. The booking was cancelled. We tried to explain that I wouldn't be giving Miss Bassey a cock attached to a football but it was too late – the damage had been done. After many notes and flowers she finally said yes. She turned out to be a great guest, and although I had promised to do nothing rude with her, she seemed only too happy to talk about sex. In the end she is a lady of simple needs – good lighting and Cristal champagne and you've got a sunny Shirley.

The day after Diana Ross did the show she personally contacted the office to say how much she had enjoyed it. Great! Was it the comedy bits, the audience, the gifts in her dressing room that she had liked? No. The reason she had felt moved to call was because she thought her skin had looked nice. Whatever.

Mariah Carey was a huge booking for us and her publicity team made sure we knew it. If Jesus himself had agreed to do the show I doubt his PR would have made such a fuss. Of course, as is often the case, once you got past all the haunted skinny women with mobile phones for earrings, the star herself was really quite fun, in her own way. There are legions of stories about how demanding Mariah Carey is, including one where she demanded a basket of puppies before a concert. I asked her if it was true. She laughed and said, 'Of course not. What actually happened was . . .' and she then went on to tell a story about how she had asked for a basket of puppies before a concert. Quite how she failed to see that both stories were exactly the same remains a mystery to me, as are her odd drinking habits. When she requires a drink she simply cocks her head to one side like a puzzled dog and a small army of people run to her side with all sorts of juices and sodas, each bottle with a straw sticking out of it. So far, so mad, but whereas anyone's natural reaction would be to take the chosen bottle and drink it, Mariah's hands don't leave her side. Like a beautiful celebrity gerbil she just suckles at her drink while a patient assistant holds it. God knows how this started, but you can't blame a baby for not being able to walk if people carry it everywhere. Somebody needs to tell her. Perhaps she'll read this book?

Because we are always on the lookout for guests and ways of getting in touch with celebrities, I was intrigued when I got a message from TalkBack to say that Shakira Caine had called. We had never had her husband Michael on the show, so although I knew she probably wanted me to help with some charity thing or other, I quickly returned the call in the hope of endearing myself to the original Alfie. The phone was answered immediately by a woman.

'May I speak to Shakira Caine, please?'

'Who?'

'Shakira Caine?'

'Oh. Who's speaking?'

'Graham Norton.'

'One moment, please, I'll see if she's available.'

A few seconds later a woman's voice came on the line.

'Hello, Shakira Caine speaking.'

The voice sounded identical to the first one and it made me laugh to think that someone like the wife of Michael Caine would pretend to be her own assistant. She explained that she wanted to meet me to discuss a project. I asked her what sort of project it might be, but she insisted that we should meet face to face and also that wherever we met there should be a video and television. We arranged that the meeting would take place at my office the next week. I warned everyone that Shakira Caine was going to be paying us a visit and that we should all be on our best behaviour; however, on the day I got a message from the receptionist to say that Mrs Caine had called to say she couldn't make it after all and could I ring her to rearrange the meeting. I did and she apologised profusely and we rescheduled for the following day at 3 p.m.

The next afternoon the receptionist called me at a little after three o'clock to tell me that Shakira Caine was in reception. I asked Jon if I looked presentable and headed downstairs. In reception there was no sign of Shakira Caine, but a middle-aged lady was sitting on the sofa. When she saw me she stood and held out her hand.

'I'm so sorry, Shakira couldn't make it, but I thought it best if I came to talk to you anyway.'

In a way I was almost relieved because I was going to feel like such a phoney sucking up to Shakira just to get to her husband. I showed my mystery visitor into our meeting room and she held out the videotape she wanted me to watch. I stuck it into the machine and a scene from the 1960s movie

The VIPs began to play. A young Maggie Smith playing a
devoted secretary persuades Richard Burton to write a
cheque for a vast sum of money in order to save her boss
and the man she loves. As soon as Richard had signed the
cheque my new friend instructed me to turn off the tape. I
simply presumed it was some new 'novelty' way of asking
people for money that the 'ladies who lunch' had come up
with. I turned to the woman sitting on the low sofa. I was
still kneeling on the floor in front of the TV. It didn't seem
as if she was going to speak.

'I'm intrigued,' I said.

'Yes, you must be,' she replied. 'I'm not Shakira Caine.'

She uttered these words in a strange and deliberate way.

'Yes,' I laughed, 'I know that.'

She shook her head. 'No, I've never been Shakira Caine.'

A horrible misshapen penny began to drop: I realised that
I had never spoken to Shakira Caine and was now sitting
alone behind a closed door with a woman who I felt fairly
certain would fit into most people's loose definition of the
word 'mad'.

I slowly got up off the floor, not wanting to startle her, and
sat on a chair. My mind was racing. True, she seemed like a
harmless lady in a pair of grey slacks with sensible shoes, but
what if my fake Shakira had a real gun? What if God had told
her to kill the vile homosexual off the telly? He'd told people
to do a lot of things more irrational than that.

'I'm sorry I lied, but I couldn't think of any other way of
getting to meet you,' she said.

'I understand,' I lied.

'You seem like a nice person.'

'I hope I am.'

'That's why I thought you might help me. I didn't know who else to turn to.'

She then went on to tell me a story so awful that it was as heartbreaking as it was hilarious. She had managed to lose all her husband's money by convincing him to invest in a novelty mattress company. I regret to say I didn't have the nerve to ask her what exactly a novelty mattress was, but it seems that they can't have been a great success. The little money he had left she then told him to invest in various shares which then crashed. I did wonder why you would take financial advice again from someone who thought amusing bedding was a good investment, but I let it go. Her plan was that she would use the £5,000 I was going to lend her to play with bank shares. If nothing else, she had certainly embraced that old piece of advice about getting back on the horse. Stocks and shares hadn't exactly been working for her so far. Now, she told me, her husband was very ill and she was desperate to do something to help.

She took out a small photo album from her handbag. She wanted to show me pictures of her husband. He was old, very old, and slumped in a chair, unable to focus on the camera lens. Someone, presumably my financial whiz-kid, had seen fit to dress him in a novelty Christmas jumper. A knitted Rudolph grinned beneath the old man's blank grey face. It was awful. Half of me wanted to give her the money, but I knew she would just throw it away on her stupid scheme.

'Well?' she asked, staring at me with eyes bigger and browner than the woolly Rudolph's.

I couldn't tell her 'No' flat out. 'Let me think about it. I have your number, I'll call you tomorrow.'

She made me promise, and then slowly, like coaxing someone off a ledge, I walked her to the door and back onto the
street.

When I went upstairs I had to tell the story of what had
just happened several times, trying to make sense of it. The
madness of it all was so random that it was very hard to get
a grip on what might be true and what might be part of a
complicated scam. In the end I think I believed her, and so
the next day I called her with my decision.

'I'm not going to lend you the money. Your husband seems
very ill and I think you should try to enjoy what time he has
left and then worry about the money.'

I knew they owned a house: perhaps they could remort-
gage that? I was trying to give sensible advice to a woman
who had pretended to be married to Michael Caine. I found
myself lecturing her like a strict parent.

'Please, never pretend to be Shakira Caine again. I didn't
mind, but some people might and you might get in trouble
with the police, and I really think that's the last thing your
husband needs.'

She promised to never do it again, thanked me for calling
and hung up.

One of the most depressing aspects of being on television
is the avalanche of begging letters that arrive the minute
your face appears on the screen. The vast majority of them
are genuine and legitimate cries for help from people with
no one else to turn to, and yet it is impossible to say yes to
them all. I tend to approach them in an emotional rather
than logical way, so that some day I'll write several cheques
and another day I'll say 'no'. The profound gratitude of the
people I help makes the thought of people I say no to all

the worse. I sent a cheque a few years ago to a young woman who was trying to pay her tuition fees for drama school, only to find out a couple of weeks later that it was a tabloid newspaper trying to see which celebs were the most generous. I was the only person who had sent money, but it didn't make me feel generous, I just felt like a fool and now thanks to that clever journalist I am much more suspicious of letters and, to be honest, probably write far fewer cheques.

Whenever I meet a journalist I'm always so glad that college rejected me for the journalism course all those years ago. I'm sure there are happy, pleasant, well-adjusted people who work for the papers, but you rarely meet them. Because I interview people as part of my job, I find being interviewed very uncomfortable. It was a wonderful revelation to me when I was talking to some journalist from the *Daily Mail* that I wasn't under oath and I could say what I liked. Knowing that you can lie takes the fear out of any question that they might ask you. There are journalists who, if they read this book, are going to be livid. One *Sunday Times* journalist had got wind of me trying to become a rent boy, but I calmly assured her that it was all a load of rubbish. I had nothing against the woman – I just didn't want her to be the one to tell that story.

When I'm doing interviews I don't exactly grill my guests – I'm no Jeremy Paxman, but then I can't afford to be. The show is a comedy show and while a rude question might get a laugh, it is going to be quite hard to sustain a happy atmosphere once I'm sitting beside someone with a face like thunder. Also, they are my guest; I have invited them on the show, they haven't asked to be there – well, apart from George Michael who just phoned my mobile out of the blue and asked if he could do the show on Friday! If only it were always that easy – but my point is, you aren't rude to guests. You wouldn't invite a vegetarian around and then force them to eat meat, and so I want my celebrities to leave happy, no matter how hateful, talentless and boring a few of them have been.

The place in the show where things do get nasty is in the monologue. I write very few of the jokes myself and sometimes their cruelty can take even my breath away, but despite this I will usually agree to do them. I know our targets seem random, but I have a fairly strict way of gauging whether or not they are defensible. Michael Douglas and Catherine Zeta-Jones are rich, successful, in love and have beautiful children. If they can't take some jokes – no matter how vile – by some guy in a shiny suit on a late-night television show, they really need to go into therapy. Similarly the Royal Family, or most politicians. When things start not to be funny is when the subject starts to seem like a victim. Mel C was funny, but when she seemed to be genuinely unhappy and depressed the jokes stopped. Jordan never seems funny to me because she has a damaged air about her. I know Leslie Ash was very upset about the jokes I did when she had the cosmetic treatment on her lips. I'm sure sitting at home listening to me trash the way you look isn't the most pleasant experience, but as far as I knew she had started the jokes herself by christening it the 'trout pout', and besides, if she was going to complain about anyone, maybe she should focus on her doctor.

I'm ashamed to admit that the monologue joke that got most complaints cannot be defended in any way. It was extremely stupid, thoughtless and insensitive of us. Maurice

Gibb had died the day before we were due back on air after our Christmas break in January 2003. Like most offices up and down the land, we amused ourselves by making jokes about his death. It sounds awful, but you probably did it yourself. It's inevitable that when someone who was famous for singing a song called 'Staying Alive' dies, there will be some humour in it. Our mistake was thinking that something that was funny in the office would be appropriate for television. I jumped through my velvet curtains and did a mild joke about the sounds his heart monitor made. 'Staying alive, oh, oh, oh. Not staying alive, ohhhhhhhhhhhhh.' It got a laugh, and unbelievably it still didn't strike us how inappropriate and hurtful it was until the next morning when the complaints started to pile in. I hate to think how any members of his family who were watching must have felt, or indeed his legions of fans. I apologised, and so did Channel 4, who had let us air the joke. There was nothing more to do. I couldn't take it back. We had been fools.

The next day we were the number-one story on the TV news in Miami, and every British paper carried the story. Unfortunately no one seemed interested in reporting how genuinely sorry we were.

A few weeks later Robin Gibb was bravely promoting his new solo album on *This Morning* with Fern Britton and Philip Schofield when he just burst into a rant about me. He wanted to rip my head off. Strong stuff, I felt, given that I hadn't actually killed his brother Maurice, but who knows how any one of us would cope with the stress of promoting an album so soon after the loss of a dear family member. I was a little surprised late in 2003 to see Robin accepting a World Day award in Germany for his contribution to world peace. Didn't they know he wanted to rip my head off? On *This Morning* he promised that he would eventually run into me at some showbiz function. Well, so far, so good. My dread is that I'll get on a plane and when I arrive at my seat there he'll be flicking through the in-flight magazine, waiting for the captain to turn off the 'No head-ripping' light.

It is hard to explain why, but the members of the public that have been involved with the show hardly ever take offence. I think the reason is that no matter how much we mock them or make them look foolish, they know that there is no malice or condemnation in it. If we let you tell your story on the show or build a comedy item or stunt around something you've done, it usually means that we are celebrating your little adventure. I like to think that people who appear on our show aren't just looking for their fifteen seconds of fame but that they genuinely want to share their favourite anecdote or funniest secrets with the audience. The studio has a real party atmosphere, and it's easy to get carried away – at least, that's the only way I can explain a man telling us about how he made a dog come by accident, or another man revealing that he managed to give his mother crabs.

After the show we very rarely hear about any fallout, but I did once bump into the sister of a woman who had told a story on the show, and she told me about its tragic consequences.

I remember meeting her because it was such an extraordinary day. I was supposed to be introducing some acts at a big concert in Trafalgar Square for Nelson Mandela. I was backstage with Richard E. Grant, chatting about nothing in particular, when we noticed a huddled group heading for a Portakabin dressing room.

'There's Nelson,' declared Richard. 'Follow me!'

I trotted behind him towards the little cabin that contained the world's favourite leader. A word with the large South African lady with the clipboard outside and suddenly we were escorted in. Richard approached Nelson first and began telling him how he had in fact gone to school with his son. I felt slightly awkward and looked at the other man standing beside Nelson. He smiled. I'd seen those teeth before – it was our own lovely leader, Tony Blair!

'Hello!' I said.

'Hello,' he replied. When Tony writes his memoirs I doubt he will find the room for a description of our meeting.

By then Richard had moved away. I stepped forward. The lady with the clipboard introduced me.

'This is Graham Norton. He is a television presenter. He is very bad.'

I hoped this was simply linguistic confusion on her part rather than an actual attack on my character. Nelson looked slightly taken aback: why was he being introduced to a bad person?

'What about "cheeky"?' I asked.

The lady considered this for a moment, but then decided on 'naughty'. I could live with that. I shook the great man's hand and told him what an honour it was to meet him. He nodded his head and then thanked me for helping to end apartheid. While this was very nice of him, I did think that he was going to be in this room for quite some time if he was personally going to thank everyone who had signed that petition outside South Africa House while they were waiting for a night bus.

It was just after this, as I was stepping out of the Portakabin, that a lady approached me and said: 'You wrecked our family!' The clipboard lady had been right, I *was* bad.

'How?' I asked, although I was dreading the answer.

She told me that her sister had told a story about her father finding her dildo in her bed. I remembered her because she had seemed very sweet and had told the story very well. Somehow the girl had imagined that neither her parents nor their friends watched my show. It turned out that the programme was more popular than she thought: her parents were so upset that they didn't speak to her for months. Finally the sister who was telling me all of this managed to broker a truce: the whole family were going to meet up and have a nice meal and forget that it had ever happened. A lovely ending to a sad story. If only it could have ended there. The night before they were all going to kiss and make-up, Channel 4 showed a compilation programme featuring highlights from the last series of *So*. Can you guess what one of the highlights was? The wound was reopened and the meal was cancelled.

Hearing this story did make me feel awful, but we do our best to make sure that this sort of situation doesn't arise. We ask everyone to sign a release form after the show, when they are no longer in the heat of the moment, and even if people call us after they have signed the form and ask us to cut things out, we always oblige.

Hopefully despite the controversy and not because of it, *V Graham Norton* was continuing to do well. Perhaps as some sort of reward, Channel 4 came up with a plan. For the last week of the series at the end of March we would take the show to New York. By a weird coincidence, at the same time the American TV giant NBC approached us about doing a pilot of a US version of the show. It was decided that we would tape the British shows from the Sunday until the Thursday and then on the Friday we would make a slightly different hour-long version of the show for the American network. The Friday was going to be 4 April, my fortieth birthday.

Dealing with American television executives is a bit like taking a shower in jelly: sickly sweet, slimy, and leaves you feeling dirtier. To begin with, our dealings with NBC were sunshine and light. They loved the show and didn't want to change a thing about it. This seemed odd given that I had recently met a producer of *The Tonight Show*, NBC's late-night comedy chat show, and he had told me that they still weren't allowed to say the word 'fart', never mind the sorts of things I say and show on my programme. NBC assured us that things were changing all the time and it would only mean minor adjustments. Mmm.

The incident that really summed up the frustration of trying to please an American network happened when we were trying to book a guest for their pilot. They sent us a list of suggested guests. One of the names on that list was Debbie Harry from Blondie. We had a good relationship with Debbie, and I thought it would be great to have a guest who was familiar with the programme when we were trying to make the show for an American audience. We booked her. Almost in passing we mentioned to NBC that we had gone ahead and confirmed one of their suggested guests. Outrage! We had no right to make the booking without getting their approval first. After that call, Graham, Jon and I just looked at each other and shook our heads. Much as we wanted to work in America, McDonald's was beginning to look like a better option than this mindless wrangling.

It sounds a ridiculous thing to say and it's an even harder thing to explain, but doing that week of shows in New York was the happiest of my life. Being in New York and witnessing the positive reaction of the audiences and guests to our silly show was thrilling. These people got it and we got them. All the staff we had brought over from Britain just mucked in and helped on every show. We went out each night but still found the energy to do the show the next day – we were all surviving on pure adrenalin. I think it was because it had all gone so well that I suddenly felt that I couldn't bear to do the pilot for NBC on the Friday. I knew it was going to be torture and that if it ever did see the light of day it would be such a misrepresentation of what was good about our show that people would hate it. On the Thursday, high on success, I announced that we weren't going to do the NBC show the next day or ever.

Melanie and Graham proceeded to have one of the most hideous meetings imaginable where they had to explain to a series of more and more senior NBC executives that there wasn't going to be a pilot the next day. We agreed to pay all the costs that had been incurred and simply walk away. If Graham and Melanie had stripped off and had full sex in front of them they couldn't have been more surprised. For me it was simply the biggest, most expensive birthday present I could ever have given myself.

On the Friday night we had our wrap party in the private room of a trendy restaurant in the Chelsea area of New York. Champagne flowed and toasts were made. We had just done five great shows in the most exciting city on earth.

Stars and Gripes

I had just stuck two fingers up to America's number-one network, a limo was waiting to take me back to the interior-designed town house I had bought in the heart of Manhattan, and yet the only fact to truly shock me that night was that somehow I had become forty years old.

17

A Dish Served Old

A Dish Served Old

A PIGEON FLYING INTO A glass door couldn't have been more shocked than I was when I hit forty. I just didn't see it coming. Obviously I saw the date in the diary: I was thirty-nine and soon I was going to be forty. What I didn't expect was that I would find it so hard to deal with. The week of my birthday in New York, *GQ* magazine named me the worst-dressed man in Britain, and while that is without question true and a great honour, it really didn't give me much confidence when I was trying to figure out what I should be wearing as a forty-year-old man. The jeans and T-shirts that had been my off-screen uniform for years suddenly seemed pathetic. 'Age appropriate' became a phrase I found myself using over and over again. I had never particularly wanted to get older, but now that I was I found I didn't know how to.

After the end of the series in New York, I headed off to Cape Town for a holiday. The moment the plane touched down I seemed to go into party overdrive. If I ran around fast enough, maybe no one would notice just how old I had become. I was hanging out with guys in their twenties, and while I could just about keep up, every now and again something would happen to remind me that even if I felt the same as I always had, things had changed. On the dance floor someone leaned over.

'I've got to hand it to you, you've got stamina!'

'What do you mean?' I asked.

'Well, you know, for a bloke your age.'

Thank you and goodnight.

Another evening I ended up snogging some guy who must have been in his mid-twenties. He came back to the house and we sat having a drink. Everything was going fine until he suddenly unleashed that question which even Siegfried fears more than tigers.

'By the way, how old are you?'

I opened my eyes as wide as my facial saddlebags allowed and replied in what I hoped was a calm voice, 'Forty.'

It was as if I had poured salt on a slug – he couldn't get out of the house fast enough. If I hadn't opened the door he would have dislocated every bone in his body in order to slither under it, and of course the worst bit was that I couldn't blame him.

Happily there are some guys who prefer older men, but that raises a whole series of other problems. Going to bed with them when you are pissed and horny is fine, but in the morning when they spring from beneath the duvet and prance around like an ad for some new product called Pert, I lie there feeling like a gay Michael Winner, and nobody, not even Michael Winner, wants to feel like that.

Towards the end of my holiday I found myself yet again with a group of twentysomethings all heading back to an after-hours party in a house that one of them was house-sitting. We piled into cars and drove up the steep, winding roads into an area of Cape Town called Fresnaye. The house was stunning, with picture-perfect views of Cape Town stretched below us like a vast carpet woven from strings of fairy lights. We raided the cellar and sat around the pool drinking expensive bottles of red wine. Soon we were splashing around in our underpants, and although it might have looked like the opening scene of a porn movie there was one thing wrong with the picture: one of the people cavorting around was forty years old, and it was me!

Suddenly the guy who was house-sitting this piece of paradise grabbed my hand.

'Follow me!'

Dripping, I was dragged along through the garden and into the house.

'I want to show you something!' He was so excited that I assumed it must be either some amazing piece of electrical wizardry or his cock.

We finally arrived in a small room at the back of the building and we stood there panting and glistening from the pool. The boy reached behind the sofa and brought out his treasure – it was a gun. He handed it to me, cold and heavy. I stared at it. I had never held a gun before. I let it lie on my open palms like a dead bird and asked, 'Is this loaded?'

'Yes.'

I carefully handed it back to him, thinking that if this were a movie one of us would not be leaving this house alive. As it happens we all did, but the incident with the gun was the wake-up call I needed. Growing old may not be the best thing in the world, but it does come with some perks. One of them is being wise enough to know when to stop. It was time to stop.

Just as I was giving myself a red flag in my personal life, professionally a major green one was waving. Given that my

job involves me being a big kid night after night, it is sometimes hard to remember that the production company I had
started with Graham and Jon had become quite a big
business. Following the debacle with NBC we had taken
on representation in America with UTA. We still wanted
to try working in the States, and this time we were going to
attempt to get it right. Our agents organised a week of meetings in LA and Graham, Jon, Melanie and I flew out to see
who would like to buy our little show.

As it turned out, quite a few people did. Each morning
we piled into a minibus and were driven through the oddly
familiar streets of LA to glass-walled offices where smartly
dressed men and women explained why their station was
the place to be. The very first meeting we had was with the
people from ABC, and it took place in one of the executive
dining rooms at Disney. We sat looking through a window
framed by the giant armpit of one of the seven dwarves that
keeps the roof aloft. As I lifted my wine glass, I noticed the
silhouette of a famous mouse etched into the glass. It
seemed unlikely that this was the home for a show that had
featured the pipes of Pam and the ping-pong-firing exploits
of Helga.

In America, television really is an industry, and it makes
the way we operate in Britain seem slightly like amateur
dramatics in comparison. Each evening we would gather by
the pool for a drink to discuss what had happened during
the day. We met lots of people we liked and a fair number
we loathed, but what we hadn't met was anyone we thought
we could have fun working with. On the last day of our trip
we had one final meeting. It was with a cable channel called
Comedy Central which produced shows like *South Park*

and was for many years the American home of *Absolutely Fabulous*. We walked into a room like all the others we had been in – glass walls and a long table with designer water on it – but the difference was that this room had people in it we instantly clicked with. After we left, UTA had lots of discussions with various people about different offers, but back in London there was no doubt in our minds: Comedy Central was our natural home.

Change was also afoot in the UK. I had just done a year of five nights a week and we were getting ready to do another year of it. Much as I still loved the show, I had to admit that I was tired. On top of that, the whole 'forty years old' thing had also had an impact. I didn't want to spend what was left of my 'active' years doing nothing but work. I wanted to spend more time with my friends, I wanted to read, travel, get drunk. I wanted my life back. The trouble with ending five nights was what to do next. No matter how we looked at it, staying at Channel 4 didn't seem like an option. Anything we could think of seemed like taking a step back. The only step forward we could see was to try something completely new on a different network. Jon and I had often talked about doing a prime-time family-friendly show, and this seemed like the perfect time to try it.

Three years after walking away from the BBC I found myself at lunch with the new people in charge. Lorraine Heggessy runs BBC 1 and Jane Lush is head of entertainment. I'd met Lorraine at various times and I'd always liked her. When she talks about television you can tell that she's not just an executive but also a fan. She'll mention what her kids enjoy, or which programmes her husband watches. It is a rare executive indeed who has the theme tune from

EastEnders as her mobile phone ringtone, but that's Lorraine.
Jane I didn't know so well, but we had sat next to each other
at the Beckhams' World Cup party, so again I knew her in
out-of-work mode. We met in San Lorenzo in Knightsbridge
and the meal was fun. We talked about holidays, restaurants
and what had been on telly the night before and then somewhere around coffee they said they'd still like me to join the
BBC and I said that I'd like to. It was as simple as that.

2004 hung in the air before us like a glittery lantern. A
series on Comedy Central followed by a new show for the
BBC. We couldn't wait. The only slight problem was that
we would have to. We had nearly a year left of the Channel
4 show. I think we were all a bit worried that it would be
difficult to maintain our enthusiasm for the programme now
that we had decided to end it, but in fact the opposite
happened. Because there was light at the end of the tunnel
we found ourselves enjoying the shows even more.

We had done what everyone had said was impossible: we
had produced a successful five-nights-a-week comedy chat
show in Britain. I'm enormously proud of that achievement,
but also slightly sorry that I didn't keep it going for longer.
I'm sure there are people who think it ended because we
had run out of ideas or guests, but the truth of the matter
is, if you can keep a show like that running for two years
you could keep it going for twenty. The weak spoke in the
wheel was me. I watch David Letterman in America, where
he has been doing his show for thirty years, and while I envy
him his talent and success, I don't envy him his life. I think
getting a job like that five nights a week needs to be your
first big break.

The trouble with me was that I was already getting paid

very well and living a very pampered life on the back of one show a week, so when I went to five nights a week, although I loved the work and the challenge, I didn't have that thing that I would have had if they'd just handed me Jack's job all those years before – gratitude. Being thankful will keep you showing up at work for many years. Like a greyhound who had been fed too many rabbits, I'd lost my hunger for the race.

Channel 4 quickly got the message that we would be doing *V Graham Norton* to the end of our contract but no longer. What they didn't know was that I would be leaving the Channel. The BBC were desperate to announce the fact that they had signed me up, presumably to get the backlash from the right-wing press out of the way as quickly as possible, but I wanted to tell Channel 4 personally. However, just like trying to tell a lover it was over, I couldn't ever find the right time.

As if there wasn't enough change and upheaval in my life, I decided to do a very odd thing. I bought a new house in London. I don't really understand why. My house in Bow was finally exactly the way I wanted it, but because I had been stupid and poorly advised I realised that it wasn't going to stay like that for long. The new bathroom which had taken nearly a year to finish – for legal reasons I can't name the company who did it, but Jesus I'd like to! – was full of a beautiful wood. It was elm that had been given an oiled finish. My toilet had been set into it, the bath was surrounded by it, even the sink was fixed into a big slab of it. It looked gorgeous. However, just as the carpenter who had installed it all was going out the door on her last day, she turned and, almost as an afterthought, said, 'Oh, do be careful not to get any water on that wood because it stains. Bye!' I rang the estate agents.

The other reason for moving was that the local children had found out where I lived. Some Sundays I would just sit for hours under the window so I couldn't be seen while children shouted through my letterbox. Even as I was doing it I asked myself, 'Why am I behaving as if I'm under siege? Why not just answer the door?' In all honesty I don't know, but there was something about the way the front door opened straight into the open-plan living room that meant the kids would have effectively been in my house, and somehow that seemed like an unacceptable invasion of my privacy. I have never invited journalists into my house, and I feel that gives me the right to keep my door closed on the world. Perhaps that is very naïve of me, but I feel as if I give both the public and the press enough access to me without them hanging around outside where I live. When I am door-stepped by a journalist, I always wonder why they feel the need to come all the way out to Bow in London's East End when they could just as well have stood outside my office, where they know I arrive and leave at exactly the same time every day.

These were the reasons I gave myself for moving, but maybe I just wanted a fresh start along with everything else in my life, or perhaps I just saw the picture of a house I preferred to the one I had in Bow. In fact, why pretend? That is exactly what happened. I was in the gym one day flicking through the paper as I waited for my trainer (I am aware that at the beginning of this book I would have been excited to find fifty pence down the back of the sofa and now I'm casually dropping in references to personal trainers.

Whether you are reading or living this book the irony is not lost), when I saw a picture of a house by the Thames. On a whim I rang and asked to see it. After the viewing I put in an offer, it was accepted, and it seemed I was on the move in my personal life as well.

I'd reached a point in my life when I didn't have to worry about the arrival of the gas or phone bill, and as a result I'd stopped reading my horoscope. All I had ever wanted it to tell me was that a windfall was coming my way, and now that it had I was no longer interested. It did strike me, however, that with all the change and new beginnings coming into my life perhaps something was written in the stars. New job, new home, could there be a new boyfriend lurking behind my moon in conjunction with Uranus?

I met Andrew in New York. I was in a club with my friend Jamie, and across the room I saw this man who I reckoned must have been about my age. What really struck me was the way he was dressed. He didn't look particularly square or fuddy-duddy, but nor was he wearing ripped jeans and a tight shiny top. He had found what I was looking for – an age-appropriate wardrobe. I was just pointing him out to Jamie when he started to walk towards me. As he got closer I realised that beyond the age-appropriate clothing he was any-age gorgeous. He smiled and reached out his hand. It turned out that he was from Scotland and was just visiting New York for the weekend. He fell in with the group of people I was chatting with. One of the women was very drunk, or maybe just naturally annoying, but at one point she opened Andrew's shirt. Hello! A well-dressed gorgeous man with a great body. My vodka and tonics were kicking in. Soon we were dancing and kissing. I couldn't believe this hunk was going to come home with me, and that was just as well because he didn't. With an 'I'm too drunk, I've got to go', he was gone, leaving me with a crumpled ball of paper with the number of his hotel. I felt like Prince Charming staring after a strangely muscular Cinderella.

The next day I called. A voice that suggested that seconds before its owner had been asleep answered. It was three in the afternoon.

'Hello. Is this Andrew?'

A wary 'Yes'.

'This is Graham. Graham Norton.'

A long pause and then, 'How on earth did you know I was staying here?'

He *had* been drunk. I explained and he told me where he would be with his friends that night if I wanted to come by. I said I'd try. When I hung up I had a brief workshop with Jamie who was staying with me. We decided that there was no point in pursuing it. The moment was over.

About two months later I was sitting at my desk. The phone rang.

'I have an Andrew you met in New York on the line. Do you want to take it?'

'Yes.'

Now it was my turn to ask how he knew my number. It turned out to be as simple as calling Channel 4 and asking for the name of the production company that made my show. Smart on top of everything else! Apparently he was coming down to London and wondered if I'd like to meet up. We arranged the when-and-wheres, and everything went like clockwork until late that night when we were kissing in a club. He suddenly pulled back.

'I can't handle this. I've got to go.' And with that he disappeared.

I stood there feeling foolish and trying to process what had just happened. Maybe I'd got it wrong and he'd just gone to the loo. Minutes passed and people had started to come over to ask me if I was all right. Unless he had a bladder as big as one of Richard Branson's hot-air balloons, I guessed he wasn't coming back. I went home alone feeling very stupid.

When we spoke the next day he explained that the pressures of London and my notoriety freaked him out. Would I like to come up to Edinburgh to see him, because he thought he'd cope better on his home turf? Given how badly this non-relationship was going, I don't quite know why the word 'yes' escaped out of my mouth, but I suppose I was very keen to make something work with someone who was in their thirties and who had a job and a car. Odd that my attempts to be a mature adult made me appear so adolescent. I got on the plane and headed north. Andrew seemed genuinely disappointed and surprised when I told him that I'd booked into a hotel.

'Given your track record,' I explained, 'I think it's best.'

Sure enough, after a really good night we got back to the hotel, and then, just before we went to bed, he let out his traditional 'Goodnight' cry of 'I've got to go'. This time I just laughed. I'd found a bolter.

Unbelievably, we did try one more time with him coming to stay with me in London. I tried not to get my hopes up, but somehow I could feel my stomach flipping. Yet again my cock and heart had conspired to make a fool of me. I knew that Andrew was deeply damaged goods and was as likely to become my boyfriend as Russell Crowe, and yet I was so desperate to make him like me that I was practically handing him the clown make-up and asking him to apply it to my face.

The London weekend was a disaster. We stayed up all night and then he headed off to some chill-out party and I never saw him again. I did get a long apologetic email from him in which he explained why he felt he had to break up with me. Break up with me? If what had gone on between us constituted a relationship then I am officially dating my postman. About six months later I walked into a bar in Cape Town and there he was. He bounded up to me, all tan and teeth.

'Great to see you. I'd love to do lunch – I'll call you tomorrow.'

Despite everything that had happened, the next day I found myself waiting for the phone to ring. He never called.

'Table for one, please. Booked under the name of Fool.'

I packed my heart away and explained to my cock that from now on it was flying solo.

Channel 4 had come up with a plan which managed to cheer me up. At the start of 2004, instead of doing one last season of five nights a week, why not take the show to New York and do a new weekly show from there? Of course I wanted to, but now that they had inadvertently forced my hand, I had to tell them about the BBC before they committed to spending a large fortune on what was to be my swansong on the station.

Kevin Lygo, having gone off to Channel Five for a while, was now back at the helm of 4. I went in to meet him, feeling nervous and wretched. Kevin's office always has six things in it: a table, a pencil, a notepad, two chairs and him. On previous occasions the effect had been very calming in a Zenlike way, but now it just meant I had nowhere to look, nothing to distract me. I explained as best as I could why I felt the time was right for me to leave, and why I thought BBC 1 was the place for me to go. We talked around it for a while, but eventually Kevin could see that my mind was made up. I brought up the subject of New York.

'I'll completely understand if you no longer want to do it.'

In the sort of gesture that would be unthinkable on American television or indeed most British TV, he waved his hand and said, 'No, it's in the schedule already, off you go.'

We shook hands and he walked me to the lifts. Why can't all break-ups be that civilised?

The shows trundled along until suddenly we were doing our last ever week of *V Graham Norton*. We would probably have been much more sentimental about it all except that for the end of this series Channel 4 had sent us to Los Angeles. Although the shows went well and we had some Hollywood royalty like Tony Curtis, Debbie Reynolds, Sharon Stone and Burt Reynolds as guests, we kept comparing it with the week we had spent in New York and it just didn't measure up. The audiences in New York for both stand-up and the TV show were the best I'd ever encountered. They don't come to judge, they come to have a good time, and if you give them a good time they are unstinting in their appreciation. Don't get me wrong, dear reader – I love British audiences too, but I think we are so familiar with each other now that often doing a show in the UK is just like performing for a group of friends. I find myself being lazy and the audiences indulge me. In America I have to up my game. It's like starting all over again and that's exciting.

After LA we all went our separate ways to spend Christmas with family and friends. I sat in the sun with my mother and Paula and a couple of friends. I very rarely discuss my work with my family, but the Saturday before we came away the *Daily Mail* had risen to the bait of the belated BBC announcement of my arrival. The headline read 'SULTAN OF SLEAZE OR COMIC GENIUS?' I wonder if you can guess which they decided I was? Short of telling people to go out and burn their TV licences in the street, I don't think they could have been any plainer in their disapproval.

We talked about it, and for the first time ever I got the sense that my mother understood what I did for a living. She seemed fully confident that I could turn my Channel 4 persona into something suitable for BBC 1. Of course this may just have been wishful thinking on her part so that she could look her friends in the eye once more. One of my mother's best friends always feels the need, every time I see her, to tell me, 'I like Graham Walker, but I don't like Graham Norton.' Each time I patiently explain that she isn't meant to. Unfortunately rural widows in their seventies aren't my target audience. Happily I know that there are plenty of such women who do like the show because they stop me in the street to tell me.

There is a real dilemma in my home town about me. They are delighted that someone from Bandon is on the television; they just wish it didn't have to be me. Even my school has never once asked me back to do a single thing, not give a speech, cut a ribbon, turn a sod – nothing. Sadly, should the invitation come now, it's too late. I'll save them the expense of stamps by stating simply here: fuck off.

Before the start of our last ever Channel 4 series we had a big party in London to thank all the people who had worked on *So* and *V Graham Norton*. The venue was near London Bridge under some railway arches, and slowly the big, dank space filled up with hundreds of people. I looked at the sea of faces and was overwhelmed by how many people it had taken to keep the show on the air over the years. Obviously I knew all the researchers and producers, but the people I really appreciated seeing at the party were the guys who opened the curtain for me night after night, the cameramen who were never afraid to let me know at rehearsal whether a joke was funny or not, all the people who didn't need to care about the show but did. I was going to miss them.

A new set, title sequence and music: we packed our bags and headed off to the States to film the final series. To say that New York was cold is like saying that Hitler was naughty. I've never experienced anything like it. We had all been warned about the city's winter, but somehow our little British coats didn't seem to work. About a week after we had arrived I was doing a photo shoot for *Hello!* magazine in order to promote the show. I stood on the roof of the Maritime Hotel in Chelsea. Snow lay all around and the wind was blowing off the Hudson river. I had never felt so cold in my entire life. I started remembering a documentary I'd heard on Radio 4 about hypothermia and how just before it killed you you began to feel warm. I was starting to feel warm. I knew that I was going to die one day, but I really didn't want it to be during a *Hello!* photo shoot. I was beginning to regret my decision not to invite them into my lovely home. The photograph ended up on the cover and I looked like a freeze-dried pig with an eye infection.

I wasn't the only one feeling the cold and the desire to be in my lovely home. One Sunday afternoon I went to put something in the bin in the kitchen. A sudden movement and there, running across the room to explore the gap behind the washing machine, was a small mouse. If an alligator had crawled out of my toilet I couldn't have been more frightened or horrified. Given that I have survived both rats and cockroaches, I don't know why it affected me so badly, but gasping and flapping my hands like a penguin chick I ran out of the room. I heard a little scuttling sound and, turning around, saw that the fucking mouse was following me. My ensuing scream seemed to convey fairly effectively to the mouse that he was not welcome. He headed for the bookshelves. I leant against the wall, frozen with fear like a teenage girl in a slasher movie. I looked around, suddenly blind to the pristine minimalism of my beautiful house; I might as well have been living in the local council dump. My first thought was that my mother was coming to stay and there was no way she was going to tolerate a room-mate with a tail and a penchant for cheese. I headed off to the corner shop and returned with a couple of traditional mousetraps. I baited them and put one by the bin and the other one where I had last seen my tiny trespasser.

A week passed and there was no sign of the mouse, alive or dead. The next weekend I was having everyone from work over for drinks and I felt that having mousetraps lying around didn't exactly scream glamour. I decided that the mouse must have gone out the same way it had come in and threw the traps away. The day after the party I was coming down the stairs and there, standing by the bottom step, was the mouse. It looked at me with a mixture of apology and embarrassment and sheepishly headed off to hide under a chair by the window. This time my fear was replaced by rage. 'Right, fucker! You are going to die!' I yelled out loud as I stormed out the front door. I returned with a series of new mousetraps, but these ones seemed much more lethal. They were glue-boards. Rather naïvely I assumed that the glue on the boards also contained some sort of poison or lethal fumes, but, as I was to discover, what they are called is exactly what they are. Boards with glue on them.

A couple of days later I came into the kitchen and there, stuck to the board, was the mouse. Apart from having a large bit of cardboard stuck to it, the little creature seemed very much alive. I considered my options. I had to kill it, but how? I guessed that you were supposed to hit it on the head with a hammer or something, but there was no way I could do that. Perhaps I should just feed it occasionally until it died of old age? It gave a great shrug and I realised that I had better act quickly or it might get away. I can't believe that animal rights protesters spend their Saturdays throwing paint on women in fur coats when they could be picketing every corner shop that sells glue-boards.

Horror upon horror, I found myself filling a bucket. I was going to drown the mouse. Using a pair of kitchen tongs I lifted up the board and threw it in the bucket. It was then that I made an interesting discovery – glue-boards float. I now had a mouse on a tiny surfboard floating aimlessly around the bucket. Although the rodent seemed more than happy to ride the waves for the time being, I needed the horror to end. I grabbed the tongs and plunged board and surfer beneath the surface. I was letting out little involuntary yelps and could hardly bear to look, but when I did the mouse was still alive, staring up at me from the depths of the bucket. I began to doubt myself. Were mice amphibians? After what seemed an eternity the answer finally came back as 'no'. The whole thing was wildly traumatic. I felt like Lucille Ball starring in *The Silence of the Lambs*. What made things even worse was that I had seen not only the first *Stuart Little* movie but also the sequel. I sat on the kitchen floor having just endured *The Passion of Stuart Little* as directed by Mel Gibson.

Apart from my cold-blooded murderer tendencies and the terrible weather, the other main shock in New York was going back to doing one show a week. I still went into the office most days, but usually all I did was check my emails and compare hangovers with everyone else. Not only had my workload decreased but I was also suddenly without my biggest excuse for not drinking – my car. My resolve to behave like a grown-up after turning forty hadn't lasted very long. On top of that, the old cliché that the city never sleeps turns out to be true. Every bar stays open until 4 a.m. and I felt it was my duty to be in all of them all the time. Every time I spoke to my mother she would say, 'You looked a bit tired on the show this week.' It became a slight concern to me which would come to an end first, the series or me.

I found myself increasingly leaving Jon and the team to get on with the day-to-day planning of the shows. I sometimes stumbled into meetings about the show, but mostly I was just told on the day what was planned and what I needed to do. At first I felt very guilty, but then I'm afraid to admit that I began to enjoy it. It felt good that after all these years of working together, Jon and I were so in sync that I could trust him completely to come up with ideas that I liked and would feel comfortable doing. Although Channel 4 was paying for these shows and we were making them for a British audience, we couldn't help but see them as ten pilots for our Comedy Central series. Yet again it was hard to feel sentimental about the end of our six-year run at Channel 4 because we were so excited about our new ventures. We went to meetings at Comedy Central where people showed us what the billboards advertising our show would look like, and yes, there would be one on Sunset Boulevard!

In Britain I have been very careful to make sure that any press I do is only about the show. I don't go to many premieres or showbiz parties, and I tend not to eat in the restaurants that have the paparazzi hanging around outside. Trying to launch a new show in the massive market that is America is a very different ball game. There are so many new shows, so many performers, so many channels that to have any chance of succeeding, you have to do a bit of jumping up and down and waving. For the first time in my life I employed a publicist to help me promote the forthcoming Comedy Central show. I'm still not very clear about what they do, but I knew that I was supposed to have one. People were asking me who my lawyer was, should they speak to my manager as well as my agent? It seemed that starting to work in the States was like learning a new language.

I was very aware that I should have been finding the whole process daunting and nerve-racking, and maybe once we started actually making the shows for America I would, but I have to admit that at that time I was just finding the whole experience exciting and surreal. I was well aware that I might be just another in a long line of British performers to fail miserably in the US, but that really didn't bother me. As my experience with the hippies taught me all those years ago, the only true failure is not making the attempt.

The last show ended with no great fanfare or fireworks. I simply thanked the viewers and Channel 4 and signed off for the last time. We had another goodbye party. I was still finding it hard to believe that I wouldn't be working with the people I'd grown to know so well over the last six years at 4. Katie Taylor, who had been our constant contact person and champion at the Channel, had never seemed like 'one of them'. She'd always fought for what we wanted and was the poor person who had had to defend us every time we crossed a line or broke some regulation or other. She was also the best present-buyer I'd ever met. Although we'd been at endless parties together over the years, it seemed really sad that she couldn't be with us for our last ever Channel 4 wrap party when we had it in New York because she had to go to her parents' fiftieth wedding anniversary. And yet she'd still found the time to send us gifts. A real class act.

In the midst of all our American excitement we would occasionally remember that we were actually supposed to be thinking up a new show to do on the BBC. At the time of writing we still have no idea what it is, but hopefully when this book is published it'll be on the air and not a complete disaster. In Jon and God we trust.

Looking forward seems like a very natural and almost healthy thing to be doing at this stage, having spent so many months delving into my past as I've worked on this book. I'm very struck by how I haven't lived my life in a straight line, but in fact I think we all do this – we're constantly passing Go and starting again. We may not pick up £200 each time, but we always seem to collect some more emotional baggage or, if we are very lucky, a little bit of wisdom. There have been so many beginnings and endings in my life so far, and where I'm at now is simply the start of a new round.

Earlier this year I went back to attend an anniversary party at Stardance in San Francisco. Maybe if I hadn't been writing this book I wouldn't have bothered, but I'm so glad I did. Everyone was there – Erica, Geoph, Mindy, Jem, Obo, even a heavily pregnant Faith Shines Help. We looked at old photos, I admired the new basement, we laughed about my cooking . . . but what struck me was that none of them remembered, because they had never known, how important they had all been in my life. To them I was just some clueless Irish boy who had passed through the house along with countless others, but to me it had been a major turning point after which, I had always believed, I became a very different person. As I picked at the vegan buffet and chatted about a new retirement home that was opening for activist pensioners, it dawned on me that in many ways I was wrong. Despite all the lessons and memories I had taken away from Stardance, I had been a fish out of water then, and, in very simple terms, I was still.

After the end of the filming in New York, I packed my laptop and headed off to Cape Town for some sun and one last burst of writing. I got back this morning, and as I write this I'm sitting tanned but tired, surrounded by boxes and dust in my new London house. I have been trying to finish this book for months, but now that I'm finally at that point

I find I'm not sure how to. There isn't a single certainty in my future, and yet I feel very calm. Perhaps the American show will fail, maybe the BBC will hate everything I do for them, but how bad can that be? Hopefully nobody will get hurt in the process and I will just get on with doing something, anything, else.

Writing the story of my life has been hugely enjoyable for me. Like everyone else I can find things to moan about, so it was wonderful to look back and see that I've lived the life of my dreams – and not many people get to say that. Yes, there has been some rain along the way, but mostly, overwhelmingly, it has been sunshine. I've won awards, I've been turned into a waxwork in Madame Tussaud's, I've leg-wrestled John Malkovich, been slapped by Sophia Loren, danced with Tony Curtis. I've loved and lost and hope to love again, and now, it seems, I've written a book.

Thank Yous

THIS BABY HAS TAKEN ME a bit over nine months to produce, but like all babies it didn't just pop out on to the shelves all by itself. Huge thanks to my übermidwife Katy Follain from Hodder & Stoughton for her incredible patience and encouragement. I'm also very grateful to Rowena Webb and all the other doctors and nurses at Hodder for the design and marketing and all the other jobs I didn't even know they were doing.

Melanie Coupland, who held my hand and yelled 'Push!', not just while I was trying to finish this book but also during all my working life; Dylan and Tracy, and everyone at Talk-Back – thank you.

Graham Stuart and Jon Magnusson, my showbusiness husbands: without you work would be work; with you it is the greatest fun in my life – well, apart from wanking.

Thanks to the legions of researchers, associate producers and producers who have given up so much of their time, energy and passion just to try and make me look good. A special thank you to my assistant Alex – it's a lonely, dirty, thankless job, but, as they say about oral sex, someone's got to do it.

My friends – old ones like Niall, Mike, Helen, Nicky, Maureen, Stephan, Gill and Darren, and new ones like Maria, Carrie, Carl, Daz, Tim, Daniel, Dennis, Jamie, Leslie,

Louise and Craig and so many more – I don't know why so few of you ended up in these pages. You are really important to me, just not when I'm writing a book, it seems.

Scott – for being there even when I thought I didn't want you to be, thank you.

And finally, the biggest thank you of all must go to all the people who have watched the show over the years. Without you there would be no book and certainly no readers. Stay tuned!